Joseph Wright

A Grammar of the Dialect of Windhill

In the West Riding of Yorkshire

Joseph Wright

A Grammar of the Dialect of Windhill
In the West Riding of Yorkshire

ISBN/EAN: 9783744661744

Printed in Europe, USA, Canada, Australia, Japan

Cover: Foto ©Andreas Hilbeck / pixelio.de

More available books at **www.hansebooks.com**

A Grammar

OF THE

DIALECT OF WINDHILL,

IN THE

WEST RIDING OF YORKSHIRE.

*Illustrated by a Series of Dialect Specimens, phonetically rendered;
with a Glossarial Index of the Words used in the
Grammar and Specimens.*

BY

JOSEPH WRIGHT, M.A., Ph.D.,

DEPUTY PROFESSOR OF COMPARATIVE PHILOLOGY
IN THE UNIVERSITY OF OXFORD.

'Nur das Beispiel führt zum Licht;
Vieles Reden thut es nicht.'

London:
PUBLISHED FOR THE ENGLISH DIALECT SOCIETY
BY KEGAN PAUL, TRENCH, TRÜBNER & CO., CHARING CROSS ROAD.
—
1892.

To My Mother

PREFACE

My chief object in writing the following Grammar has been to furnish specialists in English philology with an accurate account of the Phonology and Accidence of one of the most interesting of the Yorkshire dialects. And in order to make the work as useful as possible to this class of scholars, I have taken special care to include in the Phonology fairly complete lists of the words which are in common use in the dialect and also exist in the literary language. This method of treatment has sometimes involved me in great difficulties; because in the case of words which seem to have had an abnormal development I could not always decide with certainty whether the seeming irregularities had arisen within the dialect itself, or whether the words in question had been introduced from the literary language at various periods, or were merely borrowings from some neighbouring dialect. These are difficulties which every writer of a scientific dialect grammar has to contend with. But it would manifestly have been dishonest on my part to have omitted any word or form which did not seem to have had a regular development. The result is that the grammar contains dozens of words the vocalism of which I have not been able to

a 3

explain satisfactorily, but I have nevertheless registered
them in separate paragraphs, as being in common use in
the dialect and of equal importance to the English philo-
logist. Out of a great many such examples I will only
mention a few here: nuez (OE. nosu) *nose*, bied (OE.
beard) *beard*, ut (OE. hāt) *hot*, friet (OE. fretan) *to fret*, for
which we should expect in the dialect noiz (§§ 105, 109),
bād (§§ 61, 68), uet (§§ 122, 126), freit (§§ 82, 87). On the
other hand, the present grammar will, I trust, help to throw
some light upon Old English vowel quantities, besides
showing how dialects still keep apart many vowel sounds
which have fallen together in the literary language. Of
the latter I will only mention a few examples, although
a great many may be found in the grammar:—jād (OE.
geard) *yard*, jied (OE. gerd) *yard, three feet.* wāk (OE.
weorc) *work*, wōk (OE. wyrcan) *to work.* meil (OE. melu)
meal, flour, miel (OE. mǣl) *meal, repast.* reit (OE. reoht,
reht) *right*, rait (OE. wrītan) *to write*, rīt (OE. wyrhta)
wright.

In the treatment of the native element contained in the
grammar I have generally started out from Old English,
which in some respects presents fewer difficulties to the
writer of a modern dialect grammar than Middle English
with its numerous dialects. Had I, however, been a
specialist in this period of our mother tongue, I should
probably have been able to settle many minor points which
remain unsolved in the present grammar. But still, in
spite of my shortcomings in this respect, I hope that the
book will be a welcome contribution to English philology.

In the treatment of the French element in the dialect
I found, after trying many experiments, that the only

satisfactory plan was to start out from the present pronunciation of literary English. The words have come into
the dialect at various periods and through various chan-
nels, and it is accordingly almost impossible to treat them
historically. I have therefore contented myself with
registering the present dialectical pronunciation of the
French element, and for this purpose I have adopted, as
the standard of literary English pronunciation, the sound-
system in Sweet's Primer of Spoken English, which is fairly
typical of the Southern pronunciation of educated people.
A comparison of the development of the French and English
elements in the dialect is interesting from many points of
view. I will only draw attention to §§ 61, 203 and §§ 58,
202 ; but many other paragraphs will be found equally interesting both to English and French philologists. Any one,
who is not thoroughly acquainted with the dialect, may
possibly think that I have introduced into this part of the
grammar many words which are not in common use; but
such is not the case. I have been particularly careful in
this respect. I will only mention one instance out of
many where I may seem to have erred: **raiet akt** *riot
act*, which is one of the commonest expressions in the
dialect, a regular household phrase. What mother has not
said to her naughty child hundreds of times, if tə duz ðat
ə·giən al rīd ðī traiet akt ən reit ən oel ?

In the chapter on the consonants the chief interest
naturally lies in the gutturals. In this part of the grammar I have tried to give complete lists of the words which
differ in their development from literary English, I mean
such words as: **flik** *flitch*, **reik** *to reach*, **brig** *bridge*, **flig**
fledge, **duef** *dough*, etc.

It was originally my intention not to give any specimens of the dialect in this volume, but to reserve them for
a second which was to contain a complete glossary of
such dialect words as are not in use in the Modern literary
language, together with extensive specimens of the dialect.
With this end in view I have been collecting materials for
a great number of years, but various circumstances prevent me from entertaining the hope of being able to
publish them for some years to come. I have therefore
decided to give a few specimens in the present volume,
trusting that they may be found useful to those readers
who may wish to make themselves familiar with the
dialect. To anyone who takes the trouble to read them
I venture to say that they will be found both amusing and
instructive.

The Index, which has been a laborious piece of work,
contains all the words occurring in the grammar.

As a guarantee for the general accuracy of the material
contained in the book, I need only state that I spoke the
dialect pure and simple until I was practically grown up.

In conclusion I have the pleasant task of expressing my
most cordial thanks to three friends—Professor Napier,
Professor Holthausen, and the Rev. A. L. Mayhew—who
have given me much valuable help in the work.

JOSEPH WRIGHT.

OXFORD,
January 1893.

CONTENTS

ABBREVIATIONS, ETC.

———•+•———

Angl. = Anglian.
Dan. = Danish.
dial. = dialect.
Fr. = French.
gen. = genitive.
Germ. = German, Germanic.
Goth. = Gothic.
Lat. = Latin.
lit. = literally.
lit. Engl. = literary English.
Low Germ. = Low German.
ME. = Middle English.
MHG. = Middle High German.
Mid. Du. = Middle Dutch.
M. Low Germ. = Middle Low German.
Norw. = Norwegian.
occ. = occasionally.
OE. = Old English.

O. Fr. = Old French.
O. Fris. = Old Frisian.
OHG. = Old High German.
O. Icel. = Old Icelandic.
O. Ir. = Old Irish.
O. Low Germ. = Old Low German.
O. Norm. Fr. = Old Norman French.
O.N. = Old Norse.
O. North. = Old Northumbrian.
O. Swed. = Old Swedish.
pl. = plural.
pret. = preterite.
pp. = past participle.
sing., sg. = singular.
Scot. = Scotch.
Swed. = Swedish.
W. = Windhill.
WS. = West Saxon.
> = has become.

The asterisk (*) prefixed to a word denotes a theoretical form.

———————

WORKS REFERRED TO IN THE GRAMMAR.

Cotgr. = A French and English Dictionary, composed by Mr. Randle Cotgrave; with another in English and French, edited by J. Howell.

EEPr. = Early English Pronunciation, by A. J. Ellis.

E.E.T.S. = Early English Text Society.

Etym. Dict. = Etymological Dictionary of the English Language, by W. W. Skeat.

Florio = A Worlde of Wordes, or most copious and exact Dictionarie in Italian and English, by John Florio, London, 1598.

Grundriss der germanischen Philologie, herausgegeben von H. Paul.

The Dialect of the Southern Counties of Scotland, by J. A. H. Murray.

N.E.D. = New English Dictionary, edited by J. A. H. Murray and H. Bradley.

P. B. Beitr. = Beiträge zur Geschichte der deutschen Sprache und Literatur, herausgegeben von H. Paul und W. Braune.

Prompt. Parv. = Promptorium parvulorum sive clericorum, dictionarius Anglo-Latinus princeps, auctore fratre Galfrido, grammatico dicto, ex ordine fratrum predicatorum, Northfolciensi, circa a. d. MCCCCXL, ad fidem codicum recensuit Albert Way, London, 1865.

Sievers, OE. Gr. = Angelsächsische Grammatik, von E. Sievers.

Stratmann = Dictionary of the Old English Language, by F. H. Stratmann (new edition, by H. Bradley).

Sweet, H.E.S. = History of English Sounds, by H. Sweet.

Sweet, NE. Gr. = New English Grammar, by H. Sweet.

Synopsis of Old English Phonology, by A. L. Mayhew.

Town. Myst. = The Towneley Mysteries (printed for the Surtees Society).

The following list of letters may be useful to those who consult the book without first reading the chapter on pronunciation :—

ə = the ə in German Gabe.

ŏ = the i in lit. Engl. bird.

j = the y   ,,   you.

ŋ = the ng, n ,,   sing, song, drink.

š = the sh   ,,   she.

tš = the ch   ,,   choose.

þ = the th   ,,   thin.

ð = the th   ,,   then.

dž = the j   ,,   just.

GRAMMAR

---·---

INTRODUCTION.

§ 1. WINDHILL is a manufacturing village in the township of Idle and parish of Calverley in the West Riding of Yorkshire, three miles North of Bradford.

The dialect belongs to the Eastern North Midland group, which embraces the whole of South Yorkshire. Dr. Ellis (EEPr. v. p. 364) distinguishes nine varieties : The Western group containing var. 1. Huddersfield and var. 2. Halifax. The North Central group containing var. 3. Keighley, var. 4. Bradford, var. 5. Leeds, var. 6. Dewsbury. The South Central group containing var. 7. Rotherham and var. 8. Sheffield. The Eastern group containing var. 9. Doncaster and the Eastern slip.

Of these nine varieties the Windhill dialect is most closely related to numbers 3. 4. 5.

B

PHONOLOGY

CHAPTER I.

PRONUNCIATION.

A. The Vowels.

§ 2. The Windhill dialect contains the following vowel sounds :—

Short vowels   a,   e,   i,   o,   u,   ǝ

Long   „   ā,   ī,   ū,   ō

Short diphthongs ai, ei,   oi, ui

                 eu, iu, ou

                 eǝ, iǝ, oǝ, uǝ

Long   „   āǝ

Triphthongs   aiǝ,   iuǝ, ouǝ

NOTE.—To these must be added l, m, n, ɹ in the function of vowels. For examples see the corresponding consonants §§ 17-19.

§ 3. In the following paragraphs will be given a brief description of the Windhill vowel-system. For which purpose I have adopted the notation as given in Sweet's Primer of Phonetics. In the autumn of 1886 Dr. Sweet was kind enough to render me considerable help in the analysis of the W. vowel sounds; thus enabling me to fix

the sounds far more accurately than would otherwise have
been the case, had it not been for his kind assistance.
The late Dr. Ellis, to whom I dictated the Dialect Test
(EEPr. v. pp. 389–90) and the dialect words in his Classified Word List (pp. 391–4), was also of some help to me.
But a comparison of his appreciation of the W. vowels
with that of Dr. Sweet and my own will show that we
differ on several minor points.

All the diphthongs and triphthongs have the stress on
the first element. In my transcription I have written iǝ,
uǝ, &c., but the first element is really a medium long
vowel, which stands in the same relation to the corresponding short vowel as the lit. Engl. vowel in feet does
to fit or seek to sick.

§ 4. a (mid-back-wide) like the a in German Mann,
but with the tongue slightly more advanced.

lat *late*, faðǝ(r) *father*, mak *to make*, as *to ask*, laðǝ(r)
ladder, dlad *glad*, tšap *chap*, ratn *rat*, pastǝ(r) *pasture*,
aprǝn *apron*, kwalǝti *quality*, vari *very*.

ā (mid-back-wide) like the a in German Name and in
lit. Engl. father, but with slightly more advanced position
of the tongue as in short a. After our ā there is also
a trace of a glide (āǝ), which however is not sufficiently
developed to be conveniently represented in print.

rām *room*, fāl *fowl*, bǎn *child*, wǎm *warm*, wǎk (noun)
work, fādin *farthing*, sǎvnt *servant*, pāðǝ(r) *powder*.

ai = a + i:
raiv *to tear*, mais *mice*, tais *to entice*.
aiǝ = ai + ǝ:
aiǝn *iron*, faiǝ(r) *fire*, raiǝt *riot*.
āǝ = ā + ǝ:
dāǝ(r) *dare*, sāǝ(r) *sour*, tāǝ(r) *tower*.

§ 5. e (low-front-narrow) like the ä in Swed. lära and the first element of the diphthong in lit. Engl. care but short. Ellis identified it as mid-front-wide, but Sweet and myself agree in the above analysis.

elp *to help*, bed *bed*, brek *to break*, emen *among*, weš *to wash*, bleg *blackberry*, geðe(r) *to gather*, ðen *then*, šepste(r) *starling*, len *to lend*, gezlin *gosling*, depþ *depth*, lek *to leak*, frend *friend*, treml *to tremble*, blenkit *blanket*, fešn *fashion*, lenit *linnet*.

ei = e + i :

feit *to fight*, beid *bead*, eit *to eat*, leitš *leech*, reik *to reach*, lein *to lean*, ei *high*.

eu = e + u :

eu *ewe*, feu *few*, seu *to sew*.

ee = e + e :

beed *to bathe*, dee *day*, breed *to resemble*, bleet *to bleat*, tlee *clay*, leek *to play*, beekn *bacon*, kweet *quart*, meeste(r) *master*.

§ 6. i (high-front-wide) like the i in lit. Engl. bit :

lig *to lie down*, wik *quick, alive*, in *to hang*, sitš *such*, fligd *fledged*, dwinl *to dwindle*, litl *little*, sili *silly*, ive(r) *ever*, rik *smoke*, divl *devil*, tšimli, *chimney*, šimi *chemise*.

ī (high-front-narrow) like the ie in German Biene. It is a pure long vowel, not like the ee in South. Engl. feed, which is a diphthong (ij) :

mīld *mild*, nīt *night*, fīld *field*, wīl (adv.) *well*, frīt *fright*, bīld *to build*, īmin *evening*, kīl *to cool*, lītnin *lightning*, sī *sigh*, nī *knee*, bīf *beef*.

ie = i + e :

bied *beard*, ieþ *earth*, swie(r) *to swear*, friet *to fret*, flie(r) *to laugh* or *sneer at*, dried *to dread*, tlien *clean*, bried *bread*, bie(r) *beer*, viel *veal*, fles *fierce*.

iu = i + u :

tliu *a ball of string* or *worsted*, spiu *to vomit*, tiuk *took*, lium *loom*, iniu (pl.) *enough*, briu *to brew*, frute(r) *future*, bliu *blue*, riubub *rhubarb*.

iue = iu + e :

siue(r) *sure,* piue(r) *pure.*

§ 7. o (low-back-wide-round) like the o in lit. Engl. not:

frozn *frozen*, lop *flea*, bodi *body*, wote(r) *water*, solt *salt*, moni *many*, jole *yellow*, sori *sorry*, tof *tough*, fotnit *fortnight*, kotn *cotton*, ont *aunt*, rost *to roast.*

oi = o + i :

þoil *to give ungrudgingly*, boil *to boil*, toist *toast.*

ou = o + u. But here the first element is low-back-narrow-round like the aw in lit. Engl. law:

koud *cold*, doute(r) *daughter*, floun *flown*, kouk *coke*, grou *to grow*, þout *thought*, loup *to jump*, out *ought*, tout *taught*, poutš *to poach*, skoud *to scald.*

oue = ou + e :

foue(r) *four.*

oe = o + e, the first element of which is the same as the o in ou :

koef *calf*, woef *insipid*, boek *beam*, boeld *bald*, poem *palm*, soev *salve*, moek *maggot*, boen *born*, noeðe(r) *neither*, snoe *snow*, goem *heed, care*, goeki *left handed*, oeðe(r) *to order*, džoenes *jaundice.*

§ 8. u (high-back-wide-round) like the u in lit. Engl. put:

fun (pp.) *found*, flute(r) *to flutter*, tul *to*, fuml *to fumble*, ut *hot*, muðe(r) *mother*, uðe(r) *udder*, butše(r) *butcher*, buzed *butterfly*, nuvl *novel.*

ū (high-back-narrow-round) like the u in Germ. gut. In

the W. dialect it is a pure long vowel and not a diphthong
(uw) like the oo in Southern Engl. food:

šūl *shovel*, əbūn *above*, būkþ *bulk, size.*

ui=u+i. The first element of which is not the u in
put. Dr. Ellis identified the first element as mid-back-
narrow-round like the o in Germ. Bote, but this is certainly not the sound. At first Dr. Sweet gave the same
analysis as Dr. Ellis, but he was afterwards inclined to
think that it might be mid-back-narrow-round with outer
rounding like the o in Swedish sol. But this too is hardly
our sound. The nearest analysis seems to me to be the
tongue position of high-back-narrow-round, like the u in
Germ. gut, ou in French sou, with the lip position of mid-
back-narrow-round:

bluid *blood*, uin *to harass, treat badly*, gruin *snout of
a pig.*

uə=u+ə. The first element is the same as the u in ui:

nuəz *nose*, smuə(r) *to smother*, duə(r) *door*, juək *yolk*,
kuəm *comb*, duəf *dough*, dluə(r) *to stare*, kuəd *cord*, tluək
cloak, puə(r) *poor.*

§ 9. ə (mid-mixed-narrow) like the e in German Gabe,
but with the tongue slightly more retracted. It is not
identical with the -er in lit. Engl. better, which is mid-
mixed-wide. It occurs in both stressed and unstressed
syllables:

jəstədə *yesterday*, stərək *heifer*, fərə *furrow*, wəri *to
worry*, bəd *but*, spərit *spirit*, valə *value.*

ȫ (low-mixed-narrow) like the i in lit. Engl. bird, but
with the tongue rather more advanced. It only occurs in
stressed syllables:

gȫs *grass*, bȫk *birch*, wȫd *word*, mȫðə(r) *murder*, wȫk
to work, kȫsmes *Christmas*, gȫt *great*, kȫnz *currants.*

B. The Consonants.

§ 10. The W. dialect contains the following consonants :
b, d, f, g, j, k, l, m, n, ɳ, p, r, s, š, t, þ, ð, v, w, z, ž.

§ 11. b (lip-stop-voice) like lit. English b. It occurs initially, medially, and finally :

bän *child*, beed *to bathe*, bun (pp.) *bound*, brig *bridge*, bleb *blister*, breed *to resemble, act like another person*, brīt *bright*. kubed *cupboard*, riubub *rhubarb*, uzbn *husband*. dub *a small pool of water*, nub *to nudge*.

§ 12. d (gum-stop-voice) like lit. English d. It occurs in all positions :

duef *dough*, dī *to die*, diu *to do*, dwinl *to dwindle*, džais *joist*, dlas *glass*. bodm *bottom*, fädin *farthing*, wide *widow*. nobed lit. *not but, only*, grund *ground*, od *to hold*, snod *smooth*, boged *ghost, apparition*.

§ 13. f (lip-teeth-open-breath) like lit. Engl. f. It occurs in all positions :

feu *few*, foil *foal*, feit *to fight*, flig *fledge*, fan (pret.) *found*. duefl *cowardly*, woefl *insipid*, fift *fifth*, druft *drought*. kaf *chaff*, duef *dough*, koef *calf*, laif *life*.

§ 14. g (back-stop-voice) like lit. Engl. g. It occurs in all positions :

geen *near, direct*, galek *lefthand*, gäl *the matter which gathers in the corner of the eye*, guid *good*, goemles *foolish, silly*. blegs *blackberries*, boged *ghost*, pigin *small water can*, flegstn *flagstone*. ig *mood, temper*, ug *to carry*, lig *to lie down*, neeg *to gnaw*.

§ 15. j (front-open-voice) like lit. English y in you. It only occurs initially :

jest *yeast*, jestede *yesterday*, jole *yellow*, juꞃ *young*. I have sometimes heard the sound medially in teelje(r), teele(r) *tailor*.

§ 16. k (back-stop-breath) like lit. Engl. k. It occurs in all positions:

kā *cow*, kest *to cast*, kei *key*, koud *cold*, koul *to rake*, kīl *to cool*. skrat *to scratch*, bake *tobacco*, beekꞃ *bacon*, oks *ox*. flik *flitch of bacon*, reik *to reach*, wik *quick, alive*, bēk *birch*.

§ 17. 1 (gum-side-voice) like ordinary English 1. It occurs as a consonant in all positions, but as a vowel in unaccented syllables only:

leek *to play*, loin *lane*, len *to lend*, leeð *barn*, luensem *lonely*, leelek *lilac*, loup *to jump*. olin *holly*, bīld *to build*, twilt *quilt*. koil *coal*, steil *to steal*, wīl (adv.) *well*.

Examples of vocalic 1 are: kitl *to tickle*, adl *to earn*, satl *to settle*, spinl *spindle*, rasl *to wrestle*.

§ 18. m (lip-nasal-voice) like lit. Engl. m. It occurs as a consonant in all positions, but as a vowel only in un-accented syllables:

meitš *to measure*, mun *must*, muin *moon*, māt *to moult*. treml *to tremble*, īmin *evening*, sīmin-dlas *mirror*. steim *to bespeak*, gam *game*, freem *to make a beginning*, goem *heed, care*.

Examples of vocalic m are: bodm *bottom*, fadm *fathom*, fipms *fivepence*, wiepm *weapon*, kindm (OE. cynedōm) *kingdom*.

§ 19. n (gum-nasal-voice) like lit. Engl. n. It occurs as a consonant in all positions, but as a vowel only in un-accented syllables:

nie(r) *kidney*, nīt *night*, neꞃ-neel *corn on the foot*, nub

to nudge, noeðe(r)*ˈneither.*   snoə *snow,* inif *enough,* moni
many, sind *to rinse, wash out,* spinl *spindle.*   gēn *to grin,*
bin *within,* fādin *farthing,* runin *running.*

Examples of vocalic n are: frozn *frozen,* brusn (pp.)
burst, ratn *rat,* seldn *seldom,* getn (pp.) *got,* tšozn *chosen,*
þāzn *thousand.*

§ 20. ŋ (back-nasal-voice) like ng, n in lit. Engl. sing,
song, drink, drunk.   As a consonant it only occurs in
accented, and as a vowel only in unaccented syllables:

bleŋk *blank,* briŋ *to bring,* teŋz *tongs* fiŋe(r) *finger,* iŋ
to hang, bleŋkit *blanket,* þiŋ *thing.*

Examples of vocalic ŋ are: brokŋ *broken,* beegŋ *bargain,*
drukŋ *drunk, drunken,* wokŋ *to waken.*

§ 21. p (lip-stop-breath) like lit. Engl. p.   It occurs
initially, medially, and finally:

poəm *palm,* poəz *to kick,* penəþ *pennyworth.*   speen *to
wean,* spitək *spigot,* api *happy,* apl *apple,* stapl *staple.* lop
flea, elp *to help,* sweəp *the handle of a machine,* saip *to ooze*
or *drain out slowly.*

§ 22. r (gum-open-voice).   Before a following vowel r
is a gently trilled sound.   Final r is also slightly trilled,
but not so strongly as before a following vowel.   This is
always the case when the word containing it is used alone,
or stands at the end of a sentence.   In these positions it is
never weakened into a mere voiced glide as in lit. Engl.
fear, nor does it disappear altogether as in lit. Engl. far.
In order to distinguish strong and weak r the latter is
uniformly written (r) in this grammar:

raiv *to tear,* roet *to bray,* roem *to roam,* reik *to reach,*
rām *room,* brek *to break,* reŋ *wrong.* sarə *to serve,* marə *to
match,* feri *first turn,* barə *barrow.* gər up *to get up.*

swie(r) *to swear*, pie(r) *pear*, smue(r) *to smother*, wee(r) *to spend money*.

§ 23. s (blade-open-breath) like the s in lit. Engl. sit. It occurs in all positions:

sal *shall*, sud *should*, sīt *sight*, seem *lard*, sāk *to suck*, snod *smooth*, steim *to bespeak*, strie *straw*, speik *to speak*, siuge(r) *sugar*, swiel *to gutter (of a candle)*. koese *causeway*, brusn (pp.) *burst*, rāst *rust*, omest *almost*, þrosl *thrush.* as *ash, ashes*, guis *goose*, ās *house*, oks *ox*, oes *horse*, ius *use*.

§ 24. š (blade-point-open-breath) like lit. Engl. sh in she. It occurs far more frequently initially and finally than medially:

šuin *shoes*, šimi *chemise*, šap *shape*, šak *to shake*, šuðe(r) *to shudder*. tšons *chance*, tšeeme(r) *chamber*, tšiuz *to choose*, fešn *fashion*. weš *to wash*, rediš *radish*, fotš *to fetch*, bleitš *to bleach*, mitš *much*.

§ 25. t (gum-stop-breath) like lit. English t. It occurs in all positions:

tak *to take*, temz *hop-sieve*, toist *toast*, teu *to work zealously*, tlueþ *cloth*. fotn (pp.) *fought*, flute(r) *future*, wāte *weekday*. gēt *great*, fouet *fourth*, ut *hot*, lat *lath*.

§ 26. þ (teeth-open-breath) like the th in lit. Engl. thin. It occurs initially and finally:

þak *thatch*, þāzn *thousand*, þout *thought*, þriep *to contradict, dispute*. broþ *broth*, māþ *mouth*, dieþ *death*, swāþ *the skin of bacon*.

§ 27. ð (teeth-open-voice) like the th in lit. English then. It occurs initially only in words which had formerly the weak stress; medially between vowels; and finally after vowels:

ðai, ði *thy,* ðis *this,* ðen *then.*   šuðə(r) *to shudder,* påðə(r) *powder* feðə(r) *feather,* soðə(r) *solder.*   buið *booth,* leeð *barn,* smuið *smooth.*

§ 28. v (lip-teeth-open-voice) like the v in lit. Engl. vine.   Initially it only occurs in words of French origin :

vari *very,* viəl *veal,* vois *voice.*   avə-meil *oatmeal,* navi *canal.*   neiv *fist,* raiv *to tear,* þraiv *to thrive.*

§ 29. w (lip-back-open-voice) like lit. Engl. w in wet. It only occurs initially and medially :

wāk (noun) *work,* wen *thong,* wen *when,* wīl *wheel,* wik *quick, alive,* wām *warm.*   ewee *away,* dwinl *to dwindle,* twais *twice,* kweet *quart,* kwaleti *quality,* swiet *to sweat,* swetš *a small sample of cloth.*

§ 30. z (blade-open-voice) like the z in lit. Engl. zeal, freeze.   Initially it only occurs in ziel *zeal.*   It is common medially and finally :

uzbn *husband,* meze(r) *measure,* rīzd *rancid (of bacon),* frozn *frozen,* fuzi *soft, spongy,* buzed *butterfly,* gizn *to choke.*   temz *hop-sieve,* ez *as,* siðez *scissors,* tšiuz *to choose.*

§ 31. ž (blade-point-open-voice) like the s in lit. Engl. measure.   It only occurs after d and n :

džoul *to knock, strike,* džais *joist,* džudž *judge,* sādžn *sergeant,* eedž *age,* tšeedž *charge,* inž *hinge,* sinž *to singe* ; but in words of French origin we have indžn *engine,* moendž *mange.*

CHAPTER II.

1. Short Vowels.

a.

§ 32. Windhill **a** corresponds to:

1. OE. **æ(a)** in originally closed syllables, § 57: **as** *ashes*,
fan (pret.) *found*, **gam** *game*, **lat** *late*, **sal** *shall*, **sam** up,
(OE. **samnian**) *to pick up*, **þak** *thatch*.

2. Rarely OE. **a(æ)** in open syllables, § 71: **faðe(r)** *futher*,
mak *to make*, **tak** *to take*.

3. Shortening of OE. **ā**, § 125: **as** *to ask*, **spatl** *spittle*.

4. Shortening of OE. **ǣ**, §§ 135, 144: **blast** *blast*.
bad *bad*, **laðe(r)** *ladder*.

5. Rarely shortening of OE. **ēa**, § 186: **tšap** *chap*.

6. Lit. Engl. **æ** in French words, § 194; **galek** (O. Fr.
galc) *left hand*, **ratn** *rat*, **vale** *value*.

7. Lit. Engl. **ā** in French words, § 195: **basted** *bastard*,
paste(r) *pasture*.

8. Rarely lit. Engl. **ei** in French words, § 196: **apren**
apron.

9. Lit. Engl. o (through the influence of the preceding **w**) in French words, § 202 : **kwaleti** *quality*, **warend** *to warrant*.

10. Lit. Engl. ə before r in French words, § 208 : **tarie(r)** *terrier*, **vari** *very*.

ə.

§ 33. Windhill ə corresponds to :

1. Germanic e, and the i-umlaut of **a** in originally closed syllables ; and also when ə was originally followed by a single consonant + a suffix containing an l, m, n, r, §§ 72–3 : **delf** *delf*, **elp** *to help*, **leðə(r)** *leather*, **melt** *to melt*, **weft** *weft*.

bed *bed*, **ketl** *kettle*, **lenþ** (by assimilation) *length*, **mens** *neatness*, **set** *to set*.

2. Rarely OE. ə in open syllables, § 88 : **brek** *to break*, **get** *to get*.

3. Germ. a before a following g, ŋ, š, §§ 59, 197 : **beg** *bag*, **bleg** *blackberry*, **emeŋ** *among*, **reŋ** *wrong*, **seŋk** *sank*. **eš** *ashtree*, **weš** *to wash*.

4. Rarely OE. a(æ) in other cases, § 60 : **eltə(r)** *halter*, **geðə(r)** *to gather*, **wesp** *wasp*.

5. Rarely OE. o, § 108 : **ðen** *then*, **wen** *when*.

6. Shortening of Germanic ǣ (W.S. ǣ, O. North. ē), § 134 : **bleðə(r)** *bladder*, **šepstə(r)** *starling*, **slept** *slept*.

7. Shortening of OE. ǣ (i-umlaut of ā), § 143 : **fleš** *flesh*, **len** *to lend*, **les** *less*.

8. Shortening of OE. ē, ȫ (i-umlaut of ō), § 148 : **bled** *bled*, **gezlin** *gosling*, **met** *met*.

9. Shortening of Anglian ēo (= WS. īe) § 192 : **depþ** *depth*, **ten** *ten*.

10. Shortening of OE. ēa, § 186 : **lek** *leak*, **red** (adj.) *red*.

11. Shortening of OE. ēo, § 192 : **brest** *breast*, **frend** *friend*.

12. Lit. Engl. **ə** in French words, § 206 : **demək** *potato disease*, **mel** *to meddle*, **treml** *to tremble*.

13. Lit. Engl. **æ** before g, ŋ, š in French words, § 197 : **dregŋ** *dragon*, **bleŋkit** *blanket*, **fešn** *fashion*.

14. Rarely lit. Engl. i in French words, § 212 : **lenit** *linnet*, **rebit** *rivet*.

i.

§ 34. Windhill **i** corresponds to :

1. OE. i, § 89 : **bin** (OE. **binnan**) *within*, **bitn** *bitten*, **find** *to find*, **lig** *to lie down*, **wik** *quick, alive*.

2. OE. **e** (i-umlaut of a) before an original ŋ (now ŋ or nǯ), § 76 : **iŋ** (ME. **hengen**) *to hang*, **sinǯ** *to singe*, **þiŋk** *to think*.

3. Rarely OE. **e** in other cases, § 77 : **kil** *to kill*, **sitš** *such*, **wilə** *willow*.

4. OE. **y** (i-umlaut of u), § 117 : **brig** *bridge*, **flig** (ME. **fligge**) *fledge*, **ig** (OE. **hyge**) *mood, temper*.

5. Shortening of OE. ī, § 160 : **dwinl** *to dwindle*, **fift** *fifth*.

6. Shortening of OE. ȳ (i-umlaut of ū), § 177 : **litl** *little*, **wiš** *to wish*.

7. Rarely shortening of Germanic ǣ, § 136 : **ridl** *riddle*, **sili** *silly*.

8. Rarely shortening of OE. ǣ (i-umlaut of ā), § 145 : **ivə(r)** *ever*, **ivri** *every*.

9. Rarely shortening of OE. ē, older īe, § 150, note : **rik** *to smoke (of a chimney)*.

10. Rarely shortening of OE. ēo, § 192 : **divl** *devil*, **sik** *sick*.

11. Lit. Engl. i in French words, § 211 : **konsiðǝ(r)** *to consider*, **livǝ(r)** *to deliver*, **tšimli** *chimney*.

12. Lit. Engl. **e** before nasals in French words, § 209 : **lints** *lentils*, **šimi** *chemise*.

o.

§ 35. Windhill o corresponds to :

1. West Germanic o in originally closed syllables ; and also when o was originally followed by a single consonant + a suffix containing an l, m, n, r, § 100 : **bodm** *bottom*, **fotn** (pp.) *fought,* **lop** *flea*, **frozn** *frozen*, **olin** (ME. holen) *holly-tree*, **snod** *smooth*, **tšozn** *chosen*, **þrosl** *thrush*.

2. Rarely OE. o in open syllables, § 110 : **bodi** *body*, **popi** *poppy*.

3. OE. a preceded by w and not followed by **g, ɳ, š**, or **r** + consonant, § 58 : **swolǝ** *swallow*, **swop** *to exchange*, **wo(r)** (accented form) *was*, **wotǝ(r)** *water*.

4. OE. **ea(a)** before **ls, lt**, § 58 : **fols** *false*, **molt** *malt*, **solt** *salt*.

5. Rarely OE. **a** in other cases, § 58 : **omest** *almost*, **olǝs** *always*, **moni** *many*.

6. Rarely OE. **eo(e)**, § 80 : **jolǝ** (OE. geolu) *yellow*, **fotš** *to fetch*.

7. Shortening from OE. ā, § 125 : **sori** *sorry*.

8. Shortening of OE. ō, § 169 : **foðǝ(r)** *fodder*, **tof** *tough*.

9. Rarely shortening from OE. ēo, § 192 : **foti** *forty*, **fotnit** *fortnight*.

10. Lit. Engl. o in French words, § 214 : **boni** *nice, pretty*, **džosl** *to jostle*, **kotn** *cotton*, **poridž** *porridge*.

11. Lit. Engl. ā before n + consonant, in French words, § 200 : **dons** *dance*, **ont** *aunt*, **tšons** *chance*.

12. Rarely lit. Engl. **ou** in French words, §' 217 : **gol** *goal*, **rost** *to roast*.

u.

§ 36. Windhill u corresponds to :

1. OE. u, § 111 : drukɒ *drunk*, fun (pp) *found,* grund *ground,* kudl *to embrace,* kum *to come,* þunə(r) *thunder,* ug *to carry,* unded *hundred.*

2. Rarely OE. o, § 107 : flutə(r) *to flutter,* uvm *oven.*

3. Rarely OE. i, § 97 : kud (OE. cwidu) *cud,* tul (ME. til) *to.*

4. Rarely OE. y, § 121 : bluš *to blush,* bunl *bundle.*

5. Shortening from OE. ā, § 126 : ut *hot,* wun *one.*

6. Shortening of OE. ō, § 169 b; munþ *month,* muðe(r) *mother,* sluf (OE. slōg) *slough.*

7. Shortening of OE. ū, § 174 : fus *fuss,* plum *plum,* uðe(r) *udder,* uzbn *husband.*

8. Lit. Engl. u in French words, § 227 : butše(r) *butcher,* puš *to push,* put *to put.*

9. Lit. Engl. ɐ in French words, § 226 : buzed *butterfly,* mutn *mutton,* uml *humble.*

10. Rarely lit. Engl. o in French words, § 215 : nuvl *novel.*

ə.

§ 37. Windhill ə corresponds to :

1. Rarely OE. e, § 81 : beri *berry.* jestede *yesterday.*

2. Rarely OE. i, § 91 : sterek (OE. stirc, styric) *heifer.*

3. OE. u before a following r, § 113 : bere *borough,* fere *furrow.*

4. OE. y before a following r, § 120, (2) : beri *to bury,* weri *to worry.*

5. Lit. Engl. i before a following r in French words, § 213 : sperit *spirit.*

2. The Long Vowels.

ā.

§ 38. Windhill ā corresponds to :

1. OE. ū, § 171: ās *house*, dāst *dust*, kā *cow*, rām *room*, rāst *rust*, slām *slumber*, þāzn *thousand*.

2. OE. medial -ug-, § 114: fāl *fowl*, kāl *cowl*.

3. Rarely OE. u before n + consonant, § 115: ānd *hound*, drānd *to drown*.

4. OE. a, ea before r + consonant, § 61: ād *hard*, bān *child*, wām *warm*.

5. OE. e, eo before r + consonant, § 74: āt *heart*, dwāf *dwarf*, wāk (noun) *work*.

6. OE. ēo before r + consonant, § 189: dālin *darling*, fādin *farthing*.

7. O. Fr. er before a following consonant, § 207: pāsn *parson*, sāvnt *servant*.

8. Lit. Engl. au in French words, § 235: dāt *doubt*, gān *gown*, pāðe(r) *powder*.

ī.

§ 39. Windhill ī corresponds to :

1. OE. i before ld, § 92: mīld *mild*, wīld *wild*.

2. OE. i before ht, § 93: brīt *bright*, nīt *night*, sīt *sight*.

3. OE. medial -ig-, § 94: stīl (OE. stigel) *stile*, tīl *tile*.

4. OE. e before ld, § 78: fīld *field*, wīld *to wield*.

5. Rarely OE. e in other cases, § 79: bīzm *besom*, wīl (adv.) *well*.

6. OE. y before ht, § 118: flīt *flight*, frīt *fright*.

7. OE. y before ld, § 119: bīld *to build*.

8. Germanic ǣ (WS. ǣ, O. North. ē), § 130: īmin *evening*, nīdl *needle*, þrīd *thread*.

9. OE. ē, § 155: ī *he*, wī *we*.

10. OE. ō, œ (i-umlaut of ō), § 147: blīd *to bleed*, gīs *geese*, kīl *to cool*.

11. Anglian ē, ēo (= WS. īe), § 150: belīv *to believe*, lītnin *lightning*, sīn *seen*.

12. Rarely OE. ī, § 158: sī *to sigh*.

13. OE. ēo, § 187; dīp *deep*, nī *knee*, trī *tree*, wīl *wheel*.

14. Lit. Engl. ij in French words, § 232: bīf *beef*, pīs *piece*.

ū.

§ **40.** Windhill ū corresponds to:

1. Rarely OE. o, § 106: šūl *shovel*, stūp (ME. stolpe) *a post*.

2. Rarely OE. u, § 112: būkþ (ME. bulke) *bulk, size*, e-būn (OE. on-bufan) *above*, wūl *wool*.

ə̄.

§ **41.** Windhill ə̄ corresponds to:

1. OE. œr before a following consonant, § 69: gə̄s (OE. gœrs) *grass*.

2. OE. ir before a following consonant, § 90: bə̄k *birch*, þə̄d *third*.

3. Rarely OE. or before a following consonant, § 104, (3): wə̄d *word*, wə̄ld *world*.

4. OE. ur before a following consonant, § 113, (1): də̄st *durst*, snə̄t (ME. snurtin) *to snort, snore*.

5. OE. yr before a following consonant, § 120, (1): bə̄dn *burden*, bə̄þ *birth*, mə̄ðə(r) *murder*, wə̄k *to work*.

6. OE. ī (?) with metathesis of r, § 161: kə̄sməs *Christmas*, kə̄sn *to christen*.

7. OE. ēa with metathesis of r, § 185: gə̄t *great*.

8. Lit. Engl. ē in French words, § 228 : fēniš *to furnish*, kēn *currant*.

3. The Diphthongs.

ai.

§ 42. Windhill **ai** corresponds to :

1. OE. ī, § 156 : **ais** *ice*, **bait** *to bite*, **raiv** *to tear*, **sail** (ME. **sīlen**) *to strain*, **swaim** *to climb a tree*, **waif** *wife*.

2. OE. ȳ (i-umlaut of ū), § 175 : **aid** *hide, skin*, **mais** *mice*.

3. Rarely OE. i, § 95 : **ai** (accented form) *I*.

4. Lit. Engl. **ai** in French words, § 229 : **paint** *pint*, **sailm** *asylum*, **tais** *to entice*.

ei.

§ 43. Windhill **ei** corresponds to :

1. OE. e (Germanic e, and the i-umlaut of a) in originally open syllables, § 87 : **beid** *bead*, **eit** *to eat*, **meit** *meat*, **neiv** *fist*, **steil** *to steal*.

2. OE. e before ht, § 86 : **feit** *to fight*, **reit** *right*.

3. Rarely OE. æ (ea), § 67 : **eit** (O. North. æhto, æhta) *eight*.

4. WS. ǣ, O. North. ē before a following k, § 132 : **leitš** *leech*, **speitš** *speech*.

5. OE. ǣ (i-umlaut of a) before a following k, § 138 : **bleitš** *to bleach*, **reik** *to reach*.

6. Rarely OE. ǣ in other cases, § 139 : **lein** *to lean*, **spreid** *to spread*, **kei** *key*.

7. Rarely OE. ēa, § 182 : **ei** *high*, **nei** *nigh, near*.

oi.

§ 44. Windhill **oi** corresponds to:

1. OE. **o** in originally open syllables, § 109: **foil** *foal*, **koil** *coal*, **oil** *hole*, **þoil** *to give ungrudgingly*, **þroit** *throat*.

2. Lit. Engl. **oi** in French words, § 216: **boil** *to boil*, **oil** *oil*.

3. Lit. Engl. **ou** in French words, § 219: **doit** *to dote*, **toist** *to toast*.

ui.

§ 45. Windhill **ui** corresponds to:

1. OE. **ō**, § 163: **bluid** *blood*, **duin** *done*, **uin** (ME. hōnen) *to treat badly, harass*, **tuiþ** *tooth*.

2. Lit. Engl. **uw** in French words, § 221: **buit** *boot*, **fuil** *fool*, **gruin** *a pig's snout*.

eu.

§ 46. Windhill **eu** corresponds to:

1. OE. **e, eo, + w**, § 85: **eu** *ewe*, **streu** *to strew*.

2. OE. **ēaw**, § 180: **deu** *dew*, **feu** *few*, **teu** (OE. tēawian) *to work zealously*.

3. Rarely OE. **ēow**, § 190: **seu** *to sew*, **tšeu** *to chew*.

iu.

§ 47. Windhill **iu** corresponds to:

1. OE. **iw**, § 96: **tlïu** (OE. cliwe) *a ball of string or worsted*.

2. Rarely OE. **u**, § 116: **þriu** *through*.

3. OE. **īw**, § 159: **spiu** *to vomit*, **tiuzde** *Tuesday*.

4. OE. **ō** before a following **k, m**, and when final, § 164: **iuk** *hook*, **tiuk** *took*.

gium *gum*, lium *loom*.

diu *to do*, iniu (pl.) *enough*.

5. OE. ēow, § 190: bliu *blew*, briu *to brew*, niu *knew*.

6. Lit. Engl. juw in French words, § 237: flute(r) *future*, ius *use*, iuz *to use*, viu *view*.

7. Lit. Engl. uw in French words, § 239: bliu *blue*, friut *fruit*, riubub *rhubarb*, siu *to sue*.

ou.

§ 48. Windhill ou corresponds to:

1. OE. al before a following d, § 64: koud *cold*, oud *old*.

2. OE. o before ht, § 101: bout *bought*, doute(r) *daughter*.

3. OE. o, older ō, before ht, § 167: brout *brought*, þout *thought*.

4. ME. ow (OE. -og-), § 102: floun *flown*.

5. OE. ol before a following consonant, § 103: bouste(r) *bolster*, kouk *coke*, out *holt*.

6. OE. ōw, § 166: flou *to flow*, grou *to grow*.

7. O. Norse au, § 184: loup *to leap, jump*.

8. Rarely OE. āw, § 123: out *aught*, soul *soul*.

9. Rarely OE. ǣ before a following ht, § 140: tout *taught*.

10. Lit. Engl. ou in French words, § 220: boul *bowl*, poutš *to poach*.

11. al before d in French words, § 199: skoud *to scald*.

ee.

§ 49. Windhill ee corresponds to:

1. OE. a in originally open syllables, § 70: beed *to bathe*, eeg (OE. haga) *the berry of the hawthorn*, neeg (OE. gnagan) *to gnaw*, reeðe(r) *rather*, speen (OE. spanan) *to wean*, teem *tame*.

2. ME. ai, ei from OE. æg, § 65 : deə *day*, eəl *hail*, sneəl *snail*.

3. ME. ei from OE. eg, O. Norse ei, § 84 : breəd (OE. bregdan) *to resemble*, reən *rain*, beən (O. Icel. beinn) *near*, *direct*.

4. Rarely WS. ǣ, O. North. ē, § 133 : bleət *to bleat*, eə(r) *hair*.

5. Rarely OE. ǣ (i-umlaut of ā), § 141 : leədi *lady*, tleə *clay*.

6. O. Norse ei, § 127 : leək *to play*, weək *weak*.

7. Lit. Engl. ei in French words, § 204 : beəkɒ *bacon*, eənšn *ancient*, pleəs *place*.

8. O. Fr. ar before a following consonant, § 203 : geəd *guard*, kweət *quart*, tšeədž *to charge*.

9. Lit. Engl. ā in French words, § 195 : meəstə(r) *master*, pleəstə(r) *plaster*.

iə.

§ 50. Windhill iə corresponds to :

1. Rarely OE. ea, æ, a, § 68 : biəd *beard*, iərin *herring*.

2. OE. e before r not followed by another consonant, § 75 : biə(r) *to bear*, swiə(r) *to swear*.

3. Rarely OE. er before a following consonant, § 74 ; iəþ *earth*, liən *to learn*.

4. Rarely OE. e in other cases, § 82 : friət *to fret*, riəp *to reap*.

5. Rarely OE. i, § 98 : fliə(r) (Norw. flira) *to laugh* or *sneer at*.

6. WS. ǣ, O. North. ē, § 131 : driəd *to dread*, miəl *meal*, *repast*, wiə(r) *where*.

7. OE. ǣ (i-umlaut of ā), § 137 : diəl *deal*. iəl *to heal*, siə *sea*, tliən *clean*.

8. OE. ēa, § 179: **briəd** *bread*, **striə** *straw*, **þriəp** (OE. þrēapiən) *to contradict*.

9. OE. ēo before a following r, § 188: **biə(r)** *beer*, **diə(r)** *clear*.

10. Lit. Engl. **ij** in French words, § 231: **biək** *beak*, **fiətə(r)** *feature*, **viəl** *veal*.

11. Lit. Engl. **iə** in French words, § 233: **fiəs** *fierce*, **tliə(r)** *clear*.

oə.

§ **51.** Windhill **oə** corresponds to:

1. OE. **eal, al** in the combinations **lf**, OE. **lh, lk, ll, lm, lv**, § 62: **koəf** *calf*, **woəf** (OE. **walh**) *sickly to the smell, insipid to the taste*, **boək** *balk, beam*, **boəld** (ME. **balled**) *bald*, **poəm** *palm*, **soəv** *salve*.

2. ME. **aw** (of various origins), § 63: **moək** (ME. **mauk**) *maggot*, **soə** *he saw*, **kroəl** *to crawl*.

3. OE. **or** before a following consonant, § 104: **boən** *born*, **oəs** *horse*, **þoən** *thorn*.

4. OE. **āw**, § 123: **bloə** *to blow*, **noə** *to know*, **snoə** *snow*.

5. O. Norse **au**, § 184: **goəm** *heed, care*, **roət** *to bray*.

6. O. Fr. **al** before **k, m, l**, § 198: **goəki** *lefthanded*, **boəm** *balm*, **boəl** *ball*.

7. Lit. Engl. long open **o** in French words, § 225: **doəb** *to daub, smear*, **džoənəs** *jaundice*, **poəz** *to kick*, **foətn** *fortune*, **oəðə(r)** *to order*.

uə.

§ **52.** Windhill **uə** corresponds to:

1. Rarely OE. **o**, § 105: **uəp** *hope*, **nuəz** *nose*, **fluət** *to float*.

2. Rarely OE. **o** before a following r or r + consonant, § 104 (2): **smuə(r)** *to smother*, **buəd** *board*, **uəd** *hoard*.

3. Rarely OE. u before a following r or r + consonant, § 113, (3): muən *to mourn*.

4. OE. eol, § 83: juək *yolk*.

5. OE. a before mb, § 66: kuəm *comb*, wuəm *womb*.

6. OE. ā, § 122: buən *bone*, duəf *dough*, nuən *none*, snəp *soap*, tluəþ *cloth*, uəm *home*, uəs, uəst (OE. hās) *hoarse*.

7. OE. ō before a following r, § 165: dluə(r) (ME. glōrən) *to stare*, muə(r) *moor*.

8. Lit. Engl. long open o in French words, § 223: kuəd *cord*, fuəs *force*.

9. Lit. Engl. ou in French words, § 218: nuətis *notice*, tluək *cloak*.

10. Lit. Engl. uə before a following r in French words, § 222: puə(r) *poor*.

āə.

§ 53. Windhill āə corresponds to:

1. OE. a, ea before a following r, § 61: dāə(r) *dare*, aə(r) (accented form) *are*.

2. OE. e, eo before a following r, § 74: wāə(r) *worse*, stāə(r) *star*.

3. OE. ū before a following r, § 172: kāə(r) dān *to bend down*, sāə(r) *sour*.

4. Lit. Engl. auə before a following r in French words, § 236: āə(r) *hour*, tāə(r) *tower*.

4.   The Triphthongs.

aiə.

§ 54. Windhill aiə corresponds to:

1. OE. ī before a following r, § 157: aiən *iron*, spaiə(r) *spire*.

2. OE. ȳ (i-umlaut of ū) before a following r, § 176: faiə(r) *fire*, aiə(r) *to hire*.

3. Lit. Engl. aiǝ in French words, § 230: **raiǝt** *riot*, **umpaiǝ(r)** *umpire*.

iuǝ.

§ 55. Windhill iuǝ corresponds to:

1. Lit. Engl. uǝ before a following r in French words, § 240: **siuǝ(r)** *sure*.

2. Lit. Engl. juǝ before a following r in French words, § 238: **kiuǝ(r)** *cure*, **piuǝ(r)** *pure*.

ouǝ.

§ 56. Windhill ouǝ corresponds to:

Rarely OE. ēow before a following r, § 190: **fouǝ(r)** *four*.

CHAPTER III.

The Vowels of Accented Syllables. ·

In treating the vowels in accented syllables it is necessary
to distinguish between vowels which were originally in
closed syllables, e. g. OE. dæg *day*, helpan *to help*; and
those which were originally in open syllables, e. g. OE.
dagas *days*, etan *to eat*. In the former case OE. æ (a), o, e,
usually appear in the W. dialect as a, o, e, whereas in the
latter case they have generally become ee, oi, ei. When
through inflexional endings the vowels æ (a), o, e were in
OE. now in a closed syllable, now in an open one, the W.
dial. has mostly generalised the vowel of the open syllable.

1. The Short Vowels.

a.

§ 57. West Germanic a (= West Saxon æ (a), and ǫ before
nasals) in originally closed syllables usually appears as a in
the W. dialect.

Examples are: adl (ME. adlen, O. Icel. ǫðla) *to earn*,
afte(r) *after*, akoen *acorn*, aks *axe*, am (Sievers, OE. Gr.

§ 427) *am*, am *ham*, *ama(r) hammer*, and *hand*, anl *handle*,
ansə(r) *answer*, **antm** *anthem*, anvil *anvil*, **ap** (ME. **happen**)
to wrap with clothes, **apl** *apple*, **arə** *arrow*, as *ashes*, as-
midin *ash-pit*, at *hat*, **avə(r)-meil** (cp. ME. **havere** *oats*) *oat-*
meal, pret. **bad** (§ 373) *invited*, **bak** *back*, pret. **ban** *bound*,
band *string, cord*, **barə** *barrow*, **bas** *door mat, hassock*, **baþ**
bath, **bə-gan** *began*, **blak** *black*, **brak** *broke*, **brakɒ** (OE.
bracce, gen. **braccan**) *a kind of fern*, **bran** (OE. **brand**)
niu *quite new*, **bras** *brass*, pret. **brast** *burst*, **brat** (O. Ir., OE.
bratt) *pinafore*, **braznt** *brazen, impudent*, **daft** *foolish, silly,*
cowardly, **dam** (O.Icel. **damr**) *large pond*, **dlad** *glad*, **dlas**
glass, **dlazn** *to glaze*, **dlaznə(r)** *glazier*, **draft** *draught, draft*,
fadm (ME. **fadme**) *fathom*, **falə** *fallow*, pret. **fan** *found*, **fan**
fun, **fasn** *to fasten, conclude a bargain by paying earnest*
money, **flaks** *flax*, **flask** *flask*, **flat** *flat*, **gab** (cp. O. Icel.
gabba) *impudence*, **gad** (cp. OE. **ge-gada** *companion*) *to*
gossip, **galəs** *gallows*, **gam** (OE. **gamnian**) *game, to gamble*,
ganə(r) *gander*, pret. **gat** *got*, pret. **ga(v)** *gave*, **jarə** *yarrow*,
kaf *chaff*, **kal** *to gossip*, **kan** *a can*, **kan** (unaccented form
kn more frequently with assimilation **kɒ**) *can*, **kani** *knowing,*
intelligent, skilful, nimble, **kanl** *candle*, **kap** *a cap*, **kasl**
castle, **kat** *cat*, **krab** *crab*, **krabd** (ME. **crabed**) *angry*, **krabi**
ill-tempered, **kraft** *craft*, **krak** *to crack*, **kram** *to cram, press*
close together, **kramp** *cramp*, **lad** (ME. **ladde**) *lad*, **laf** (with
a from the pp.) *to laugh*, **laftə(r)** *laughter*, **lam** *lamb*, **land**
land, **lap** *lap, lappet*, **lap** (ME. **lappen**) *to wrap up*, **las**
(ME. **lasse**) *lass*, **last** *last, latest*, **lat** *late*, **lat** (OE. **lætt**) *lath*,
latə(r) *latter, later*, **man** *man*, **marə** *marrow*, **nap** *nap*,
narə *narrow*, **nat** *gnat*, **pak** (ME. **pakke**) *a pack, bundle*,
pan *pan*, **paþ** *path*, **pratli** *gently, softly*, **raftə(r)** *rafter*, **ram**
ram, **rami** (cp. OE. **hramsa** *wild garlic*) *having a strong*
taste or smell, **raml** *to ramble*, **ran** *ran*, **sad** *sad*, **sakləs**
(OE. **saclēas** *innocent*) *simple, silly*, **sam** *up* (OE. **samnian**)

to pick up, gather together, **sal** (emphatic form, see § 391)
shall, **sale** *sallow*, **sand** *sand*, **sap** *sap*, pret. **sat** *sat*, **satl**
(OE. **sahtlian** *to make peace, reconcile*) *to settle*, **skaftin**
shafting, **skab** *scab*, **skraml** *scramble*, **skrat** (ME. **scrattin**)
to scratch, **slafte(r)** *to slaughter*, **slak** *slack*, **slave(r)** *slaver*,
spak (§ 372) *spake, spoke*, **span** *to span*, pret. **span** *span*,
spare *sparrow*, **staf** *staff*, pret. **stak** *stuck*, **stamp** *to stamp*,
stand *to stand*, **šade** *shadow*, **šaft** *shaft*, **šale** *shallow*, **šap**
shape, **tale** *tallow*, **tan** *to tan*, **tap** *tap*, **tate(r)** *tatter*, **tlam**
(see N.E.D. sub **clem**) *to famish*, **tlap** *clap*, **tlate(r)** *to clatter*,
trap *trap*, **tšavl** *to nibble at, gnaw, chew*, **þak** *thatch*, **ðat**
(see § 354) *that*, pret. **þrast** (§ 367, 4) *thrust*.

§ 58. **a** preceded by **w** and not followed by **r** + consonant (§ 61), **g**, **ɒ**, **š** (§ 59), has become **o**. It has also
become **o** when followed by **ls, lt** :

swole *swallow*, **swom** *swam*, **swon** *swan*, **swop** *to exchange,
barter*, **wokɒ** *to waken*, **woks** *wax*, **wonde(r)** *to wander*,
wont *want*, **wo(r)** (emphatic from § 396) *was*, **wot** *what*,
wote(r) *water*, **wotš** *watch*.

fols *false*, **molt** *malt*, **olt** *halt*, **solt** *salt*.

a has also become **o** in **omest** *almost*, **oles** *always*, **moni**
many.

§ 59. **a**, followed by **g**, **ɒ**, **š**, has become **e** :

benɒ (cp. O.Icel. **banga** *to hammer*) *to throw violently*,
benk *bank*, pret. **brenɒ** *brought*, pret. **denɒ** (§ 367) *reviled,
reproached*, **drenk** *drank*, pret. **enɒ** (§ 367) *hung*, **enɒ** *to hang*,
enk *hank*, **enkl** *ancle*, **enke(r)** *anchor*, **emenɒ** *among*, pret.
flenɒ (§ 367) *threw*, **genɒ** *gang*, **genɒ-wee** *thoroughfare, passage*,
kenke(r) (ME. **cancren**) *to become rusty*, **krenk** *crank*, **lenɒ**
to long for, **lenɒ-setl** *a long bench with a high back*, **lenɒ**
(this form is gradually going out of use. The younger

people say loŋ) *long*, neŋ to *gnaw as a pain*, neŋ-neel (sec
N.E.D. sub **agnail**) *corn on the foot*, preŋk *prank, trick*,
pret. reŋ (§ 367) *rang*, reŋ *wrong*, reŋk *rank*, reŋl (ME.
wrangleŋ) *to pull the hair of the head*, pret. seŋ *sang*, seŋ
(this form is now seldom heard among the younger people.
Its place is gradually being supplanted by soŋ) *song*, seŋk
sank, pret. sleŋ *slung*, pret. sleŋk *slunk*, speŋk *to beat, hit*,
spreŋ *sprang*, pret. steŋk *stunk*, pret. steŋ *stung*, streŋ
(archaic, stroŋ is now generally used) *strong*, pret. sweŋ
swung, sweŋki *small beer*, šeŋk *shank*, pret. šreŋk *shrunk*,
teŋ (cp. ME. tange, O.Icel. tangi *sting, dagger*) *a sting, to sting*,
teŋz *tongs*, pret. tleŋ *clung*, tleŋk *to beat, flog*, þreŋ *busy*,
þeŋk *to thank*, weŋ *thong*. muŋe(r) *monger* is a loan-word.

beg *bag*, bleg *blackberry*, breg *to brag*, deg (cp. Swed.
dagga *to bedew*) *to sprinkle with water*, dreg *to drag*, fleg
flag, geg (ME. **gaggin**) *to gag*, reg *rag*, seg (ME. **saggin** *to
sink down*) *to distend*, stege(r) *to stagger*, šeg *shag*, tleg
(Lowland Scot. **clag**) *to stick to, as thick mud to the boots*,
tlegi *sticky, dirty (of roads), stopped up with dirt*, weg *to
wag*, wegŋ *wagon*.

eš *ash-tree*, leš (ME. **laschin**) *to comb*, meš (cp. § 125)
mash, peš (ME. **paschen**) *to dash, strike hard*, pleš (Swed.
plaska) *to splash*, reš *rash*, smeš *smash*, weš *to wash*.

§ 60. In the following words we have e which in
many of the examples is no doubt the i-umlaut of a : besk
to bask, elte(r) (Prompt. Parv. heltir, Town. Myst. heltere,
Stratmann) *halter*, esked (cp. ME. **aske** *lizard*) *newt, eft*,
espin *aspin*, etš (ME. **hacchen**) *to hatch*, fest *fast*, geðe(r),
to gather, te-geðe(r) *together*, kest (ME. **kesten**) *to cast*, kredl
cradle, swetš (OE. **swæcc** *taste*) *a small sample of cloth,
cotton*, etc., weðe(r) *whether*, wesp *wasp*, ev *have*, ez *hast,
has*, ed *had*.

§ 61. a + medial r has become ā before consonants :
ād *hard*, ādn *to harden*, ām *harm*, ām *arm*, āp *harp*, āt
thou art, āvis(t) *harvest*, bāk *bark*, bāli *barley*, bān *child*,
dān *to darn*, fān *fern*, jād (OE. geard) *yard*, jān *yarn*, kăt
cart, māk *mark*, pāk *park*, spāk *spark*, stāk (always used
in combination with some other word, as stāk mad *very
angry*, stāk neekt *quite naked*, cp. OE. stearc *strong, severe*),
stākɒ (OE. stearcian) *to grow stiff, stiffen*, swăm *swarm*,
swāþ (OE. sweard) *the skin of bacon*, swūþi *swarthy*, šăp
sharp, tādz *towards*, wād *ward*, wāf *wharf*, wāk (OE wærc)
pain, as verb *to ache*, wăm *warm*, wăn *to warn*, wāp *warp*,
wāt *wart*.

But it has become āə before medial and final r in : āə(r)
are, dāə(r) *dare*.

§ 62. eal, al has become oə in the combinations lf,
OE. lh, lk, ll, (l), lm, lv :

lf : koef *calf*, koef *calf (of the leg)*, oef *half*, oəpni *halfpenny*, oəpəþ *halfpennyworth*.

lh : woef, woefl (OE. walh *sickly taste*) *sickly to the smell,
insipid to the taste*.

lk : boek (OE. balca) *balk, beam*, stoek *stalk, stem*, toek
to talk, woek *to walk*, tšoek *chalk*.

ll, (l) : boeld (ME. balled) *bald*, foel *to fall*, foel *a veil*,
goel *gall*, koel (cp. kal § 57) *to call*, oel *all*, oel *hall*, smoel
small, stoel *stall*, woel *wall*.

lm : poem *palm*. lv : soəv *salve*.

§ 63. ME. aw (of various origins) has become oə :
doən *dawn*, droe *to draw*, kroel *crawl*, loe *law*, moek
(ME. mauk Stratmann) *maggot*, oek *hawk*, oel *awl*, pret.
soə *saw*, tloe *claw*.

§ 64. al has become ou before a following d :
boud *bold*, foud *fold*, foud *to fold*, koud *cold*, oud *old*.

The regularly developed form oud *to hold* is now only used
in the phrase **oud on** *stop!* The usual form **od** *to hold*, is a
new formation from the past participle **odn**, where the stem
vowel has been regularly shortened before the following n.

§ **65.** ME. **ai, ei** from OE. **æg** has become **ee** :
breen *brain*, **dee** *day*, **deezi** *daisy*, **eel** (OE. **hægl**) *hail*,
feen (OE. **fægen**) *glad, fain, gladly*, **fee(r)** *fair*, **mee**
(shortened in **mebi** *perhaps, possibly*) *may*, **meen** *main*,
neel *nail*, **peel** *pail*, **slee** (a new formation from the past
participle) *to slay* ; **sleen** *slain*, **sneel** *snail*, **teel** *tail*.

§ **66.** **a** became lengthened to **ā** before **mb** already in
early ME., as is shown by the forms in the Ormulum. This
ā fell together with OE. **ā** = Germanic **ai**, and has accordingly become **ue** (see § 122) in the Windhill dialect :
kuem *comb*, **wuem** *womb*. **lam** *lamb* is a new formation
from the plural, where the short vowel was regularly
retained, cp. Ormulum acc. sing. **lamb** (i. 274) beside acc.
plural **lammbre** (ii. 109). The word-lists in vol. v of
Ellis' Early English Pronunciation show that all English
dialects have a short vowel in this word.

§ **67.** **a** has become **ei** in **eit** *eight*, **eit'** (with suspended
t) *eighth*. In **meitš** *to measure* the **ei** seems to point to an
OE. **ǣ** (cp. §§ 132, 138).

§ **68.** **a** has become **ie** in **bied** *beard*, **gie(r)** *gear*, **ierin**
herring.

§ **69.** **æ** (**a**) has become **ē** in **gēs** (OE. **gærs**, ME. **gers**)
grass ; and **oi** in **loin** (OE. **lane, lone**) *lane*, which has had
the same development as old **o** in open syllables. See § 109.

§ **70.** Short **a** in originally open syllables has usually
become **ee** But see § 71.
Examples are : **beed** *to bathe*, **beek** *to bake*, but **bak-stn** (lit.

bake-stone) *the iron plate on which oat cakes are baked,*
beə(r) *bare*, pret. bee(r) *bore*, bleed *blade*, bleez *to blaze,*
deel *dale*, dleə(r) (ME. glarin) *to stare hard*, dreeg (OE.
dragan) *to drawl*, dreek *drake*, eeg (OE. haga) *the berry
of the hawthorn* (the tree is called tšīz en brīed trī lit.
cheese and bread tree), eekə(r) *acre*, eel *ale*, ee(r) *hare,*
eet *to hate*, be-eev *to behave*, fee(r) *to fare*, fleek *flake,*
freem (OE. framian) *to make a start or beginning*, nītin-
geel *nightingale*, geep *to gape*, e-geet *in action, at work,*
geet *gate*, greev *grave*, greez *to graze*, keek *bread of
every kind*, kee(r) *care*, kreev *to crave*, leedl *ladle*, leem
lame, leeð (O.Icel. hlaða) *barn*, meed *made*, meeg (OE.
maga) *maw*, meen *mane*, nīt-mee(r) *nightmare*, meet (M.
Low Germ. mate) *mate*, neeg (OE. gnagan) *to gnaw*, neekt
naked, neem *name*, preet (cp. Swed. prata) *to prate, babble,*
reek *rake*, reeðe(r) *rather*, seeg (OE. sage) *a saw*, seek *sake,*
seel *sale*, seem *same*, skeelz *scales*, skreep *to scrape*, sneek
snake, snee(r) *snare*, speed *spade*, speen (OE. spanan) *to
wean*, spee(r) *to spare*, steek *stake*, steel (pret.) *stole*, stee(r)
to stare, steevz *staves*, sweep *the handle of a machine*, šeed
shade, šeem *shame*, šee(r) *share*, šeev *to shave*, teel *tale,*
teem *tame*, teen *taken*, weed *to wade*, weel *whale*, ween *to
wane*, wee(r) (ME. waren) *to spend or lay out money,*
weev *wave*, weeve(r) *to waver.*

§ 71. æ (a) appears as a in: gavlek (OE. gafoluc *spear*)
crowbar, mak *to make*, ransak (O.Icel. rannsaka *to search a
house*) *to ransack*, tak (O.Icel. taka) *to take*, šak *to shake,*
šakl *shackle*, sadl *saddle*, stapl *staple*, faðe(r) *father*, laðe(r)
foam, froth. On the stem-vowel in the last five words cp.
the similar double development in German in such words as
Schemel, Vater, nehmen, beside Semmel, Vetter, kommen.
See Paul-Braune's Beiträge, vol. ix. pp. 101–135.

e.

§ 72. West Germanic e and the OE. e which arose from the i-umlaut of a(o) have fallen together in the W. dialect as also in all other Mod. Engl. dialects, at least so far as can be ascertained from the word-lists in Ellis' EEP. vol. v.

§ 73. e (= old e and the i-umlaut of a(o)) in originally closed syllables usually appears as e in the W. dialect; and also when e was originally followed by a single consonant + a suffix containing an l, m, n, r.

I. Old e:

beg (OE. bedecian) *to beg*, bele *to bellow*, bel *bell*, delf *a stone quarry*, delv *to delve*, elde(r)-trī *elder*, elm *elm*, elp *help*, etn *eaten*, enent *anent, opposite*, evm *heaven;* felt *felt*, feðe(r) *feather*, freš *fresh*, getn (pp.) *got*, jel *yell*, jelp *yelp*, kres *cress*, leðe(r) *leather*, melt *to melt*, nest *nest*, nevi (OE. nefa, gen. nefan) *nephew*, rekn *to reckon*, sel(sen) *self*, seldn (OE. seldon) *seldom*, sevm *seven*, skelp (ME. skelpen) *to beat, flog*, skep (O. Icel. skeppa) *a large wicker basket for holding spinning bobbins*, etc., smel *to smell*, smelt *to smelt*, spek *speck*, swel *to swell*, swelt (OE. sweltan) *to faint, be overpowered by heat*, twenti *twenty*, þreš *to thresh*, þrešld *threshold*, weft *weft*, west *west*, weðe(r) (OE. weder) *weather*, weðe(r) (OE. weðer) *the wool of a sheep which has already been shorn at least once before*.

2. i-umlaut of a(o):

bed *bed*, bef (Germ. bäffen *to bark*) *to cough*, bek (O. Icel. bekkr) *beck*, beli *belly*, belesez *bellows*, belt *belt*, bend *to bend*, benk *bench*, best *best*, bete(r) *better*, blend *to blend*, dregz *dregs*, drenš *to drench*, eb *ebb*, edž *edge*, edž *hedge*, eft (O. Icel. hepti) *haft*, eg (O. Icel. eggia) *to urge, incite*,

D

eg (O. Iccl. egg) *egg*, el *hell*, els *else*, em *hem*, en *hen*, end
end, esp (O. Icel. hespa) *hasp*, evi *heavy*, fel *to fell*, kemp
(ME. kempe) *short coarse white hairs in wool*, ketl *kettle*,
leg (O. Icel. leggr) *leg*, lenþ (by assimilation) *length*, men
men, mens (OE. mennisc *dignity, honour*) *neatness*, neb
bill, beak, nek *neck*, net *net*, netl *nettle*, pen *pen*, peni
penny, rest *rest*, retš *wretch*, seg *sedge*, sek (O. Icel. sekkr)
sack, sel *to sell*, send *to send*, sent *sent*, set *to set*, slek
small coal, slek (OE. ge-sleccan) *to extinguish a fire*, etc.
with water, snek (ME. snekke) *the latch of a door*, spend *to
spend*, stem *stem*, step *step*, strenþ (by assimilation) *strength*,
stretš *to stretch*, šel *shell*, šelf *shelf*, tel *to tell*, temz (cp. OE.
temsian *to strain, pass through a sieve*) *a coarse hair sieve*,
tletš (cp. O. Icel. klekia *to hatch, bring forth*) *brood of
chickens*, twelft *twelfth*, twelv *twelve*, web *web*, wed (OE.
weddian) *to wed, marry*, wedž *wedge*, wel (noun) *well*,
welp *whelp*, oue(r)-welt (O. Icel. velta) *to turn over, upset*,
went *went*, wet-stn *whet-stone*.

§ 74. er in the combination er + consonant has partly
become ā and partly iə. The reasons for this twofold
development are not clear. It is probable that the words
belonging to the latter category have been influenced by
the literary language :

āt *heart*, bāk *to bark*, bākm (OE. beorg + ham N.E.D.
sub bargham) *collar of a horse*, bām *barm*, bān (OE. bern)
barn, dāk *dark*, dwāf *dwarf*, fāt (ME. ferten) *pedere*, kāv
to carve, smāt *smart*, stāv *to starve*, wāk (noun) *work*, wāte
(lit. work-day) *week-day*.

Before final r we have āə : fāə(r) (OE. feorr) *far*, stāə(r)
(OE. steorra) *star*, wāə(r) (O. Icel. verre) *worse*.

iənist *earnest*, iəþ *earth*, jiəd (3 feet) *yard*, jiən *yearn*,
liən *learn*.

The following words seem to have been borrowed from the literary language : bēn to *burn*, gēn (with metathesis) to *grin*, wēþ *worth*, sued (older swēd) *sword*.

§ 75. e has become ie before r not followed by another consonant: bie(r) to *bear*, pie(r) *pear*, smie(r) to *smear*, spie(r) *spear*, swie(r) to *swear*, wie(r) to *wear*, šie(r) to *shear*. The only exceptions are : tāe(r) *tar*, mee(r) *mare*.

§ 76. e (i-umlaut of a) has become i before original ꬻ (now ꬻ or nž): iꬻ (ME. hengen, O. Icel. hengia) to *hang*, inž *hinge*, iꬻlnd *England*, iꬻliš *English*, diꬻ *up* (O. Icel. dengia to *beat, strike*) to *reproach*, fliꬻ (ME. flingen) to *fling, throw*, krinž to *cringe*, liꬻe(r) to *linger*, miꬻl to *mingle*, sinž to *singe*, sliꬻ to *sling*, striꬻ *string*, þink to *think*, wiꬻ *wing*.

§ 77. e has become i in : giv, gi to *give*, kil to *kill*, milk *milk*, rid *rid*, siks *six*, sikst *sixth*, silve(r) *silver*, siste(r) (probably from O. Icel. syster) *sister*, šil (ME. schellen, but Prom. Parv. p. 446 has schillin, Stratmann) to *shell peas*, etc., wile *willow*, witš *which*.

§ 78. e has become ī before ld : fīld *field*, jīld to *yield*, šīld *shield*, wīld to *wield*.

§ 79. The following words also have ī : bīzm *besom*, dī (ME., Ormulum deჳen) to *die*, wīl (adv.) *well*, but see § 399, wīzl *weazel*, and gīn *given*.

§ 80. e has become o in : fotš (OE. feccan, Town. Myst. fetche, foche, inf. fott, Sweet, HES. p. 315) to *fetch*, jole *yellow*, jon *yon*, swole (OE. swelgan, ME., Ormulum swollჳhen) to *swallow*. We have oe in joen (OE. geonian, also gānian) to *yawn*.

§ 81. e has become ə in : beri *berry*, (ə)levm *eleven*, jəst *yeast*, jestede *yesterday*, jet *yet*.

§ 82. e has become ie in: estied *instead*, friet *to fret*, bewail, *mourn over*, riep *to reap*, but cp. Sievers, OE. Gr. § 382, 3.

§ 83. OE. eol has become ue in : juek *yolk*.

§ 84. ME. ei from OE. eg, O. Icel. ei has become ee :

breed (OE. bregdan) *to resemble, act like another person*, geen (OE. gegn) *near, direct*, lee *to lay*, leed *laid*, leen *lain*, reen *rain*, see *to say*, seel *sail*, wee *way*, ewee *away*.

been (O. Icel. beinn) *near, direct*, beet *bait*, nee *nay*, steek *steak*, ðee (accented form) *they*, ðee(r) (accented form) *their*.

e has also become ee in feevr(r) *fever*.

§ 85. e(eo) + w has become eu: eu *ewe*, streu *to strew*.

§ 86. The combination eht has become eit: feit *to fight*, reit *right*, streit *straight*.

§ 87. Short e in open syllables has generally become ei :

beid *bead*, breitš (O. Fris. breke) *a breach*, eit *to eat*, bried-fleik (O. Icel. fleki *hurdle*) *a hurdle on which oat-cakes are dried*, meil *meal-flower*, meit *meat*, neid *to knead*, neiv (O. Icel. knefi) *fist*, pei (ME. pese) *pea*, speik *to speak*, bed-steid *bedstead*, steil *to steal*, steil (OE. stel) *the handle of a pot* or *jug*, steim (OE. ge-stefnian, a-stemnian *to give voice for, appoint*) *to bespeak*, treid *to tread*, wei (OE. wegan) *to weigh*, weik (ME. weke) *the wick of a lamp* or *candle*, weiv *to weave*.

§ 88. Short e in open syllables has remained in : brek *to break*, get (O. Icel. geta) *to get*, lek (O. Icel. leka) *to leak*.

i.

§ 89. OE. i has generally remained :

bid *to invite to a funeral*, pp. bidn, big *big, large*, bil *bill*, bin (OE. binnan) *within*, bind *to bind*, biŋ (ME. biŋg, O. Icel. biŋgr) *a bin*, bit *a bit*, bitə(r) *bitter*, bitn *bitten*, bitš *bitch*, biznəs *business*, blind *blind*, blis *bliss*, brim (ME. brimmən, cp. O. Icel. brimi *burning heat*) *to put the boar to the sow*, briŋ *to bring*, dig *to dig*, dim *dim*, diš *dish*, diðə(r) (ME. diderin) *to tremble, shiver with cold*, dlitə(r) *to glitter*, drift *drift*, driŋk *to drink*, drivṃ *driven*, fidl *fiddle*, fikl *fickle*, film *film*, fin *fin*, find *to find*, fiŋə(r) *finger*, fiš *fish*, fit *ready, prepared*, flik *flitch*, flikə(r) *to flicker*, flint *flint*, gidi *giddy*, gift *gift*, gilt (OE. gilte, O. Icel. gilta) *a young female pig*, bə-gin *to begin*, grind *to grind*, grip *grip*, if *if*, ik *to hitch*, il *ill*, ilt *hilt*, im *him*, in, i *in*, ində(r) (occ. inðə(r)) *to hinder*, bi-int *behind*, it *it*, it *to hit*, iðə(r) *hither*, iz *is*, iz *his*, kid *kid*, kiŋ-kof *whooping-cough*, kiŋk (ME. kinken *to pant, gasp*) *to cough* (of whooping-cough), kist (O. Icel. kista) *chest, box*, kit (ME. kitte) *a pail*, kitl (ME. kitelen) *to tickle*, krisp *crisp*, lid *lid*, lig (OE. licgan) *to lie down*, lik *to lick*, lim *limb*, lip *lip*, liv *to live*, livə(r) *liver*, midl *middle*, miks *to mix*, mil-deu *mildew*, mint *mint*, mis *to miss*, mizl-tuə *mistletoe*, mist *mist*, mitš *much*, nibl *to nibble*, niml *nimble*, nit (OE. hnitu) *nit*, pig *pig*, pigin *a small water-can*, pitš *pitch*, piþ *pith*, prik *to prick*, prikl *prickle*, rib *rib*, ridl (ME. ridil Prom. Parv. p. 433, Stratmann) *sieve*, ridn *ridden*, rift (ME. riftən) *to belch, eructate*, rim *rim*, rind *rind*, riŋ *ring*, riŋ *to wring*, riŋkl *wrinkle*, rist *wrist*, rizn *risen*, ritn *written*, sift *to sift*, sikl *sickle*, grun-sil *groundsel*, silk *silk*, sin *since*, sində(r) *cinder*, siŋ *to sing*, siŋk *to sink*, sit *to sit*, siv *sieve*, skift *to shift, remove*, skin *skin*, skil *skill*, slidn (pp.) *slid*, sliŋk *to slink*, slip *to slip*, slipi *slippery*, slitn (pp.) *slit*, smitl *to infect*, smitn *smitten*, smiþ *smith*, smiði *smithy*, spil *to spill*, spin *to spin*, spinl *spindle*, spit *to spit*, spitək *spigot*, spriŋ *to spring*, stik *stick*, stik *to stick*, stil *still*, stiŋ *to sting*, stiŋk *to stink,* stitš *stitch,* strikᴅ *stricken,* swift *swift,* swil (OE. swilian) *to rinse, wash out,* swilinz *thin liquid food for pigs,* swim *to swim,* swiᴅ *to swing,* šift *chemise,* šilin *shilling,* šin *shin,* šip *ship,* šrimp *shrimp,* šriᴅk *to shrink,* tik *tick,* til *to till,* tin *tin,* tit, titi (OE. tit) *breastmilk,* tlim *to climb,* tliᴅ *to cling,* tlip *to clip,* tšikin *chicken,* tšildə(r) (only used in the plural, for the sing. bān is always used) *children,* tšin *chin,* twig *twig,* twin *twin,* twiᴅkl *to twinkle,* twist *twist,* þik *thick, friendly, in love with,* þiᴅ *thing,* þisl *thistle,* þrift *thrift,* ðis *this,* wi *with,* widə *widow, widower,* wik (O. Icel. vik *stirring, moving) quick, alive,* wik *week,* wil (accented form) *will,* win *to win,* wind *wind,* wind *to wind,* wində *window,* wintə(r) *winter,* wiᴅk *to wink,* wispə(r) *to whisper,* wisl *to whistle,* wit *wit,* witl (ME. þwitel) *large carving knife,* witš *witch,* wizn (OE. wisnian *to dry up) to wither.*

§ 90. ir + consonant has become ə̄ + consonant:
bə̄d *bird,* bə̄k *birch,* gə̄sl *gristle,* ə̄d *herd,* tšə̄tš (but kə̄-gət *kirkgate) church,* þə̄d *third,* þə̄ti *thirty,* wə̄l *to whirl.*

§ 91. i has become ə in: gosəp *gossip,* jəs *yes,* stərək (OE. stirc, styric) *heifer,* ə(r) *her,* tšərəp *to chirp.*

§ 92. i has been lengthened before ld: mīld *mild,* wīld *wild.* But tšildə(r) (only used in the plural, for the sing. bān is used) *children,* owing to the following suffix.

§ 93. ME. iht has become īt: brīt *bright,* līt *light, levis,* līts *the lungs of animals,* mīt (noun) *might,* nīt *night,* shortened in fotnit *fortnight,* plīt *plight,* sīt *sight,* slīt *slight,* tīt *tight.* weit (OE. gewihte) has been influenced by wei *to weigh.*

§ 94. Medial OE. ig has become ī in: stī *sty, ladder,* stīl (OE. stigel) *stile,* tīl *tile.*

§ 95. i has become **ai** in: **ai** (accented form, see § 350) *I*.

§ 96. iw has become iu: **tliu** (OE. **cliwe**) *a ball of string* or *worsted*.

§ 97. i has become u in: **kud** (OE. **cwidu**) *cud*, ruš *rush*, **tul** *to*.

§ 98. i has become ie in: **flie(r)** (Norw. **flira**) *to laugh* or *sneer at*, **striek** *streak, stripe*, ðiez *these*.

§ 99. i has become e in: **lenit** (ME. **lynet**, probably from Fr. **linotte**) *linnet*.

O.

§ 100. OE. o (= West Germanic o) in originally closed syllables has usually remained **o**; and also when **o** was originally followed by a single consonant + a suffix containing an l, m, n, r :

blob (see N.E.D.) *a bubble, bulb,* **bodm** *bottom,* **boks** *box,* **bore** *to borrow,* **brokᴅ** *broken,* **broþ** *broth,* **dof** *to undress,* **dog** *dog,* **dokᴅ** (OE. **docce**) *a dock,* **dolt** *lump of dirt,* **don** *to dress,* **drop** *drop,* **džogl** (cp. ME. **joggen**) *to shake,* **flok** *flock,* **fog** (ME. **fogge**) *aftergrass,* **foks** *fox,* **fole** *to follow,* **fond** (ME. **fonned**, pp. of **fonnen** *be foolish*) *fond,* **fotn** (pp.) *fought,* **frog** *frog,* **frost** *frost,* **froþ** *froth,* **frozn** *frozen,* **god** *god,* **gospl** *gospel,* **kob-web** *cob,* **kod** *cod,* **kof** *cough,* **kok** *cock,* **kokl** *cockle,* **kolep** (ME. **colop,** cp. O. Swed. **kollops**) *slice (of bacon),* **kope(r)** *copper,* **kroft** (OE. **croft**) *a small field,* **krop** *crop,* **kros** *cross,* **loft** *loft,* **lok** *lock,* **loks** *small pieces of wool which have been detached from the fleece,* **lop** (OE. **lopp**) *flea,* **loped** (ME. **lopren** *coagulate*) *clotted, covered with dirt,* **lopste(r)** *lobster,* **lost** *lost,* **lot** *lot,* **mos** *moss,* **moþ** *moth,* **nod** (ME. **nodden**) *nap, short sleep,* **nok**

to knock, not *knot*, **notš** *notch*, **od** *odd*, **ofl** *offal*,. **oft** *oft*,
often, **og** (ME. **hog**) *the first year's wool of a sheep*, **oks** *ox*,
olə *hollow*, **olin** (OE. **holen**) *the holly-tree, twig of the holly-
tree*, **on** (accented form) *on*, **op** *to hop*, **opm** *open*, **otə(r)**
otter, **otšəd** *orchard*, **ovl** *hovel*, **plot** *plot*, **poks** *pox*, **prod** *to
prick, goad*, **rok** *rock*, **rot** *to rot*, **slop** (O. Icel. **sloppr**) *the
leg of a pair of trousers*, **slot** (ME. **slot**) *bolt of a door*,
smok *smock*, **snod** (O. Icel. **snoðinn** *smooth (of hair)*),
smooth, even, **snodn** *to make smooth*, **snot** *snot*, **sod** *sod*,
sodnd *saturated, wet through*, **sok** *sock*, **sorə** *sorrow*, **spokṇ**
spoken, **spot** *spot*, **stok** *stock*, **stop** *to stop*, **šop** *shop*, **šot** *shot*,
šotn (pp.) *shot*, **tlog** *a shoe with wooden soles*, **tlok** *the common black beetle*, **tlok** *to cluck*, **tlot** *clot*, **tlovm** *cloven*, **top**
top, **topin** (ME. **topping**) *the front part of the hair of the
head*, **topl** *to fall over*, **tot** *a small beer glass*, **trodn** *trodden*,
trof *trough*, **tšozn** *chosen*, **þrosl** (OE. **þrostle**) *thrush*, **þrotl**
(ME. **þrotlen**) *to press on the windpipe*, **wovm** *woven*.

§ 101. **oht** has become **out**: **bout** *bought*, **doutə(r)**
daughter, **rout** *wrought*. We have however **o** in **fotn**
(§ 100) *fought*.

§ 102. ME. **ow** (=OE. **og**) has become **ou**: **reen-bou**
rain-bow, **floun** *flown*.

§ 103. **ol**+consonant has become **ou**+consonant: **boul**
bowl, **boustə(r)** *bolster*, **bout** *bolt*, **fouk** *folk*, **goud** *gold*,
kouk (see N.E.D. sub. **colk**) *coke, cinder*, **kout** *colt*, **out** *holt*,
moud-wāp *a mole*, **stoun** *stolen*, **toul** *toll*.

But we have **o** in **wod** (accented form) *would*; and **u** in
sud (accented form) *should*; and **oe** in **noep** (ME. **nolpen**
to strike) *to beat, strike*.

§ 104. The development of **o** before a following **r**:
(1) **oe**: **boen** *born*, **foek** *fork*, **koen** *corn*, **tə-moen** *to-*

morrow, moən, moənin *morning,* noəþ *north,* oən *horn,*
oəs *horse,* stoəm *storm,* swoən *sworn,* šoen *shorn,* šoet
short, toən *torn,* þoən *thorn.*

(2) uə: ə-fuə(r) *before,* smuə(r) (OE. smorian) *to smother,*
suffocate.

buəd *board,* ə-fuəd *afford,* uəd *hoard.*

(3) ō̆: spə̄(r) *spur,* wə̄d *word,* wə̄ld *world.*

§ 105. o has become uə in: buekɒ (ME. bolkin) *to
belch, retch,* fluet *float,* kuev *cove,* juek *yoke,* uep *hope,* nuez
nose, puek (OE. poca) *sack,* pueni *pony,* puest (OE. post
from Lat. postis) *post,* ruez *a rose,* stuev *stove,* suek *to soak,*
suep (OE. sopa *sup, small quantity (of water))* *a little tea*
or *beer,* etc., tšuek *to choke.*

NOTE.—Most, if not all, of the above words are early borrowings from the
literary language.

§ 106. o has become ū in: smūk *to smoke,* šūl *shovel,*
stūp (ME. stolpe) *a post.*

§ 107. o has become u in: dul *dull,* foks-dluv *fox-
glove,* flute(r) *to flutter,* kus (noun, also used as verb)
kiss, uvm *oven.* It is very probable that the u in some of
these words goes back to OE. y (§ 121), as has been
pointed out by Prof. Napier in the Academy, May 7,
1892, p. 447.

§ 108. o has become ə through loss of stress in: ð̌en
then, wen *when.*

§ 109. o in originally open syllables has generally
become oi: boil (O.Icel. bolr, ME. bole) *bole of a tree,* foil
foal, goit (ME. gote) *channel, mill-stream,* koil *coal,* pig-
coit (OE. cot, cote) *pig-sty,* loin (OE. lone) *lane,* loiz (OE.
losian) *to lose,* moit *mote,* oil *hole,* roid (mostly used in the
plural roidz) *a clearing (of a wood),* soil (OE. sol) *ground,*

earth, soil (OE. sole, Lat. solea) *sole*, tlois (OE. close) *a field*, toidi *very small*, þoil (OE. þolian *to endure*) *to give ungrudgingly*, þroit *throat*.

§ 110. Short o in open syllables has remained in : bodi (OE. bodig) *body*, popi (OE. popig) *poppy*.

u.

§ 111. Short u has generally remained unchanged :

bluðe(r) *to cry, weep*, buk *buck*, bul *bull*, bulek *bullock*, bun (pp. of bind) *bound, obliged, beholden*, bute(r) *butter*, busl *to bustle*, drukŋ (pp.) *drunk*, dub *a small pool of water*, dum *dumb*, dun *to urge for payment*, duŋ *dung*, ful *full*, fule(r) *fuller*, fun (pp.) *found*, grunsil *groundsel*, grunt *to grunt, grumble, find fault*, grund *ground*, grunz (pl.) *sediment*, be-gun *begun*, gust *gust*, guts (OE. gutt) *entrails, belly*, juŋ *young*, krudl (cp. ME. cruddin) *to curdle*, krudz (ME. crudde) *curds*, krum *crumb*, krumpl *to crumple*, kudl *to embrace*, kuf (kuft) *cuff*, kum *to come*, kunin *cunning*, kup *cup*, lug (ME. luggen, Swed. lugga *to lug, drag*) *to pull the hair of the head*, luŋ *lung*, luv *love*, muml *to mumble*, mun (accented form, O.Icel. muna *will, shall*) *must*, musl *mussel*, num *numb*, nut *nut*, pluk *to pluck*, pund *a pound*, rudi *ruddy*, ruŋ *wrung*, skuft *the nape of the neck*, skul *skull (of the head)*, skute(r) *to spill*, sluŋ *slung*, spruŋ *sprung*, spun *spun*, stubi (cp. O.Icel. stubbi *stock of a tree*) *short and stiff*, stump *stump*, stun *to stun*, stuŋ *stung*, stut (cp. ME. stutten *to cease, stay*) *to stutter*, sum *some*, sume(r) *summer*, sumet (lit. somewhat) *something, anything*, sump *a puddle or dirty pool of water*, sun *son*, sun *sun*, sunde *Sunday*, sukŋ *sunk*, suŋ *sung*, swum (pp.) *swum*, swuŋ *swung*, šrukŋ *shrunk*, šun *to shun*, šŭðe(r) (ME. schuderen) *to shudder*, tluɒ *clung*, tluste(r) *cluster*, tub (ME. tubbe) *tub*, tug (ME. tuggen) *to tug, plod*, tuml *to tumble*, tun *tun*, tuɒ *tongue*, tup (ME. tuppe) *a ram*, tusk *tusk*, tšuf *proud, haughty*, ug *to carry*, ugli *ugly*, ugɒ (see Notes and Queries i. 10. 400, Nov. 18, 1854) *hip*, ulz (ME. huls) *bean-swads*, unded *hundred*, unde(r) *under*, uni *honey*, unt *to hunt*, uɒe(r) *hunger*, þune(r) *thunder*, wud *wood*, wulzi *wollen*, wun (pp.) *wound*, wun (pp.) *won*, wund *wound*, wunde(r) *wonder*.

§ 112. u has become ū in : būk, būkþ (ME. bulke, O.Icel. bulki) *bulk, size*, e-būn (OE. on-bufan) *above*, mūfin *muffin*, pūl *to pull*, šūlde(r) (this word has been influenced by the literary language. Most old people still say šūðe(r)) *shoulder*, wūl *wool* (but wulzi *wollen*).

§ 113. u before a following r.

(1) ē : dēst *durst*, kēs *to curse*, skēf *scurf*, snēt (ME. snurtin, cp. Low Germ. snurten *to snort, snore*) *to sneeze, giggle*, tēn *to turn*, tēf *turf*.

(2) e : bere *borough*, eri *row, disturbance, noise*, fere *furrow*.

(3) ue : due(r) *door*, muen *to mourn*. It is highly probable, however, that muen has nothing to do with OE. murnan, but is simply muen *to moan* (§ 122).

§ 114. Medial ug has become ā : fāl (OE. fugol) *fowl*, kāl (OE. cugle) *cowl*, sā (OE. sugu) *sow*.

§ 115. u underwent early lengthening, and then had the same further development as old ū (§ 171) in : ānd *hound*, bāns (ME. bunsen) *to bounce*, drānd (OE. druncnian) *to drown*.

§ 116. u has become iu in : þriu (þrift) *through, from, on account of.*

y.

§ 117. y (= the i-umlaut of u) has generally become i :
bizi *busy*, brig *bridge*, brim *brim*, brimstn *brimstone*, did
did, didl (cp. OE. dyderian) *to cheat*, din *din*, dip *to dip*,
dizi *dizzy*, fil *to fill*, flig (ME. fligge, cp. OHG. fiukke *able
to fly*) *to fledge*, flit *to remove*, kiln *kiln*, ekin *akin*, kinl *to
bring forth (of rabbits)*, kinlin *firewood*, kiᴅ *king*, kripl
cripple, kitšn *kitchen*, ig (OE. hyge *mind*) *mood, temper*,
il *hill*, inš *inch*, ip *hip*, ipin *a cloth placed round the hips of
children*, lift *to lift*, liᴅ (O.Icel. lyng) *heather*, lisn *to listen*,
mig *midge*, miln *mill*, nit *to knit*, pile *pillow*, pit *pit*, rig
(OE. hrycg) *back*, rigin *ridge of a house*, sil *sill*, sin *sin*,
kā-slip *cowslip*, snift *to sniff, scent*, stint *to stint*, tlik (OE.
clycc(e)an, see N.E.D. sub clitch) *to seize, snatch, catch hold*,
tlip *to clip*, trim *to trim*, þin *thin*.

§ 118. yht has become īt : flīt *flight*, frīt *fright*, rīt
wright.

§ 119. y has become ī before ld : bīld *to build*, gīld *to
gild*.

§ 120. y before a following r.

(1) ō̄: bōdn *burden*, bōl āt (OE. byrlian) *to draw or
pour out (drink to or for anyone)*, bōþ *birth*, ōdl *hurdle*,
fōst *first*, gōdl *girdle*, kōnl *kernel*, mōþe(r) *to murder*, mōki
mirky, šōt *shirt*, tōd (cp. OE. tyrdel, Stratmann) *turd*,
wōk *to work*, wōm *worm*.

(2) e: beri *to bury*, meri *merry*, sperinz (cp. OE.
spyrian) *banns of marriage*, ste(r) *to stir*, weri *to worry*,
fig-wet *figwort*.

§ 121. y has become u in : bluš *to blush*, bruslz *bristles*,
bunl *bundle*, krutš *crutch*, muk *muck*, stubl *stubble*, šut
to shut, šutl *shuttle*, trunl *trundle*.

2. The Long Vowels.

ā.

§ 122. The normal development of OE. ā in the W. dialect is uə:

bruəd *broad*, buən *bone*, buə(r) *boar*, buət *boat*, buəþ *both*, druən *drone*, druəv (noun) *drove*, duə *doe*, duəf *dough*, duəfl *cowardly*, duəl *dole*, fuəm *foam*, guəd *goad*, gruən *to groan*, gruəp *to grope*, gruəv *grove*, guə *to go*, ə-guə *ago*, guən *gone*, guə(r) *gore*, guəst *ghost*, guət *goat*, kruək *to croak*, luəd *load, burden*, luəf *loaf*, luən *loan*, əluən *alone*, luənsm *lonely*, luəþ *loath*, luəð *to loathe*, muən (OE. mǣnan, ME. mǣnen, mānen) *to moan*, muə(r) *more*, muəst *most*, nuə *no*, nuən *none*, ruəd *road*, ruəp *rope*, ruə(r) *to roar*, struək *to stroke*, struək (OE. strāc) *half a bushel*, stuən *stone*, suə *so*, suəp *soap*, suə(r) *sore*, tluəþ *cloth*, tluəz *clothes*, tluəð *to clothe*, tluəvə(r) *clover*, tuə *toe*, tuəd *toad*, tuəkn *token*, tuən (lit. *the one*) *one of two*, uə *who*, uək *oak*, uəli *holy*, uəl *whole*, uəm *home*, uənli *lonely*, uə(r) *oar*, uə(r) *hoar*, uəs(t) (OE. hās) *hoarse*, uəts *oats*, uəþ *oath*, wuə *woe*.

§ 123. āw has become oə:

bloə *to blow*, kroə *crow*, kroə *to crow*, moə *to mow*, noə *to know*, sloə *slow*, snoə *snow*, soə *to sow*, þoə *to thaw*, þroə *to throw*, oəðə(r) *either*, noəðə(r) *neither*.

But we have ou in: out (OE. āwiht) *aught*, nout (OE. nāwiht) *naught*, soul (OE. sāwol) *soul*.

§ 124. ā has become ou in:

lou (O.Icel. lāgr) *low*, ou (OE. āgan) *to owe*, out (OE. āhte) *ought*; but oe in: oen (OE. āgen) *own*.

§ 125. ā was shortened to a at an early period in: as, aks (OE. āscian, ācsian) *to ask*, alidə (OE. hālig-dæg) *holiday*, **lavrek** (OE. **lāwerce**, ME. **laveroc**) *lark*, **spatl** (OE. **spātl**) *spittle*. To e in **meš** *mash*, cp. § 59.

And to o in **sori** (OE. **sārig**) *sorry*. But this word has probably been influenced by **sore** (OE. **sorg**) *sorrow*.

§ 126. ā has become u in **ut** *hot*, **wun** *one*, **wuns** *once*.

§ 127. O.Norse **ei** (=OE. ā) has become **ee**: **feek** (O.Icel. **feikr**) *trick, deception*, **leek** (O.Icel. **leika**) *to play*, **week** (O.Icel. **veikr**) *weak*. It is not absolutely necessary to assume that these words are of Norse origin; they may be regularly developed from OE. **fācen, lācan, wāc** with early shortening of the ā before the following k, cp. words like **leitš** *leech* (§ 132), **teitš** *teach* (§ 138), which cannot be of Norse origin.

§ 128. ā has become e in the unaccented particles: **en** *an*, **e** *a*, **an**, **e(r)** *or*, **ne(r)** *nor*, **net** *not*.

§ 129. The following words remain unclassed: **poul** *pole*, probably an early borrowing from the lit. language; the same is probably the case with **rees** *race*, **swīp** *to sweep* (OE. **swāpan**, pret. **swēop**) with the vowel of the pret. transferred to the present, **tū** *two*.

Germanic ǣ.

§ 130. Germanic ǣ (=WS. ǣ, O.North. ē) has become ī in: **grīdi** *greedy*, **īmin** (OE. **ǣfnung**, ME. **ǣfening**) *evening*, **nīdl** *needle*, **rīd** *to read*, **sīd** *seed*, **slīp** *to sleep*, **strīt** *street*, **šīp** *sheep*, **tšīz** *cheese*, **þrīd** *thread*.

§ 131. It has become **ie** in:
brieþ *breath*, **brieð** *to breathe*, **dried** *to dread*, **fie(r)** *fear*, **e-fied** *afraid*, **iel** *eel*, **iernd** *errand*, **jie(r)** *year*, **miel** *meal, repast*, **swiel** (OE. **swǣlan**, O.Icel. **svǣla**) *to gutter (of a candle)*, **ðie(r)** *there*, **wiepm** *weapon*, **wie(r)** *where*, **wiez** *to wheeze*.

§ 132. Before c(k) it became shortened to e, and then underwent the same further development as old e in open syllables (§ 87): leitš *leech*, speitš *speech*.

§ 133. It has become ee in : bleet *to bleat*, gree *gray*, ee(r) *hair*, weev *wave*.

§ 134. It underwent early shortenings to e in : bleðe(r) *bladder*, let *to let*, mede *meadow*, red (OE. rædde) *read*, sed (OE. sæde, older sægde, Sievers, OE. Gr. § 214, 3) *said*, setede (OE. sæterdæg) *Saturday*, slept *slept*, sez *sayest*, *says*, šeped *shepherd*, šepste(r) *starling*, wet *wet*.

§ 135. It has become a in : blast *blast*.

§ 136. It has become i in : ridl *riddle*, sili *silly*.

OE. ǣ (= i-umlaut of ā).

§ 137. The normal development of the i-umlaut of ā is ie :

briedþ *breadth*, diel *deal*, dliem *gleam*, iel *to heal*, ielþ *health*, iet *heat*, ieðn *heathen*, lied *to lead*, liede(r) *tendon*, lien *lean*, liest *least*, liev *to leave*, mien *mean*, mien *to mean, intend*, rie(r) *to rear*, rieþ *wreath*, sie *sea*, siet *seat*, swiet *to sweat*, šieþ *sheath*, tiez *to tease*, tlien *clean*, wiet *wheat*.

§ 138. Before c(k) it became shortened to e, and then underwent the same further development as old e in open syllables (§ 87), cp. also § 132 : bleitš *to bleach*, reik *to reach*, teitš *to teach*.

§ 139. ǣ has also become ei in :

(1) lein *to lean*, spreid *to spread*.

(2) kei *key*, nei *neigh*.

140. ǣht has become out : tout (OE. tǣhte) *taught*.

§ 141. ǣ has become ee in: leedi *lady*, steez *stairs*, tlee *clay*.

§ 142. It has become oe in: noeðe(r) *neither*, oeðe(r) *either*. These examples rather belong to § 123. See Sievers, OE. Gr. §§ 346, 348.

§ 143. It underwent early shortening to e in: emti *empty*, fleš *flesh*, left (pret. and pp.) *left*, lent (pret. and pp.) *lent* (len *to lend* has its vowel from the pret.) les *less*, ment *meant*.

§ 144. It was shortened at an early period to a in: bad *bad*, fat *fat*, laðe(r) *ladder*, mad *mad*, madlin *a bewildered or confused person, stupid fellow*, rasl *to wrestle*, spat (pret.) *spat*.

§ 145. It has become i in ive(r) *ever*, ivri *every*, nive(r) *never*.

§ 146. oni (OE. ǣnig) has been influenced by moni (OE. manig) *many*.

ē.

1. ē (=i-umlaut of ō).

§ 147. ē, the i-umlaut of ō, has become ī: blīd *to bleed*, brīd *to breed*, dīm *to deem*, fīd *to feed*, fīl *to feel*, fīt *feet*, gīs *geese*, grīn *green*, grīt *to greet*, īd *heed*, īl *heel*, kīl (OE. cēlan) *to cool*, kīn *keen*, kīp *to keep*, kwīn *queen*, mīt *to meet*, sīk *to seek*, sīm *to seem*, slī *sly*, swīt *sweet*, tīm (O. Icel. tœma) *to pour out*, tīp *teeth*, wīp *to weep*.

§ 148. It was shortened early to e before consonant combinations in: bled *bled*, bles *to bless*, bred *bred*, gezlin *gosling*, fed *fed*, felt (pret.) *felt*, kept *kept*, met *met*, tem (pret. of tīm § 147) *poured out*, tem-ful *brimful*.

§ 149. The following forms are irregular: britšez (OE.

brōc) *breeches*, weest (OE. wēste) *waste*, wieri (OE. wōerig) *weary*.

2. ē (=older īe, partly arising from the i-umlaut of ēa, ēo, and partly arising from ecthlipsis).

§ 150. This ē has also generally become ī: dī *to dye*, drī *dreary*, lītnin *lightning*, be-līv *to believe*, nīd *need*, sīn *seen*, slīv *sleeve*, stīl *steel*, stīpl *steeple*, šīt *sheet*, tī *to tie*, siks-tīn *sixteen*.

NOTE.—This ē has been shortened to i in: rik *reek, smoke*, strip *to strip*.

§ 151. It has become ie before a following r in: ied *heard*, ie(r) *to hear*, nie(r) (OHG. nioro) *kidney*, stie(r) *to steer*.

§ 152. ē has been shortened to e at an early period in: nekst *next*.

§ 153. It has become ee in: ee *hay*; and ei in: eit *height*.

3. Germanic ē.

§ 154. let (pret.) *let*, ie(r) *here*. Here may also be placed: mīdles (cp. OE. mēd, older meord *pay, reward*) *troublesome, tiresome, to no purpose*.

4. The OE. ē which arose from lengthening in mono-syllables (Sievers, OE. Gr. § 121).

§ 155. This ē has become ī in the following accented forms (§ 350): ī *he*, jī *ye*, mī *me*, ðī *thee*, wī *we*.

ī.

§ 156. OE. ī has regularly become ai: aidl *idle*, aim (OE. hrīm?) *hoarfrost*, ain *hind*, ais *ice*, aivi *ivy*, baid (OE. bīdan) *to endure, put up with, wait, stay, remain*, bait *to bite*, **braidl** *bridle*, **daik** *dike, dyke*, **dlaid** *to glide*, **draiv** *to drive*, **fail** *file*, **faiv** *five*, **graip** *to gripe*, **graim** (ME. **grīm**) *soot (on the kettle)*, **kraist** *Christ*, **laif** *life*, **laik** *like*, **laim** *lime*, **lain** *line*, **ə-laiv** *alive*, **mai** (accented form) *my*, **mail** *mile*, **main** *mine*, **mait** *mite*, **naif** *knife*, **paik** *pike*, **pail** *pile*, **pain** *to pine*, **paip** *pipe*, **raid** *to ride*, **raip** *ripe*, **rait** *to write*, **raiv** (O. Icel. **rīfa** *to break*) *to tear*, **raiz** *to rise*, **said** *side*, **sail** (ME. **sīlen**) *to strain through a sieve*, **saip** (cp. MHG. **sīfen**) *to ooze or drain out slowly*, **saið** *scythe*, **slaid** *to slide*, **slaim** *slime*, **slaip** *to take away the skin or outside covering*, **smait** *to smite*, **snaip** *snipe*, **straid** *to stride*, **straik** *to strike*, **swaim** *to climb up a tree or pole*, **swaip** (cp. MHG. **swīfen**) *to sweep off, remove hastily*, **šain** *to shine*, **šait** *cacare*, **šaiv** (ME. **schīve**) *slice*, **taid** *feast time*, **taidin** *a present from the feast*, **taik** (O. Icel. **tīk** *dog*) *a low fellow*, **taim** *time*, **tait** (in the phrase: **es tait** *as soon*, comp. **taite(r)** *sooner, rather*, ME. **tīt**, O. Icel. masc. **tīðr**, neut. **tītt**) *soon*, **twain** *twine*, **twais** *twice*, **ðai** (accented form) *thy*, **ðain** *thine*, **þraiv** *to thrive*, **waid** *wide*, **waif** *wife*, **wail** *a while, time*, **wain** *wine*, **waip** *to wipe*, **wait** *white*, **waiz** *wise*, **fraide** *Friday*.

§ 157. ī before a following r : **aien** *iron*, **spaie(r)** *spire*, **waie(r)** *wire*.

§ 158. Old ī appears as ī in : **sī** *to sigh* (§ 318, *b*), **skrīk** (O. Low Germ. **scrīcōn**, Swed. **skrīka**) *to shriek*. And possibly in **stī** (OE. **stīg**, OHG. **stīga**) *ladder*, but see § 94.

§ 159. īw has become iu : **spiu** (OE. **spīwan**) *to spew*, **tiuzdə** (OE. **tīwesdæg**) *Tuesday*.

§ 160. ī underwent early shortening to i in : **bi** (unaccented form) *by*, **dwinl** *to dwindle*, **fift** *fifth*, **fifti** *fifty*, **fipms** *fivepence*, **linin** *linen*, **linsīd** *linseed*, **stif** *stiff*, **wimin** *women*, **midif** *midwife*, **wizdm** *wisdom*.

§ 161. rī has become ō through metathesis in : kōsmes *Christmas*, kōsn *to christen*.

§ 162. ī has become u in : wumn *woman*; ie in: sniek *to sneak*; ə in : sterəp *stirrup*.

ō.

§ 163. The normal development of ō is ui : bluid *blood*, bruid *brood*, buin *boon*, buit *to boot*, buiδ *booth*, buizm *bosom*, duin *done*, fluid *flood*, fuid *food*, fuit *foot*, guid *good*, guis *goose*, kruidl *to shrink* or *cower with cold, fear* or *pain*, kuil *cool*, muid *mood*, muild *confusion, bad temper*, muin *moon*, nuin *noon*, pruiv (OE. prōflan from Lat. probāre) *to prove*, ruid *rood*, ruif *roof*, ruit *root*, skuil *school*, smuiδ *smooth*, spuin *spoon*, stuid *stood*, stuil *stool*, suin *soon*, suit *soot*, tuil *tool*, tuiþ *tooth*, šuin *shoes*, uid *hood*, uif *hoof*, uin (ME. hōnen) *to harass, treat badly*.

§ 164. ō has become iu before k, m, and when the vowel has come to stand finally in the mod. dialect.

(a) Before k : briuk *brook*, iuk *hook*, kriuk *crook*, liuk *to look*, niuk *nook*, riuk *rook*, šiuk *shook*, tiuk *took*.

būk *book*, and kūk *cook* have been borrowed from the literary language.

(b) Before m : blium *bloom*, brium *broom*, dlium *gloom*, dium *doom*, gium *gum*, lium *loom*.

(c) When final in the mod. dialect: biu *bough*, diu *to do*, driu *drew*, iniu (plural) *enough*, pliu *plough*, sliu *slew*, tiu *too*.

šū *shoe* has been borrowed from the literary language, cp. the pl. form šuin § 163. ō appears as i in inif (sing.) *enough*.

§ 165. ō has become uə before r: dluə(r) (ME. glōrən) *to stare*, fluə(r) *floor*, muə(r) *moor*.

§ 166. ōw has become ou: dlou *to glow*, flou *to flow*, grou *to grow*, stou *to stow*.

§ 167. ōht became oht already in OE. (Sievers, OE. Gr. § 125), and has become out in the W. dialect, cp. § 101: brout *brought*, sout *sought*, þout *thought*.

§ 168. ō has become ou in: skoup *scoop*.

§ 169. Shortenings of old ō.

(a) To o: blosm *blossom*, fostə(r) *foster*, foðə(r) *fodder*, kom (OE. cōm) *came*, soft *soft*, šod *shod*, tof *tough*.

(b) To u: bruðə(r) *brother*, dluv *glove*, duz *dost, does*, mundə *Monday*, munþ *month*, muðə(r) *mother*, sluf (OE. slōg) *slough*, tuðə(r) *the other*, uðə(r) *other*.

§ 170. ō has become e in wednzdə (OE. wōdnes-dæg) *Wednesday*.

ū.

§ 171. ū has generally become ā: ā *how*, āl *owl*, āmivə(r) *however*, ās *house*, āt *out*, bā *to bow*, bān (O. Icel. būenn, lit. *bound*; generally used in the sense of *going*, as wiə(r) tə bān? *where art thou going?* am bān dān tloin *I am going down the lane*), brā *brow*, brān *brown*, bāt (OE. būtan, beūtan) *without*, ə-bāt *about*, dān *down*, dāst *dust*, dlāmi (not the same word as *gloomy* which is dliumi § 164) *sad, downcast*, drāzi *drowsy*, fāl *foul, ugly*, kā *cow*, krād *crowd*, lād *loud*, lās *louse*, mās *mouse*, māþ *mouth*, nā *now*, rām *room*, rāst *rust*, prād *proud*, sāk *to suck*, sāþ *south*, slām (OE. slūma) *slumber*, sprāt (cp. ME. sprūte, M. Low Germ. sprūtə) *to sprout*, šrād *shroud*, tān *town*, tlād *cloud,* tlāt *clout,* trāst (ME. trūsten) *to trust,* ðā (accented form) *thou,* þāzn *thousand.*

§ 172. ū has become āe before a following r: āe(r) (accented form) *our,* kāe(r) dān (ME. couren, Swed. kūra *to cower) to bend down, sit down,* sāe(r) *sour,* šāe(r) *shower.* But we have ō in þēzde *Thursday.*

§ 173. doen *down, feathers,* seems to have been borrowed from the literary language.

§ 174. ū was shortened to u at an early period in: busk (ME. busken from O. Icel. būask *to get oneself ready) to go about from place to place singing and playing for money,* druft *drought,* duv *dove,* fus *fuss,* kud (accented form) *could,* plum *plum,* ruf *rough,* uni-sukl *honeysuckle,* sup *to drink, sup,* šuv *to shove,* þum *thumb,* ulet *owl,* up *up,* uðe(r) *udder,* uz (accented form) *us,* uzbn *husband.*

It has been weakened to e in the unaccented particle bed *but.*

ȳ.

§ 175. ȳ, the i-umlaut of ū, has become ai: aid *hide, skin,* aiv *hive,* braid *bride,* brain *brine,* drai *dry,* draip *to drip,* daiv *to dive,* kait *kite,* lais *lice,* mais *mice,* praid *pride,* skai *sky.*

§ 176. It has become aie before a following r: aie(r) *to hire,* faie(r) *fire,* maie(r) *mire.*

§ 177. It underwent early shortening to i in: filþ *filth,* idn (pp. from which was formed a new present id *to hide),* litl *little,* lits (retained only in the game of lits en gōts *lit. littles and greats,* a game played by boys with brass buttons, clog clasps, or small pieces of brass of any kind. Two lits

have the value of one **gĕt**; cp. P. B. Bcitr. ix. p. 365–7).
þiml *thimble*, **wiš** *to wish*.

§ 178. **ȳ** (?) has become u in **þrust** *to thrust*.

3. The Diphthongs.

ēa.

§ 179. OE. **ēa** has generally become iə:. **biəm** *beam*,
biən *bean*, **biət** *to beat*, **briəd** *bread*, **diəd** *dead*, **diəf** *deaf*,
diəþ *death*, **driəm** *dream*, **ə-giən** *again, against*, **iəd** *head*,
iəp *heap*, **iə(r)** *ear*, **iəst** *east*, **iəstə(r)** *Easter*, **liəd** *lead*, **liəf**
leaf, **bə-liəf** *belief*, **niə(r)** *near*, **piə-kok** *peacock*, **siəm** *seam*,
stiəm *steam*, **stiəp** *steep*, **striə** (WS. **strēa**, O. North. **strē**,
Sievers, OE. Gr. § 250, note 2) *straw*, **striəm** *stream*, **šiəf**
sheaf, **tiəm** *team*, **tšiəp** *cheap*, **þriəp** (OE. **þrēapian** *to rebuke*) *to contradict*, **þriətn** *to threaten*.

§ 180. **ēaw** has become eu: **deu** *dew*, **eu** *to hew*, **feu**
(OE. **fēawe**) *few*, **šeu** *to show*, **teu** (OE. **tēawian**) *to work
zealously*.

But we have oə in **roə** (OE. **hrēaw**) *raw*; which pre-
supposes a form **hrāw** (§ 123).

§ 181. It has become ī in: **ī** (plural **īn**) *eye*, **tšīk** *cheek*.
The latter word has probably been borrowed from the
literary language.

§ 182. It has become ei in: **ei** (OE. **hēah**) *high*, **nei**
(OE. **nēah**) *nigh, near*. The ME. forms **heh** and **neh** would
regularly become diphthongized to ei, see § 87.

§ 183. It has become eə in: **fleə** (OE. **flēan**, Skeat,
Etym. Dict. p. 211) *to skin*, **neəbə(r)** *neighbour*.

§ 184. O. Norse au has become ou in : loup (O. Icel. hlaupa) to *leap, jump*, lous (O. Icel. lauss) *loose*; and oe in: goem (O. Icel. gaum) *heed, care, attention*, goemles *silly, stupid*, root (O. Icel. rauta to *roar*) to *bray*.

§ 185. ēa has become ō through absorption of r in: gōt *great*.

§ 186. Shortenings of ēa :
(a) To e in: efə(r) *heifer*, lek *leek*, red *red*.
(b) To a in: laðə(r) *lather*, tšap *chap*.

ēo.

§ 187. OE. ēo has generally become ī: bī *bee*, bī (accented form) to *be*, bīn *been*, dīp *deep*, dlī *glee*, fīnd *fiend*, flī to *fly*, flī *fly*, flīs *fleece*, frī *free*, frīz to *freeze*, krīp to *creep*, lī to *lie*, līf (OE. lēof) *soon*, līvə(r) *sooner, rather*, līt a *light*, nī *knee*, nīz (O. Icel. hniósa) to *sneeze*, rīd *reed*, rīl *reel*, prīst *priest*, sī to *see*, sīð to *seethe*, snīz to *sneeze*, tlīv to *cleave*, trī *tree*, bə-twīn *between*, þī *thigh*, þīf *thief*, prī *three*, wīd *weed*, wīl *wheel*.
But we have tšiuz to *choose* (§ 366).

§ 188. It has become iə before a following r : biə(r) *beer*, diə(r) *dear*, driəri *dreary*.

§ 189. Before r + consonant it became shortened to e already in ME., and then had the same further development as old e before r + consonant (§ 87): dālin (OE. dēorling, ME. derrling) *darling*, fādin (OE. fēorðung, ME. ferthing) *farthing*.

§ 190. ēow has become iu: bliu *blew*, briu to *brew*, griu *grew*, jiuþ *youth*, kriu *crew*, niu *new*, niu *knew*, riu to *rue*, **sniu** (§ 377) *it snowed*, **tliu** *clew*, **triu** *true*, **triuþ** *truth*, **siu** *sowed*, **þriu** *threw*.

But in the following words we have **eu** which points to an old **ēaw** (§ 180): **eu** *yew*, **seu** *to sew*, **t̆ʃeu** *to chew*. We have **ouə** in: **fouə(r)** (OE. **fēower**, but ME. **fōwer**, which would regularly become **fouə(r)** in the dialect, § 166) *four*, **fouet** (OE. **fēowerða**) *fourth*, **fouetīn** (OE. **fēowertēne**) *fourteen*. And **āə** in: **jāə(r)** (accented form) *your*. This last word has been influenced by **āə(r)** *our*, § 172.

§ 191. The following two words remain unclassed: **ʃū** (accented form) *she*, **ʃuit** *to shoot*.

§ 192. Early shortenings of **ēo**:

(*a*) To **e** in: **brest** *breast*, **fel** (pret.) *fell*, **frend** *friend*, **step-faðə(r)** *step-father*. Anglian **ēo** (=WS. **īe**) has been shortened to **e** in: **depþ** *depth*, **ten** *ten*.

(*b*) To **o** in: **foti** *forty*, **fotnit** *fortnight*.

(*c*) To **i** in: **divl** *devil*, **sik** *sick*, **e tūþri** lit. *a two* (or) *three, a few*.

(*d*) To **e** in: **se ðe** lit. *see thou, look!* **þrepms** *threepence*.

Elision of ə.

§ 193. The **ə** is elided in the diphthongs and triphthongs **eə, iə, oə, uə, āə, aiə, iuə, ouə**, when they occur finally and the next word begins with a vowel; thus **guə** but **gu uem** *go home*, **me ai** *may I*, but **mee wī** (§ 393), **noə** but **a no im** *I know him*, and similarly for the others.

CHAPTER IV.

In the following treatment of the French element in the W. dialect, the present pronunciation of literary English has, in most cases, been taken as the starting point. The transcription of the lit. English vowel sounds is based on that given in Sweet's Primer of Spoken English, pp. 7–8, and is as follows:—

ʋ	as in	just, dozen, double.
ā	,,	grant, art, master.
ai	,,	fine, pie, try.
au	,,	doubt, powder.
æ	,,	value, rat.
e	,,	debt, measure.
ei	,,	bacon, bailiff, pay.
eə	,,	pair, chair.
ō	,,	furnish, journey.
i	,,	dinner, pity.
ij	,,	beak, secret, beef, grief.
iə	,,	fierce, clear.
o	,,	jolly, profit.
oi	,,	boil, poison.
ou	,,	roast, notice.

ŏ „ pork, daub, false.

u „ put, butcher.

uw „ fruit, blue.

uə „ sure, poor.

§ 194. Lit. Engl. æ (written a) appears as a : abit *habit*, aktli *actually*, ali *aisle*, *alley*, arend (ME. araine, O. Fr. araigne) *spider*, avek *havoc*, baril *barrel*, damidž *damage*, faks *facts*, galək (O. Fr. galc) *lefthand*, galəp *to gallop*, galn *gallon*, garit *garret*, gran-faðe(r), gram-faðe(r) *grand-father*, kap *cap*, kapil (Fr. capel *a little hat*, Cotgr.) *a piece of leather sewn over a hole in a boot or shoe*, karit *carrot*, lamp *lamp*, mane(r) *manner*, map (see Skeat, Etym. Dict. sub mop) *a mop*, mare *to match a pattern*, natrel (natre-bl) *natural*, pantri *pantry*, ratn (O. Fr. raton) *rat*, salit *salad*, skafl *scaffold*, skaflin *scaffolding*, stati *statue*, tali *to agree, be right*, tə liv tali *to live together without being married*, tšapil *chapel*, vali *valley*, vale *value*.

§ 195. Lit. Engl. has ā where the W. dial. has a in: basted *bastard*, branš *branch*, grant *to grant*, paste(r) *pasture*, plant *plant*.

But ee in : bees *bass*, leerem *alarum*, meeste(r) *master*, pleeste(r) *plaster*.

§ 196. Lit. Engl. has ei (written a), but W. dial. a in : aprən *apron*, stapl *staple*.

But we have moendž *mange*.

§ 197. a has become ə before a following g, n, š, cp. § 59 :

dregn *dragon*.

blenk *blank*, blenkit *blanket*, kenke(r) (ME. cancren) *to corrode*, lenwidž *language*, plenk *plank*, renk *rank*.

bešfl *bashful*, fešn *fashion*, pešn *passion*, seš *sash*.

§ 198. al has become oe in the combinations lk, lm, ll, cp. § 62.

goeki (but galek § 326) *left handed*, boem *balm*, oeminak *almanac*, oemend *almond*, boel *ball*.

§ 199. al in the combination ld has become ou, cp. § 64: skoud *to scald*.
The same sound also occurs in fout (ME. faute) *fault*.

§ 200. a has become o before a following n in: dons *dance*, ont *aunt*, trons *trance*, tšons *chance*, tšont *chant*.

§ 201. a has become e in: rediš *radish*.

§ 202. a has been retained where in the lit. language it has become o through the influence of the preceding w in: kwaleti *quality*, kwari *stone-quarry*, warend *to warrant*, walep (cp. Fr. galoper *to curry, use rudely*, Cotgr.) *to beat, flog*.

§ 203. ar in the combination r + consonant has become ee, which shows that ar in this combination was pronounced differently in Engl. and Fr. words in the ME. period; cp. § 61.

beebe(r) *barber*, beedž *barge*, beegɒ *bargain*, beete(r) *to barter*, deet *to dart*, eet *art, skill*, geed *guard*, geedn *garden*, geete(r) *garter*, keed *card*, keekes (Fr. carquasse, Cotgr.) *body, carcase*, kweet *quart*, kweete(r) *quarter*, peedn *pardon*, peesl *parcel*, peet *part*, peetne(r) *partner*, skeelet *scarlet*, tšeedž *charge*.

§ 204. Lit. Engl. ei (written a, ai (ay), ei) appears in the W. diäl. as ee: beekɒ *bacon*, beel *bale*, beeli (bumbeeli, cp. O. Fr. baili) *bailiff*, beet *to abate*, bleem *blame*, bree (ME. braiin, O. Fr. breier) *to beat, pound*, deendže(r) *danger*, deenti *dainty*, deet *date*, deevi *affidavit*, eebl *able*, eedž *age*, eem *to aim, intend*, eenšn *ancient*, feed *fade*, feel

to fail, **feent** *to faint*, **fees** *face*, **feeþ** *faith*, **feeve(r)** *to favour,
resemble in appearance or manners*, **fleem** *flame*, **gee** *gay*,
iᵑgeedž *to engage*, **greenz** (pl.) *malt which has been used in
brewing beer*, **grees** *grace*, **greet** *grate*, **keedž** *cage*, **kees**
case, **lees** *lace*, **meesn** *mason*, **neete(r)** *nature*, **pee** *pay*,
peedž *page*, **peel** *pale*, **peen** *pain*, **peen** *pane of glass*, **peent**
paint, **pees** *pace*, **peest** (but **pasti** *pasty*) *paste*, **pleen** *plain*,
plees *place*, **pleet** *plate*, **pree** (but **pre-ðe** (*I*) *pray thee*) *to
pray*, **preet** *to prate, babble*, **preez** *to praise*, **reedž** *rage*,
reet *rate*, **seef** *safe*, **seekrid** *sacred*, **seem** (often called **swain-
seem**, Ancren Riwle **seim**, OE. **seime** *adipe*, Ps. lxii. 6,
E. E. T. S. No. 92, from O. Fr. **sain**) *lard*, **seent** (but before
names **sant**) *saint*, **seev** *to save*, **skeelz** *scales*, **steebl** *stable*,
streendž *strange*, **teebl** *table*, **teele(r)**, **teelje(r)** *tailor*, **teest**
taste, **tleem** *to claim*, **treel** (Fr. **trailler**) *to drag*, **treen**
train, **tšeef** *to chafe*, **tšeeme(r)** *chamber*, **tšeendž** *change*, **veen**
vein, **weet** *to wait*.

NOTE.—*contrary* is **kontréeri**.

§ 205. Before a simple r we have the same development
as the lit. language : **pee(r)** *pair*, **pee(r)** *to peel*, **tšee(r)**
chair.

e.

§ 206. e (written e, ea) in the lit. language has generally
remained in the W. dialect : **bezl** *to embezzle*, **demek** (from
epidemic) *potato disease*, **demekt** *diseased (of potatoes)*, **det**
debt, **dželes** *jealous*, **dželi** *jelly*, **e-seml** *to assemble*, **fend** *to
provide for oneself*, **fent** *remnant of a piece of cloth*, **fezn**
pheasant, **ges** *to guess*, **lete(r)** *letter*, **letis** *lettuce*, **mel** (Fr.
mail) *mallet*, **mel** (ME. **mellen, medlen**, O.Fr. **medler**) *to
meddle*, **mend** *to mend*, **meze(r)** *measure*, **pleze(r)** *pleasure*,
prentis *apprentice*, **sens** *sense*, **ses** *assessment, tax*, **spekteklz**

spectacles, **treml** *to tremble,* **treze(r)** *treasure,* **vente(r)** *to venture,* **vesl** *vessel.*

But **fliem** *phlegm,* **siene** *senna.*

§ **207.** **er** has become **ā** before a following consonant: **konsắn** *concern,* **pāsn** *parson,* **sādžn** *sergeant,* **sāmen** *sermon,* **sāvnt** *servant,* **sāvis** *service,* **tlāk** *clerk,* **vāment** *vermin,* **vāniš** *varnish.*

In the following two words we have **a**: **arend** (O.Fr. **errant**) *notoriously bad,* **sare** (rarely **sāv**) *to serve.* On **sare** see Behrens, Beiträge zur Geschichte der französischen Sprache in England, p. 91. **ie** in: **ieb** *herb,* and **e** in: **tšeri** *cherry.*

§ **208.** **e** has become **a** before a following **r** in **tarie(r)** (ME. **terrere**) *terrier dog,* **vari** *very.*

But **pie(r)** *pear.*

§ **209.** **e** has become **i** before a following nasal in: **indžói** *to enjoy,* **indžn** *engine,* **ɪngeedž** *to engage,* **ɪɲk** *ink,* **lints** *lentils,* **simetri** *cemetery,* **šimi** *chemise.*

tribl *treble* (in music) from contamination with **triple,** and **þribl** *threefold* from contamination with **þrī.**

§ **210.** **e** has become **a** in **saleri** *celery,* cp. **sallary** sub **celery** in N.E.D.

i.

§ **211.** **i** has generally remained in the W. dialect: **dine(r)** *dinner,* **dizml** *dismal,* **finiš** *to finish,* **gimlek** (this word has now almost gone out of use, its place being taken by **gimlit**) *gimlet,* **gizn** *to choke,* **gizn** (Fr. **guisern,** Cotgr. sub **gesier**) *gizzard,* **konsiðe(r)** *to consider,* **limit** *limit,* **list** *list,* **list** *to enlist,* **live(r)** *to deliver,* **mínɪste(r)** *minister,* **mins** *mince,* **mistšif** *mischief,* **pidžn** *pigeon,* **pik** *pickaxe,* pinien *opinion*, piti *pity*, rivə(r) *river*, siɒl *single*, siðez *scissors*, skriptə(r) *scripture*, tift (cp. ME. tiffen from O. Fr. tiffer *to adorn*) *condition, state, order*, tšimli *chimney*, twilt *quilt*.

§ 212. i has become ə in : lenit *linnet*, rebit *rivet*, redžeste(r) *to register*, rens *to rinse*.

§ 213. i has become ə in sperit *spirit*; and a in krakit *cricket (game)*.

o .

§ 214. Lit. Engl. short o = W. dial. o : boni *nice, pretty*, džoli *jolly*, džosl *to jostle*, kole(r) *collar*, kotn *cotton*, lodž *to lodge*, mot, moti (French motte, Cotgr., edit. 1673) *a mark at quoits*, obstakl *obstacle*, oke-daik (Fr. oker Cotgr.) *small stream of iron-water*, onə(r) *honour*, rok *rock*, poridž *porridge*, posnit (O. Fr. poçonet) *saucepan*, pot *pot*, profit *profit*, soðe(r) *solder*.

§ 215. o has become u in : nuvl *novel*, nuvis *novice*.

§ 216. Lit. Engl. oi = W. dial. oi : boil *to boil*, džoi *joy*, džoint *joint*, ə-noi *to annoy*, koit *quoit, coit*, loin *loin*, moist *moist*, moistə(r) *moisture*, noiz *noise*, oil *oil*, oint- ment *ointment*, oistə(r) *oyster*, point *point*, poizn *poison*, soil *soil, ground*, spoil *to spoil*, tšois *choice*, vois *voice*, voiðe(r) *large clothes' basket*.

§ 217. Lit. Engl. ou (written oa) = W. dial. o in : gol (only used in the game of lits en gēts § 177, O. Fr. gaul) *goal*, rost *to roast*.

§ 218. Lit. Engl. ou (written, o, oo, oa) = W. dial. ue in : bruetš *brooch*, kuetš *coach*, nuəbl *noble*, nuetis *notice*, pueni *pony*, puest *post*, puezi *nosegay*, rueb *robe*, rueg *rogue*, tluek *cloak*.

§ 219. Lit. Engl. ou (written o, oa)=W. dial. oi in: broitš *to broach*, doit *to dote*, koit *coat*, loitš *loach*, tloiz *close, narrow*, tloiz *to close*, toist *to toast*.

§ 220. Lit. Ẹngl. ou (written o, oa, ou, ow)=W. dial. ou in: boul *bowl*, koul (O. Fr. coillir) *to rake;* moud *mould, model*, poutri *poultry*, poutš *to poach*, roul *to roll*, soudžə(r) *soldier*.

But we have pŭltis *poultice*.

NOTE.—The first element of the W. diphthong is not the o in not. See § 7.

§ 221. Lit. Engl. uw (written oo)=W. dial. ui: buit *boot*, fuil *fool*, gruin (ME. groin, O. Fr. groing) *snout of a pig*.

§ 222. Lit. Engl. uə (written oor)=W. dial. uə: puə(r) *poor*, puəli *poorly, ill*.

§ 223. Lit. Engl. long open ō sound (written or before a following consonant)=W. dial. uə in: fuədž *forge*, fuəs *force*, kuəd *cord*, puək *pork*, puəšn *portion*, puətə(r) *porter*.

But we have foəfit *to forfeit*, foəm *form*, foətn *fortune*, koənə(r) *corner*, oəðə(r) *order*.

§ 224. uə occurs before single r in dluəri *glory*, stuəri *story*. And ə in ferin *foreign*.

§ 225. Lit. Engl. long open ō (written au, aw)=W. dial. oə in: doəb (ME. daubin, O. Fr. dauber) *to daub, smear*, džoəm (Fr. jaumbe, Cotgr.) *the side post of a door or chimney piece*, džoənəs *jaundice*, froəd *fraud*, koəsə *causeway*, poə *paw*, poəz (O. Fr. poulser, posser) *to kick*, soəs *sauce*.

But we have short o in bə-kos, ə-kos, kos *because*, fols *false; in reference to a child, implying that it is shrewd and witty beyond its years.*

u.

§ 226. Lit. Engl. ʊ (written u, o, ou)=W. dial. u:
bukit *bucket*, buldž *to bulge*, butn *button*, buzəd (O. Fr.
busart) *butterfly*, dlutn *glutton*, dubl *double*, duzn *dozen*,
džudž *judge*, džust *just*, frunt *front*, gruml *to grumble*, gulit
gullet, channel for water, gutə(r) *gutter*, guzl *to swallow
greedily*, krust *crust*, kruš *to crush*, kulə(r) *colour*, kumfət
comfort, kumpni *company*, kuntri *country*, kupl *couple*,
kusted *custard*, kustm *custom*, kuvə(r) *to cover*, kuzin, kuzn
cousin, muni (a commoner word is bras) *money*, muʊril
mongrel, musted *mustard*, mutn *mutton*, muzl *muzzle*,
numə(r) *number*, plumə(r) *plumber*, pulp *pulp*, rikuvə(r)
to recover, rubiš *rubbish*, sudn *sudden*, sufə(r) *to suffer*,
sumən *to summon*, supə(r) *supper*, stuf *stuff*, trubl *trouble*,
truʊk *trunk*, tšuk *to throw, pitch*, tun *tun*, tutš *to touch*,
uml *humble*, uniən *onion*, uʊkl *uncle*.
But we have foisti *fusty*.

§ 227. Lit. Engl. u (written u, and mostly occurring
after labials)=W. dial. u: bušl *bushel*, butšə(r) *butcher*,
bulit *bullet*, puli *pulley*, pulit *pullet*, puš *to push*, put
to put.
But we have siugə(r) *sugar*, see § 310, 1; puilpit
pulpit.

§ 228. Lit. Engl. ə̄ (written ur, our before a following
consonant)=W. dial. ə̄, see § 113 a: bə̄l (ME. burlə) *to
pick out small pieces of straw*, etc. *from flannel or cloth*,
distə̄b *to disturb*, džə̄ni *journey*, fə̄niš *to furnish*, fə̄nite(r)
furniture, kə̄n *currant*, nə̄s *nurse*, pə̄s *purse*, tə̄n *to turn*,
tə̄nəp *turnip*, ə̄t *to hurt*.

ai.

§ 229. Lit. Engl. ai (written i, ie, y)=W. dial. ai: ed-vais *advice*, ed-vaiz *to advise*, e-plai *to apply*, fain *fine*, frai *to fry*, kontráiv *to contrive*, krai *cry*, nais *nice*, pai *pie*, paint *pint*, prais *price*, praiz *to lift with a lever*, rais *rice*, sailm *asylum*, sain *sign*, saizez *assizes*, straiv *to strive*, tais *to entice*, trai *to try*, traifl *trifle*.

But tšiene *china ware*.

ai also occurs in: džais (O. Fr. giste) *joist*, paik *to pick, select*.

e-blīdž (pp. e-blītšt) *to oblige*, and leelek *lilac*, still remain to be explained.

§ 230. Lit. Engl. aie=W. dial. aie: dizaie(r) *desire*, kwaiet *quiet*, raiet *riot*, umpaie(r) *umpire*, vaielet *violet*.

ij.

§ 231. Lit. Engl. ij (written ea, ei, e, ee, ie) appears in the W. dial. as ie in: biek *beak*, biest *beast*, but bies *cows*, disiet *deceit*, disiev *to deceive*, fiebl *feeble*, fiet *feat*, fiest *feast*, fiete(r) *feature*, gries *grease*, iege(r) *eager*, iegl *eagle*, iekwl *equal*, iez *ease*, nies *niece*, niet *neat, tidy*, piel *to appeal*, pies *peace*, plied *to plead*, pliez *to please*, riel *real*, riezn *reason*, risiet *receipt, recipe*, risiev *to receive*, siekrit *secret*, sies *to cease*, siezn *season*, tie *tea*, triet *treat*, trietl *treacle*, tšiet *to cheat*, viel *veal*.

§ 232. Lit. Engl. ij=W. dial. ī in: bīf *beef*, e-grī *to agree*, grīf *grief*, pīp (pp. pept) *to peep*, pīs *piece*.

§ 233. Lit. Engl. ie=W. dial. ie in: fies *fierce*, tlie(r) *clear*.

§ 234. Lit. Engl. ij W. dial. ei in: dein *dean*, preitš *to preach*.

F

ai in : **bastail** (Fr. **bastille**) *workhouse, union.*

ee in : **konseet** *conceit.*

i in : **pil** *to peel,* **pilinz** *the peels of potatoes,* etc.

e in : **mezlz** *measles.*

au.

§ 235. Lit. Engl. **au** (written **ou, ow**) appears in the W. dial as **ā**: **āl** *to howl,* **āns** *ounce,* **bānti** *bounty,* **dāt** *doubt,* **e-kānt** *account,* **e-lā, lā** *to allow,* **e-mānt** *amount,* **frān** *to frown,* **gān** *gown,* **gāt** *gout,* **kānsl** *to counsel,* **kānt** *to count,* **kātš** *couch,* **krān** *crown,* **lāns** *an allowance of refreshment* or *money,* **mānt** *to mount,* **māt** (Lat. **mūtāre**) *to moult,* **pāǒe(r)** *powder,* **rānd** *round,* **sānd** *sound, noise,* **stāt** *stout,* **tǎ-il** (also **tail**) *towel,* **trǎ-il** *trowel,* **trāns** *to beat, flog,* **vā** *vow.*

au appears as **ū** in : **trūzez** *trousers.*

§ 236. Lit. Engl. **aue** = W. dial. **āe** : **āe(r)** *hour,* **divāe(r)** *to devour,* **flāe(r)** *flower, flour,* **pāe(r)** *power,* **tāe(r)** *tower.*

juw.

§ 237. Lit. Engl. **juw** (written **eau, ue, u, ui, ew, iew**) is **íu** in the W. dialect : **biuti** *beauty,* **diu** *due,* **diuti** *duty,* **fiuil** *fuel,* **fiute(r)** *future,* **ius** *use,* **iuneti** *unity,* **iunien** *union,* **iusfl** *useful,* **iusles** *useless,* **iuz** *to use,* **miul** *mule, donkey,* **miuzik** *music,* **piu** *pew,* **pius** *puce colour,* **rifíuz** *to refuse,* **siut** *suit,* **stiupid** *stupid,* **viu** *view.*

But we have **ā** in : **kākume(r)** *cucumber.*

jue.

§ 238. Lit. Engl. **jue** (written **ure**) = W. dial. **íue** : **kiue(r)** *cure,* **meniue(r)** *manure,* **piue(r)** *pure.*

uw.

§ **239.** Lit. Engl. uw (written ue, ui, u, and mostly occurring after l, r, s) is íu in the W. dialect : **bliu** *blue*, **bliuz** (pl.) *delirium tremens*, **fliu** *flue*, **fliut** *flute*, **seliut** *to salute*.

friut *fruit*, **griuil** · *gruel*, **rikriut** *to recruit*, **riubub** *rhubarb*, **riul** *rule*, **riume(r)** *rumour*, **riuin** *ruin*.

siu *to sue*, **siuit** *suet*.

ue.

§ **240.** Lit. Engl. ue = W. dial. iue : **siue(r)** *sure*, **siueli** *surely*, **unsiue(r)** *uncertain*.

CHAPTER V.

§ 241. Diphthongs and short and long vowels in un-accented syllables have regularly been weakened to ə, i, or the vowel has disappeared altogether. In the latter case, when an l, m, n followed, it has become vocalic.

1. ə.

§ 242. *a.* In initial syllables followed by the principal accent:

befuə(r) *before*, begin *to begin*, and similarly in all other words containing this prefix ; fegetn (pp.) *forgot*, əbāt (also bāt) *about, without*, əbūn *above*, əfled *afraid*, əfued *to afford*, əfuə(r) *before*, əgeet *in action, at work*, əgien *again, against*, əgrī *to agree*, əgue *ago*, əkin *akin*, əkos (also kos) *because*, əlaiv *alive*, əluən *alone*, əmeɒ *among*, ənent *opposite*, ənoi *to annoy*, əplai *to apply*, əseml *to assemble*, əstied *instead*, əwee *away*, məniuə(r) *manure*, səliut *salute*, tə-moən *to-morrow*.

But we have edikéet *to educate*, əkuədinlái *accordingly*, kontréeri *contrary*, redžéstə(r) *to register*, siuelĭ *surely*, spektéklz *spectacles*.

§ **243.** *b.* In syllables preceded by the principal accent :

basted *bastard,* **baleks** *testiculi,* **bulek** *bullock,* **buzed** *butterfly,* **dželes** *jealous,* **džoenes** *jaundice,* **figwet** *figwort,* **galep** *to gallop,* **gimlek** *gimlet,* **kēsmes** *Christmas,* **kolep** *slice of bacon,* **koese** *causeway,* **kubed** *cupboard,* **kusted** *custard,* **lavrek** *lark,* **leelek** *lilac,* **loped** *clotted, covered with dirt,* **mare** *to match a pattern,* **musted** *mustard,* **otšed** *orchard,* **omest** *almost,* **oles** *always,* **sakles** *silly, foolish,* **sare** *to serve,* **siene** *senna,* **simetri** *cemetery,* **siðez** *scissors,* **spitek** *spigot,* **šeped** *shepherd,* **sterep** *stirrup,* **tēnep** *turnip,* **ulet** *owl,* **unded** *hundred,* **vale** *value,* **winde** *window.*

are *arrow,* **bare** *barrow,* **bore** *to borrow,* **fale** *fallow,* **fole** *to follow,* **fere** *furrow,* **jare** *yarrow,* **jole** *yellow,* **mare** *marrow,* **mede** *meadow,* **nare** *narrow,* **ole** *hollow,* **pile** *pillow,* **sale** *sallow,* **sore** *sorrow,* **spare** *sparrow,* **swole** *to swallow,* **swole** *swallow,* **šade** *shadow,* **šale** *shallow,* **tale** *tallow,* **wide** *widow,* **wile** *willow.*

ame(r) *hammer,* **bleðe(r)** *bladder,* **bute(r)** *butter,* **faðe(r)** *father,* **gane(r)** *gander,* **geðe(r)** *to gather,* **kenke(r)** *to rust, corrode,* **neebe(r)** *neighbour,* **oeðe(r)** *either,* **pleeste(r)** *plaster,* **skute(r)** *to spill,* **slume(r)** *slumber,* **šuðe(r)** *to shudder,* **tarie(r)** *terrier,* **þune(r)** *thunder,* **unsiue(r)** *uncertain,* **une(r)** *hunger,* **wote(r)** *water.*

fēnite(r) *furniture,* **flute(r)** *future,* **moiste(r)** *moisture,* **neete(r)** *nature,* **paste(r)** *pasture,* **pikte(r)** *picture.*

meze(r) *measure,* **pleze(r)** *pleasure,* **treze(r)** *treasure.*

But we have **óeminak** *almanac,* **bástail** *union, workhouse,* **óbstakl** *obstacle,* **ríubub** *rhubarb.*

In compounds, some of which have been given above : **beekes** *bakehouse,* **koiles** *coalhouse,* **wākes** *union, workhouse,* **wešes** *washhouse,* **alide** *holiday,* **jestede** *yesterday,* **wāte** (lit. work-day) *week-day,* **sunde** *Sunday,* and similarly for the other days of the week, nek-ləþ *neck cloth, hand-kerchief*, bakəd *backward*, forəd *forward*, tādz *towards*, forədiš *rather forward*, oekəd *awkward*, oepəþ *halfpenny worth*, penəþ *pennyworth*, sumət *something, anything*.

2. i.

§ **244.** *a.* In initial syllables followed by the principal accent :

indžoi *to enjoy*, iŋgeedž *to engage*, disiet *deceit*, disiev *to deceive*, ministe(r) *minister*.

§ **245.** *b.* In´ syllables preceded by the principal accent :

āvis(t) *harvest*, bleŋkit *blanket*, bulit *bullet*, damidž *damage*, ienis(t) *earnest*, inif (sing.) *enough*, pl. iniu, ferin *foreign*, fotnit *fortnight*, gulit *water channel*, karit *carrot*, lenit *linnet*, letis *lettuce*, olin *holly*, posnit *saucepan*, puil-pit *pulpit*, pūltis *poultice*, salit *salad*, sperit *spirit*, rebit *rivet*, rediš *radish*.

bāli *barley*, beeli *bailiff*, beli *belly*, beri *berry*, beri *to bury*, bodi *body*, but nuebdi *nobody*, boni *nice, pretty*, dizi *dizzy*, emti *empty*, evi *heavy*, eri *hurry, row, disturbance*, kani *knowing, intelligent, skilful, nimble*, leedi *lady*, meri *merry*, moni *many*, nevi *nephew*, oepni *halfpenny*, but oepəþ *halfpenny worth*, oni *any*, peni *penny*, but penəþ *pennyworth*, popi *poppy*, pratli *gently, softly*, rudi *ruddy*, sili *silly*, slipi *slippery*, sori *sorry*, snikit *a small passage*, stati *statue*, šabi *shabby*, šimi *chemise*, tali *to agree*, þēti *thirty*, ueli *holy*, uenli *lonely*, vali *valley*, vari *very*, weri *to worry*.

fādin *farthing*, gezlin *gosling*, īmin *evening*, ipin *a cloth placed round the hips of children*, kunin *cunning*, skaftin *shafting*, speriŋz *the banns of marriage*, swiliŋz *thin liquid food for pigs*, **šilin** *shilling*, **topin** *the front part of the hair of the head*, **runin** *running*, and similarly in all present participles and words ending in the lit. language in -**ing**.

3. Loss of Vowel or Syllable.

§ **246.** *a.* Initial syllables followed by the principal accent:

bāt *without*, **beet** *to abate*, **kros** *across*, **levm** *eleven*, **pinien** *opinion*, **prentis** *apprentice*, **sailm** *asylum*.

bezl *to embezzle*, **bake** *tobacco*, **kos** *because*, **lāns** *allowance*, **list** *to enlist*, **live(r)** *deliver*, **lotments** *allotments*, **piel** *to appeal*, **saieti** *society*, **saizez** *assizes*, **ses** *to assess, tax*, **tais** *to entice*, **twīn** *between*, **vantidž** *advantage*.

deevi *affidavit*, **demek** (lit. epidemic) *potato disease*.

§ **247.** *b.* In syllables preceded by the principal accent:

aktli *actually*, **dif-rnt** *different*, **džen-rl** *general*, **kumpni** *company*, **n̦at-rl**, **n̦at-re-bl** *natural*, **nuebdi** *nobody*, **navi** (lit. navigation?) *canal*, **oepeþ** *halfpenny worth*, **peneþ** *pennyworth*, **reg-le(r)** *regular*, **sumdi** *somebody*.

Vocalic l:

anl *handle*, **apl** *apple*, **ginl** *a long narrow uncovered passage*, **gruml** *to grumble*, **kanl** *candle*, **ketl** *kettle*, **kredl** *cradle*, **kudl** *to embrace*, **sinl** *single*, **smitl** *to infect*, **spinl** *spindle*, **þiml** *thimble*, **uml** *humble*.

Vocalic m:

bodm *bottom*, **buism** *bosom*, **evm** *heaven*, **fadm** *fathom*, **fipms** *five pence*, **kustm** *custom*, **luensm** *lonely*, **wizdm** *wisdom, wise*, **wiepm** *weapon*.

Vocalic n:

ādn *to harden*, **brimstn** *brimstone*, **eenšn** *ancient*, **fasn** *to* *fasten*, **feš̌n** *fashion*, **frozn** *frozen*, **indž̌n** *engine*, **inlnd** *England*, **fotn** (pp.) *fought*, **foetn** *fortune*, **mutn** *mutton*, **pidž̌n** *pigeon*, **ratn** *rat*, **sāvnt** *servant*, **seldn** *seldom*, **slidn** (pp.) *slid*, **tš̌ozn** *chosen*, **pāzn** *thousand*.

Vocalic ɒ :

beegɒ *bargain*, **beekɒ** *bacon*, **brokɒ** *broken*, **dokɒ** *dock*, **drukɒ** *drunk, drunken*, **rekɒ** *to reckon*, **spokɒ** *spoken*, **sukɒ** *sunk*, **tuekɒ** *token*, **ugɒ** *hip*, **wegɒ** *wagon*, **wokɒ** *to waken*.

Svarabhakti.

§ 248. A vowel has been developed between l, r, and a following consonant in: **galɘk** (O. Fr. **galc**) *left hand*, **sterɘk** (OE. **stirc**, also **styric**) *heifer*, **tš̌erɘp** (ME. **chirpen**) *to chirp*.

Weak Forms and Particles.

§ 249. The following is a fairly complete list, arranged alphabetically, of words which have weak forms caused by the sentence accent. Any other unaccented forms not given here will be found under the headings of pronouns, auxiliary verbs, adverbs, conjunctions, and prepositions.

The auxiliary verb **diu** is never used in asking questions, except when it begins the sentence: **dije** (**deje**) **þiɒk il** (**el**) **diut?** *do you think he will do it?* but **wile diut, þiɒk je?** *will he do it, do you think?* The auxiliary verb *have* (**ev, e ; ɘv, ɘ**) is often omitted entirely, or perhaps rather has disappeared through assimilation ; thus **a dunt** *I have done it*, **we funt** *we have found it* ; here **fun** is the pp. and not the pret., *we found it* is **we fant**.

a = *I*.   Chiefly used in direct assertions: **a fan ɘm** *I found them*.

abed *yes but* : **abed ठa men ger up suin** *yes but thou must get up soon.*

am, aim, im *I am.* **aim, am** are used in principal and **im** in subordinate sentences : **aim** or **am nuen bān te stop hie(r)** *I am not going to stop here.* **if im wīl inif** *if I am well enough.*

    bi = 1. *be* : **wil ठe bi wi em?** *will they be with them?*

    = 2. *by* : **bi nā** *by now.*

    bin *been.*

    bed *but.*

    —d = 1. *had* : **ठed** *they had,* **ad** *I had.*

        = 2. *would, wouldst* : **ठad e te diut** *thou wouldst have to do it.*

de, di *do* : **deje** or **dije þiɴk el kum?** *do you think he will come?*

duz, dus (voiceless before the **t**) *does, dost* : **þa duz** *thou dost,* but **dus te?** *dost thou?*

e, ev *have* : **wis et** *we shall have it,* but **wis ev em** *we shall have them.*

ez, es *hast, has* : cp. **duz, dus.**

    e = 1. *a* : **e boni bān** *a pretty child.*

    = 2. *he* (in subordinate sentences and interrogatively, in other cases it is **ĭ**).

    = 3. *her* (before consonants) : **e faठe(r)** *her father.*

    = 4. *have* (weakest form) : **ast e dunt if id ed e tšons** *I should have done it, if I had had a chance.*

    = 5. *on* : **e ठi rig** *on thy back.*

    = 6. *of* (may be used before a vowel or a consonant, **ev** only before vowels) :

e pund e or **ev aplz** *a pound of apples.*

NOTE.—Through **e** being also the unaccented form of **on**, it often happens that **on** is used where we should expect **ev**, as **toef on em** *the half of them.*

ed = 1. *had.*

= 2. *would*: it ed or ted tak ə lot *it would take a lot.*

em or rather m (vocalic) *them*: sam em up *pick them up.*

en *an*: en apl *an apple.*

en or rather n (vocalic) =

    1. *and*: Doed en Eels *George and Alice.*

    2. *one*: it wer ə guid en *it was a good one.*

ə(r) = 1. *or.*

    = 2. *are.*

et = 1. *at.* et uem *at home.*

    = 2. *that* (cj.): a sī et im reɒ *I see that I am wrong.*

    = 3. *who, whom* (rel.): im et sed sue *he who said so,*
      ðem et we soe dān trued *those whom we saw*
      down the road.

ev = 1. *have* (weakest form before vowels): ðe med ev ed
      it bi nā *they might have had it by now.*

    = 2. *of* (before vowels): toef ev ə keek *the half of a*
      tea-cake.

ez = 1. *us*: giv ez ə tūþri *give us a few* (lit. *two or three*).

    = 2. *he has*: wen ez weŏt isen *when he has washed*
      himself.

    = 3. *he is*: wol ez bān *until he is going.*

    = 4. *as.*

fe(r) *for.*

fre *from.*

i = 1. *in*: i tās *in the house.*

    = 2. *I* (in subordinate and interrogative sentences,
      see a): sali et? *shall I have it?* if i ger it *if I*
      get it.

    = 3. *he* (in direct assertions): i sez *he says.*

inte *into.*

iz *his,* but is before voiceless sounds: a mer iz muŏe(r)
I met his mother, but is faŏe(r) *his father.*

je = 1. *ye, you.*

= 2. *your* (before consonants).

= 3. *you are* (before consonants) je bān, äje? *you are going, are you?*

jet = 1. *yet.*

= 2. *you it*: al sel jet *I will sell you it.*

ked *could.*

kɒ (vocalic ɒ) *can*: ðɑ kɒ see wot te laiks *thou canst say what thou likest.*

l *will*: al *I'll*, wil *we will*, etc.

me = 1. *me* gi(v) me e feu *give me a few.*

= 2. *may*: ame wŏk wol i drop fer out te keez *I may work until I drop for anything thou carest.*

med *might.*

men or rather mn (with vocalic n)

= 1. *must*: a men gue *I must go.*

= 2. *man*: diu it, men *do it, man.*

mi *my.*

ne(r) = 1. *nor.*

= 2. *than* (after a comparative).

net, nt (the form net is seldom used. The usual form is nt) *not.*

s *us* (after voiceless consonant): lets ev em *let us have them.*

s, el: ðasl, ðas et *thou shalt have it.*

sänt *shall not.*

sant *saint* (before proper names).

se *so.*

sed, st *should, shouldst*: ðɑ sed or ðast e dunt *thou shouldest have done it.*

še *she* (in subordinate and interrogative sentences, in other cases šŭ).

t = 1. *the* : **tman** *the man.*

    = 2. *it* : **len met** *lend me it.*

    = 3. *art* : **ðat e fuil** *thou art a fool.*

ta, te *thou* (in subordinate and interrogative sentences, in other cases **ðä**).

te, tev (before vowels) *to.*

ðe *there* : **ðez** *there is, there has, there are.*

ðe = 1. *thee* : **a spak te ðe** *I spoke to thee.*

    = 2. *they* : **mun ðe stop?** *must they stop?*

    = 3. *they* (*are*) : **ðe nuen se ritš** *they are not so rich.*

    = 4. *they* (*have*) : **wen ðe funt** *when they have found it.*

    = 5. *their* (before consonants).

ði *thy.*

v *have* : **wiv sīnt** *we have seen it.*

wa *why.* The unaccented form of **wai**, cp. **a** beside **ai** *I,* **wol** beside **wail** *while, until.* It is always used when speaking in an encouraging manner to a person : **wa lad, ða men trai** *why lad, thou must try.*

we = 1. *we* : **sal we gue?** *shall we go?*

    = 2. *our* (before consonants) **we faðe buits** *our father's boots,* but **we soe wer ont** *we saw our aunt.*

    = 3. *we* (*are*) : **we bān te d'len** *we are going to the Glen.*

    = 4. *was, were* : **a we liukin foje** *I was looking for you.*

wed *would.*

wi = 1. *with.*

    = 2. *we* (in direct assertions).

    = 3. *wilt* : **wite** *wilt thou.*

wol *until,* unaccented form of **wail** (noun) *while.*

z = 1. *is* : **iz** *he is.*

    = 2. *has, hast* : **ðaz** *thou hast,* **iz** *he has.*

CHAPTER VI.

The Semi-vowels.

w.

a. Initially.

§ 250. OE. initial w has remained before vowels: **waip** *to wipe*, **weed** *to wade*, **wee(r)** *to spend money*, **wāk** *work*, **wiðe(r)** *to hurl, throw*, **woef** *insipid*, **wote(r)** *water*.

It also appears as w in words of Norse origin: **weeve(r)** *to waver*, **winde** *window*, **wik** *quick, alive*, **wiɒ** *wing*, **wont** *want*.

In words of French origin we have w in some words and v in others, just as in the lit. language: **warend** *to warrant*, **weedž** *wage*, **weet** *to wait*, **walep** *to beat, flog*, **vari** *very*, **viel** *veal*, **vois** *voice*, **voiðe(r)** *a large clothes' basket*.

It has disappeared in the combination wr : **rait** *to write*, **reɒ** *wrong*. Examples for wl- are wanting.

It has also generally remained in the OE. combinations hw, dw, þw, tw, sw, as **wot** *what*, **wīl** *wheel*, **dwinl** *to dwindle*, **dwāf** *dwarf*, **witl** (ME. þwitel) *large carving knife*, **weɒ** (OE. þwang) *thong*, **wak** *to beat, flog*, **twais** *twice*, **twot** *pudendum fem.*, **swiet** *to sweat*, **sweep** *the handle of a machine*.

kw mostly occurs in French words: **kweet** *quart*, **kwari**
quarry, **kwaleti** *quality*.

Initial **w** has disappeared in the weak forms of **wil** *will*,
wod *would*, as **al gue** *I will go*, **id diut, if e kud** *he would
do it, if he could*.

w has also disappeared in: **kil** *to kill*, **kud** *cud*, **sued**
sword, **sitš** *such*, **sump** *a puddle* or *dirty pool of water*. **tū**
two, **ue** *who*.

b. Medially.

Medial **w** + final vowel have become **e** after consonants:
swole (OE. **swalwe**) *swallow*, **spare** (OE. **spearwa**) *sparrow*,
jare *yarrow*, **wide** (OE. **widwe**) *widow, widower*.

aw > oe: **tloe** (OE. **clawu**) *claw*, § 63.

āw > oe: **bloe** *to blow*, **noe** *to know*, **sloe** *slow*, **snoe** *snow*,
§ 123.

eow, ew > eu: **eu** (OE. **eowu**) *ewe*, **streu** (OE. **strewian**)
to strew, § 85.

ēaw > eu: **deu** (OE. **dēaw**) *dew*, **feu** *few*, **eu** (OE. **hēawan**)
to hew, § 180.

ēow > iu, eu: **triu** *true*, **riu** *to rue*, **briu** *to brew*   **eu** *yew*,
seu *to sew*, § 190.

īw > iu: **spiu** *to spew*, § 159.

ōw > ou: **dlou** *to glow*, **grou** *to grow*, **flou** *to flow*, § 166.

§ **251. w** has disappeared in words compounded with
ward: **bakedz** *backwards*, **fored** *forward*, **oeked** *awkward*,
tādz *towards*, § 243; as also in those compounded with
worth: **oepeþ** *halfpenny worth*, **peneþ** *pennyworth*, **siks-
peneþ** *sixpenny worth*, etc.

It has also disappeared in: **midif** *midwife*, **oles** *always*,
sumet (**et** may here however be the rel. pr.) *something*,
anything, **anse(r)** *answer*, **grunsil** *groundsel*.

j.

§ **252.** OE. initial j, mostly written g, has had the same development as in lit. Engl.: **jĭ, je** *ye, you,* **jie(r)** *year,* **jon** *yon,* **juek** *yoke,* **jun** *young.*

§ **253.** French **ü**, which has become **juw** in lit. Engl., appears in the W. dial. as a falling diphthong initially, medially, and finally: **ius** *use,* **iuneti** *unity,* **flute(r)** *future,* **viu** *view,* § 237.

The Liquids.

1.

§ **254.** l has generally remained unchanged: **lap** *to wrap up,* **lat** *late,* **lig** *to lie down,* **loin** *lane,* **lium** *loom.*

boeld (ME. **balled**) *bald,* **molt** *malt,* **fĭld** *field,* **mĭld** *mild,* **wĭld** *wild,* **bĭld** *to build,* **flik** *flitch of bacon,* **jole** *yellow,* **tšelte(r)** *to clot, coagulate (of blood),* **twilt** *quilt,* **nozl** *to beat, thrash,* **blob** *bubble,* **galesez** *braces.*

džoul *to knock, strike,* **kāl** *to frown,* **foel** *to fall,* **koil** *coal,* **teel** *tale,* **swiel** *to gutter (of a candle).*

§ **255.** **al** has become **oe** in the combinations **lf,** OE. **lh, lk, lm, ll, lv.** For examples see §§ 62, 198. To these add: **omest** *almost,* **oeminak** *almanac,* **oemend** *almond.*

al has become **ou** before a following **d.** For examples see §§ 64, 199.

ol has become **ou** before a following consonant. For examples see §§ 103, 220.

§ **256.** l has also disappeared before a following consonant in: **witš** (OE. **hwelc**) *which,* **sitš** (OE. **swelc**) *such,* **būk** *bulk,* **stūp** (ME. **stolpe**) *a post.*

It has also disappeared in: **wod, wed, -d** (§ 397) *would,* sud, sed, st (§ 391) *should*, sänt *shall not*, s (§ 391) *shall*, wite ? (§ 397) *wilt thou?* wient *will not*.

In fout (ME. faute, Fr. faute) *fault*, māt (cp. Lat. mūtāre) *to moult*, there probably never was an l in the dialect forms.

§ 257. Consonantal l, when it came to stand finally, has become vocalic after consonants: adl *to earn*, kitl *to tickle*, nibl *to nibble*, ridl *sieve*, satl *to settle*. For further examples see § 247 *b*.

r.

§ 258. r, which is a gently (not strongly as in Scotch) trilled sound, has only remained intact before a following vowel:

raiv *to tear*, reit *right*, ram *to thrust, press*, rīzd *rancid (of bacon)*, briɒ *to bring*, brek *to break*, beri *to bury*, fere *furrow*, sore *sorrow*, sare *to serve*, vari *very*.

r has probably been lost in aim (OE. hrīm?) *hoarfrost*.

§ 259. Before a following consonant it has entirely disappeared: bān (§ 61) *child*, bied (§ 68) *beard*, wāk (§ 74) *work*, bēk (§ 90) *birch*, boen (§ 104, 1) *born*, bued (§ 104, 2) *board*, dōst (§ 113, 1) *durst*, bēþ (§ 120, 1) *birth*, aien (§ 157) *iron*, dālin (§ 189) *darling*, kweet (§ 203) *quart*, sāvnt (§ 207) *servant*, oeðe(r) (§ 223) *order*, kēn (§ 228) *currant*, faðe(r) *father*, pl. faðez, swie(r) *to swear*, but i swiez *he swears*.

NOTE.—The above list contains one example only of the various vowels which have been influenced through the absorption of the r; for full lists of examples, see the paragraphs enclosed in parentheses.

§ 260. r, which has come to stand finally in the modern dialect, is still slightly trilled, but not so strongly as before a following vowel. This is always the case when

the word containing it is used alone, or stands at the end
of a sentence. In these positions it is never weakened into
a mere voiced glide as in lit. Engl. **fear**, nor does it disappear altogether as in lit. Engl. **far**. We thus make a
distinction between **pee** *pay*, and- **pee(r)** *pair*, **kā** *cow*, and
kāe(r) *to cower*.

r disappears, of course, altogether in the sentence when
the next word begins with a consonant: **aje bān ?** *are you
going ?* **wi we leekin** *we were playing.*

Examples of final r are: **wāe(r)** *worse*, **dlue(r)** *to stare
hard*, **smue(r)** *to smother*, **bie(r)** *to bear*, **pie(r)** *pear.*

§ 261. In addition to the examples in which r has
undergone metathesis in the lit. language as, **bēd** *bird*, **bēn**
to burn, **brīt** *bright*, **frīt** *fright*, **oes** *horse*, **pēd** *third*, we
have **brust** *to burst*, **gēn** *to grin*, **gēs** (also OE. **gærs**) *grass*,
gēsl *gristle*, **gēt** *great*, **kēsmes** *Christmas*, **kēsn** *to christen.*

§ 262. r has disappeared in **pim-ruez** *primrose.*

The Nasals.

m.

§ 263. m has generally remained unchanged: **muml**
to mumble, **muin** *moon*, **mistl** *cow-house*, **mizl** *to drizzle* (*of
rain*), **mun** *must*, **mūd** *crowded, crammed.*

gami *lame*, **kākume(r)** *cucumber*, **niml** *nimble*, **treml** *to
tremble*, **tšeeme(r)** *chamber*, **tuml** *to tumble*, **uml** *humble.*

brim *to put the boar to the sow*, **gam** *to gamble*, **krum**
crumb, **rām** *room*, **sam up** *to pick up.*

§ 264. m has become vocalic after consonants: **bodm**
bottom, **fadm** *fathom*, **film** *film*, **kindm** *kingdom*. m is also
vocalic in **em** (= m) *them.*

n.

§ 265. Initial n has remained unchanged: nate(r) *to gnaw*, *nibble*, nati *neat*, *tidy*, *dexterous (of old people)*, navi *canal*, nīt *night*, nie(r) *kidney*, noilz (pl.) *the short hairs taken out of wool by the combing machine.*

§ 266. When n has remained medial in the W. dial., it has generally undergone no change: dwinl *to dwindle*, kanl *candle*, sind *to rinse*, *wash out*, spinl *spindle*, þune(r) *thunder.*

§ 267. Medial n has disappeared before s in unaccented syllables without compensation lengthening: estied *instead*, Robisn *Robinson*, Adkisn *Atkinson.*

§ 268. n has remained when it has come to stand finally after vowels or was already final in OE.: ain (ME. hīne) *hind*, bin (OE. binnan) *within*, bleen *blain*, *boil*, gruin *a pig's snout*, don *to put on one's clothes*, len (OE. lænan) *to lend*, nuin *noon*, olin *holly*, speen (OE. spanan) *to wean.*

§ 269. n has become vocalic after dentals and sibilants: eenšn *ancient*, fešn *fashion*, fezn *pheasant*, frozn *frozen*, miln (OE. myln) *mill*, ratn (O. Fr. raton) *rat*, seldn (OE. seldon) *seldom*. For other examples see § 247 *b*.

§ 270. n has become vocalic m after labials by assimilation:

apm (lit. *happen*) *perhaps*, fipms *fivepence*, þrepms *three pence*, etc., opm *open*, wiepm *weapon*. For further examples see § 247 *b*.

evm *even*, īmin *evening*, sevm *seven*, uvm *oven*, wovm *woven.*

§ 271. n has become vocalic ŋ after gutturals: beegŋ *bargain*, ugŋ *hip*, wegŋ *wagon*.

brokṇ *broken*, buəkṇ (ME. bolkin) *to retch, belch*, kṇ (weak form of kan *can*, akṇ diut *I can do it*), spokṇ *spoken*, stākṇ *to stiffen*, wokṇ *to waken*.

§ 272.• n generally disappears in ə *on*, i *in*. It has also disappeared in oepəþ *halfpenny worth*. It has also disappeared by assimilation in amət *am not*.

ṇ.

§ 273. The guttural ṇ, written n in OE., only occurred before the gutturals g and c.

It has generally remained in accented syllables in the W. dialect: biṇ (O. Icel. bingr *heap*) *bin*, briṇ *to bring*, driṇk *to drink*, iṇ (ME. hengen) *to hang*, liṇ (O. Icel. lyng) *heather*, teṇz *tongs*, þiṇ *thing*, þiṇk *to think*, weṇ *thong*.

fiṇə(r) *finger*, never fiṇgə(r) as in lit. Engl., iṇliš *English*, miṇl *to mingle*, uṇə(r) *hunger*, siṇl *single*.

Note.—kindm (OE. cynedōm) but lit. Engl. *kingdom*, through association with *king*.

§ 274. ṇ has disappeared through assimilation before the following kṇ in the pp. of verbs ending in ṇk : drukṇ *drunk, drunken*, sukṇ *sunk*, slukṇ *slunk*, šrukṇ *shrunk*. But see § 368.

§ 275. ṇ has become n before the following dental in : lenþ *length*, strenþ *strength*.

§ 276. ṇ has regularly become n in unaccented syllables : fādin *farthing*, gezlin *gosling*, īmin *evening*, iəzinz *the eaves of a building*, midin (ME. midding) *dunghill*, runin *running*, and similarly in all present participles.

§ 277. Palatal ṇ, written n in OE., only occurred before the palatal forms of g and c.

In the W. dial. it has become dental n as in lit. Engl.: drenš (OE. drencan) *to drench*, sinž (OE. sengan) *to singe*.

The Labials.

p.

§ 278. p has remained in all positions:

pei *pea*, **pimruez** *primrose*, **piek** *perch*, **pāk** *a kind of blain*, **poem** *palm*, **poez** (O. Fr. **poulser**) *to kick*, **poutri** *poultry*, **prog** *to collect wood for the bonfire on the fifth of November*, **preet** *to prate, babble*, **put** *to put*.

lopste(r) (OE. **loppestre**) *lobster*, **speed** *spade*, **speen** *to wean*.

dolep *lump of dirt*, **draip** *to drip*, **elp** *to help*, **flep** *to beat, flog*, **kep** *to catch (a ball)*, **kraps** *the renderings of lard*, **lop** *flea*, **noep** (ME. **nolpen**) *to hit on the head*.

§ 279. Assimilation has taken place as in lit. Engl. in **emti** (ME. **empti**, but OE. **æmet(t)ig**) *empty*, **kubed** *cupboard*.

b.

§ 280. The voiced explosive **b** has generally remained in the W. dialect:

bān *child*, **bef** (ME. **beffin**) *to cough*, **bek** *beck*, **ben** (O. Icel. **banga** *to hammer*), *to throw, hit violently*, **bid** *to invite to a funeral*, **boged** *ghost*, **brig** *bridge*, **bun** *bound*.

bleb *blister*, **bluðe(r)** *to weep*, generally used in the phrase **te bluðe(r) en rue(r)** lit. *to blubber and roar*, **gab** (cp. O. N. **gabba**) *impudence*, **kubed** *cupboard*, **neb** *beak*, **nub** *to nudge*, **nuebdi** *nobody*, **web** *web*.

§ 281. b has disappeared after **m**: **kuem** *comb*, **lam** *lamb*, **tlim** *to climb*, **wuem** *womb*. Also in **sumdi** *somebody*.

§ 282. b never occurs between m—l or m—r, as in lit. Engl.: əseml *to assemble*, fuml *to fumble*, muml *to mumble*, niml *nimble*, raml *to ramble*, treml *to tremble*, tuml *to tumble*, þiml *thimble*, uml *humble*.

kākumə(r) *cucumber*, numə(r) *number*, slumə(r) *slumber*, tšeemə(r) *chamber*.

f.

§ 283. OE. f was used to re resent both the voiceless (= Mod. Engl. f) and the voiced (= Mod. Engl. v) spirant.

1. Initially it was voiceless and corresponds to Germanic f.

2. Medially it was voiced, except in the combinations ff, ft, fs. See Sievers, OE. Gr. § 192.

3. Finally it was probably voiceless in the historic period even when it corresponded to Germanic ƀ. But when OE. f came to stand medially through being followed by a case, or personal ending, etc., it was voiced, thus wīf *wife*, gen. wīfes, pret. sing. geaf *I, he gave*, pl. gēafon. In this case the W. dial., like lit. Engl., has sometimes generalized the one form, sometimes the other. We shall here treat the sounds in the above order.

1. faðe(r) *father*, feu *few*, flee *to frighten*, flumeks *to confound, cheat*, foil *foal*, foud *fold*, fouk *folk*, fout *fault*, freem *to make a start*, fudl *to confuse*, fuzi *soft, spongy*.

2. eft *haft*, gift *gift*, rift *to belch, eructate*, sift *to sift*, weft *weft*, kuf *cuff*.

delv *to delve*, daiv *to dive*, draiv *to drive*, duv *dove*, evm *heaven*, ivə(r) *ever*, kāv *to carve*, kuəv *cove*, live(r) *liver*, neiv (O. Icel. knefl) *fist*, nivə(r) *never*, raiv (O. Icel. rīfa *to break*) *to tear*, siv *sieve*, stāv *to starve*, stuəv *stove*, šeəv *to shave*, šuv *to shove*, þraiv *to thrive*, weiv *to weave*.

ev, əv, ə *have*, and liv *to live* are, of course, not directly
developed from OE. habban, libban but from the forms
without gemination, as hafað *he has*, hæfdə *he had*, liofað
he lives, lifdə *he lived*.

It has disappeared as in lit. Engl. in such words as: ez
hast, has, eltə(r) (OE. healfter) *halter*, ənent *opposite*, iəd
head, krœl *to crawl*, oək *hawk*, leedi *lady*, loəd *lord*, wimin
women, wumən *woman*.

It has also disappeared in: əbūn *above*, īmin *evening*,
steim (ME. stefnen, OE. ge-stefnian and a·stemnian *to give
voice for, appoint*) *to bespeak a thing*, šūl *shovel*, gīn *given*,
ouə(r) beside ovə(r) *over*, niə(r) beside nivə(r) *never*, and
generally also in the present gi, pret. ga and ə, ə *have*,
when the next word begins with a consonant.

The voiced spirant has become b in rəbit *rivet*, if the
dial. word is etymologically the same as the lit. Engl. word.

3. delf *stone quarry*, kaf *chaff*, oəf *half*, ruif *roof*, tēf
turf, þīf *thief*, uif *hoof*, waif *wife*. ·

aiv *hive*, faiv *five*, greəv *grave*, twelv *twelve*.

f has disappeared in: oəpni *halfpenny*, ə *of*, sel, sen *self*.

§ 284. tə *to* appears as təv when the next word begins
with a vowel: təv ə man *to a man*.

The Dentals.

t.

§ 285. Initial t has remained: taid *feast-time*, teem
tume, temz (ME. temse) *hop-sieve*, teu (OE. tēawian) *to
work zealously*, toe *a marble of any kind*, toidi *small,
little*, troləp *a dirty, untidy person*, tul (O. Icel. til) *to*.

§ 286. Medial t has mostly remained unchanged:

antm (OE. antefn) *anthem*, getn *got*, nati *neat, tidy, dex-terous (of old people)*, ratn *rat*, tluste(r) *cluster*.

It has become d in bodm *bottom*, praid *pride*. It has become r in poreəts *potatoes*, has undergone metathesis in witek *wicket*, and disappeared before the b in nobed (lit. *not but*) *only*.

§ 287. t is dropped between s and a following l or n in :

busl *bustle*, bruslz *bristles*, gēsl *gristle*, kasl *castle*, rasl to *wrestle*, þrosl *thrush*, wisl *whistle*, dēsnt *durst not*; but mistl (O. Icel. mjalta-sel *shed for milking*) *cow-house*.

brusn (pp.) *burst*, fasn to *fasten*, lisn to *listen*, ouə-kesn *overcast, gloomy (of the sky)*, þrusn (pp.) *thrust*.

ts > ss > s in wisnde *Whitsuntide*. Whitsunday is wisnde sunde.

§ 288. The t in French words which has become tš in lit. Engl. through the influence of the following ü has remained in the W. dialect :

flete(r) *feature*, fēnite(r) *furniture*, flute(r) *future*, foetn *fortune*, kriete(r) *creature*, moiste(r) *moisture*, neete(r) *nature*, natrəl *natural*, paste(r) *pasture*, pikte(r) *picture*, vente(r) to *venture*.

§ 289. When t came to stand finally in the W. dial., or was final already in OE., it has generally remained :

fift (OE. fīfta) *fifth*, sikst *sixth*, toist *toast*, twelft *twelfth*.

bāt *without*, feit to *fight*, gēt *great*, goit (ME. gote) *water channel*, mīt to *meet*, out *holt*, slāt to *bedabble*, suit *soot*.

bit *bit*, fat *fat*, it *it*, kot *staples of wool tightly entangled together*, lat (OE. lætt) *lath*, lat *late*, mat *mat*, net *net*, wet *wet*.

§ 290. The t in all verbal forms ending in t preceded by a short vowel, appears as r when the next word begins with a vowel. We regularly say : amīt im ivri dee *I meet*

him every day ; but **amer im ivri dee** *I met him every day.*
Similarly with **get me wun** *get me one*, **ger up** *get up*, **gar**
got, **ir** *to hit*, **ler** *to let*, **pur** *to put*, **sar** *sat*, **ser** *to set*, **sir** *to
sit*, **šur** *to shut*, etc.   Also in all the present participles, as
gerin *getting*.

> NOTE.—This phenomenon is widely spread in Mod. English dialects. See
> EEPr. vol. v. p. 420.

The same is also the case with the pronoun **wot** *what*:
wotste dun ? *what hast thou done ?* but **wor iz it** ? *what is it?*

§ 291. **t** has become **d** in : **abed** *yes but*, **bed** *but*, **prād**
proud, **buzed** (O. Fr. **busart**), *butterfly*, **Adkisn** *Atkinson*,
warend *to warrant*.

§ 292. It has been dropped in **kēn** *currant*, **sādžn**
sergeant, **džais** (O. Fr. **giste**) *joist*.   The older generation
also say **omes** *almost*, **āvis** *harvest*, **bies** (lit. *beast*) *cow*,
cows.

§ 293. A **t** is never pronounced in **eenšn** (Fr. **ancien**)
ancient, **fezn** (O. Fr. **faisan**) *pheasant*, **tairen** *tyrqnt*.

§ 294. **t** is excrescent in **vāment** *vermin*.

d.

§ 295. Initial **d** has remained : **daiv** *to dive*, **deu** *dew*,
dī *to die*, **died** *dead*, **dof** *to undress*, **don** *to dress*, **dreet** *to
drawl*.

§ 296. Medial **d** has also generally remained unchanged :

fidl *fiddle*, **inde(r)** *to hinder*, **midin** (ME. midding, Dan.
mögdynge) *dunghill*, **midl** *middle*, **nīdl** *needle*, **ridn** *riden*,
wide *widow*, **sadl** *saddle*, **redi** *ready*.

§ 297. Intervocalic **d** followed by **r** in the next syllable

has become ð: bleðe(r) *bladder*, bluðe(r) *to cry, weep*,
diðe(r) (ME. diderin) *to shiver*, faðe(r) *father*, foðe(r) *fodder*,
geðe(r) *to gather*, te-geðe(r) *together*, iðe(r) *hither*, konsiðe(r)
to consider, laðe(r) *ladder*, moiðe(r) *to ponder, be anxious
about a thing*, muðe(r) *mother*, pāðe(r) *powder*, šuðe(r) *to
shudder*, tluðe(r) *to get closely together*, uðe(r) *udder*,
voiðe(r) (O. Fr. voider *to void*) *a large clothes' basket*,
weðe(r) *weather*.

NOTE.—The words *thither* and *whither* are not used in the dialect.

The law also holds good when an l or r has disappeared
before the d: soðe(r) *solder*, māðe(r) *murder*, oeðe(r) *to
order*.

NOTE.—The ð in māðe(r) is probably not the þ in OE. myrþran, but rþ
became rd (§ 306, 2) and then ð by the above law.

§ **298.** d never occurs between n—l, n—r, as in lit.
English :

anl *handle*, dwinl *to dwindle*, kanl *candle*, kinlin *firewood*, spinl *spindle*.

gane(r) *gander*, þune(r) *thunder*.

§ **299.** d has disappeared in ansem *handsome*, anfl
handful, grunsil *groundsel*, gran-faðe(r), gram-faðe(r)
grandfather, lanloed *landlord*, unded *hundred*, but undet
(by assimilation of dt) *hundredth*.

§ **300.** OE. final d and the medial d which has come
to stand finally in the W. dial. have generally remained :
bid *to invite to a funeral*, find *to find*, grund *ground*, od
to hold, oud *old*, pund *pound*, roid *a clearing (of a wood)*,
sind *to rinse, wash out*, wund *a wound*, blier-īd *blear-
eyed*.

§ **301.** d has disappeared after n in : bran (OE. brand)
niu *quite new*, en *and*, þāzn *thousand*, uzbn *husband*,

and also in the pret. and pp. of the verbs **bind** *to bind*, **find** *to find*, **wind** *to wind*, thus : **ban, bun ; fan, fun ; wan, wun**.

d has also been dropped in **skafl** *scaffold*, **skaflin** *scaffolding*.

§ 302. Final **ndz** has become **nz** : **anz** *hands*, **frenz** *friends*, **senz** *sends*, **grunz** (lit. *grounds*) *sediment*. **þāzn** and **uzbn** may accordingly be new formations from the plural forms.

§ 303. A **d** is never pronounced in **ain** (ME. **hīne**) *hind*, **bān** (O. Icel. **būenn**) *going*, as **wie te bān ?** *where art thou going ?*, **len** (OE. **lǣnan**) *to lend*.

§ 304. **d** is excrescent in **arend** (ME. **aranie**, O. Fr. **araigne**) *spider*, **drānd** *to drown*.

§ 305. **d** has become **t** in **wāte** (lit. *work-day*), *week-day*, **wōsit** *worsted*, **st** the weak form of **sud** *should*. In **be-int** *behind*, the **t** is probably due to the **t** in **frunt** *front* ; for similar examples see Paul-Braune's Beiträge, xiii. p. 590. In the phrase **iust te wod** or **wed** *to be wont* or *willing*, the **t** is due to assimilation with **te** : **ða iust te wed diu e bit e wāk** *thou wast formerly wont to do a bit of work*.

þ.

§ 306. OE. **þ**, also written **ð**, was a voiceless spirant like the **th** in lit. Engl. *thin*, initially, finally as also medially except probably between voiced sounds. Between voiced sounds it was probably voiced like the **th** in lit. Engl. *breathe*. See Sievers, OE. Gr. § 201.

We shall here adopt the following order : 1. Initially. 2. When the sound or its further development has remained medial in the W. dialect. 3. When it has become final in

the W. dialect. In this case two subdivisions are necessary according as we have now the voiceless or the voiced
sound. Cp. § 283, 3.

Fifty years ago f for þ and v for ð were quite general
throughout the Township of Idle, but they have now practically disappeared except as an individualism. When I
was a boy þ and ð were regularly used among the younger
Windhill people, but f and v were still generally used in
Thackley and Idle, which are only about a mile distant
from W. I well remember how we used to twit the
Thackley and Idle people about their pronunciation of
these sounds: **fakle** *Thackley*, **fiŋk** *think*, **fēd** *third*, **leev**
barn, **smivi** *smithy*, etc.

1. þ has remained voiceless except in pronouns and the
adverbs derived from them:

þak *thatch*, **þiŋk** *to think*, **þoil** *to give ungrudgingly*,
þraiv *to thrive*, **þriep** (OE. **þrēapian** *to rebuke*) *to contradict*,
dispute.

In the pronouns and the adverbs derived from them
there originally existed double forms: the stressed forms
with þ and the unstressed forms with ð. The W. dial., like
lit. Engl., has generalised the latter, which are now used
both as the stressed and unstressed forms. See the Chapter
on the pronouns:

ðä *thou*, **ði** *thy*, **ðat** (only as demonstrative, the rel. pr.
and cj. is **et** which is of Norse origin) *that*, **ðem** (mostly
as demonstrative, the pers. pr. is **em**) *those*, **ðis** *this*, etc.;
ðie(r) *there*, **ðen** *then*, etc.

The def. art. is generally t and is attached to the following
word, thus **tman** *the man*, **toudn** *the old one*, **tkoilz** *the
coals*. We make a clear distinction between **teebl** *table*
and **t'teebl** *the table*, **eit** *eight* and **eit'** *eighth*, the former is
the ordinary Engl. t and the latter is a suspended t. ð has

become t in the nom. of the second pers. sing. of the pers.
pronoun when used interrogatively and in subordinate
sentences (§ 350): es-te ? *hast thou?* sal-te ? *shalt thou?* wite ? *wilt thou?* kante diut ? *canst thou do it?* þa kɒ gue
wen tet redi *thou canst go when thou art ready.*

þ has disappeared before w in : wak *to beat severely,* see
Skeat, Et. Dict., witl (ME. þwitel) *large carving knife,*
weɒ (OE. þwang) *thong.*

Occasionally the þ is omitted in the pres. tense of þiɒk,
as a iɒk *I think.*

2. Between vowels we have ð: feðe(r) *feather,* laðe(r)
foam, froth, leðe(r) *leather,* reeðe(r) *rather,* smiði *smithy,*
weðe(r) (OE. weðer) *the wool of a sheep which has already
been shorn at least once before.*

It has become d medially after r in : bēdn *burden,* fādin
farthing, efued *to afford.*

It has also become d in : fadm *fathom,* snodn *to make
smooth,* snod (O. Icel. snoðenn *smooth (of hair), bald)
smooth, even.*

ð has disappeared in moek (O. Icel. maðkr) *maggot,* and
besk (O. Icel. baðask) *to bask.*

3. baþ *bath,* dieþ *death,* froþ *froth,* gēþ *girth,* ielþ *health,*
paþ *path,* smiþ *smith,* swāþ (O. Icel. swörðr) *the skin of
bacon,* wēþ *worth.*

brieð *to breathe,* buið *booth,* leeð (O. Icel. hlaða) *barn,*
saið *scythe,* smuið *smooth.*

§ 307. It has disappeared before the s, z in muns
months, tluez *clothes.* And also in wi *with.*

§ 308. The d in beed *to bathe* has probably been influenced by weed *to wade.*

§ 309. The ordinal numerals, except seknd *second,* þēd
third, all end in t. Regular forms are fēst (OE. fyresta),

first, **fift** (OE. **fīfta**) *fifth*, **sikst** (OE. **siexta**) *sixth*, **twelft**
(OE. **twelfta**) *twelfth*, after the analogy of which have
been formed **fouet** (OE. **fēowerða**) *fourth*, **naint** *ninth*, **tent**
tenth, etc.

Sibilants.

s.

§ **310.** Initially and finally as also medially (except
between voiced sounds) OE. **s** was a voiceless spirant like
the **s** in Mod. English **sin**. Medially between voiced
sounds it was possibly voiced like the **s** in Mod. English
rise. See Sievers, OE. Gr. § 204.

The development of **s** in the W. dialect is parallel with
that of **f** (§ 283) and **þ** (§ 306), so that we shall here
distinguish the three positions: 1. Initially. 2. When
the sound has remained medial in the W. dialect. 3. When
the sound was already final in OE. or has become final in
the W. dialect. Here two subdivisions are necessary
according as we have now the voiceless or the voiced
spirant. Cp. § 283.

1. Initial **s** has remained both before vowels and consonants: **sā** *a drain, sough*, **sāk** *to suck*, **sam up** *to pick up*,
seem *lard*, **set** *to set*, **sī** (OE. **sēon** = OHG. **sīhan**) *to stretch*,
sin *since*, **sind** *to rinse, wash out*, **slate('r)** *to spill*, **smuið**
smooth, **snod** *smooth, even*, **snikit** *a small passage*, **speik** *to
speak*, **spitek** *spigot*, **steim** *to bespeak*, **stedi** *steady*, **strie**
straw, **swāþ** *the skin of bacon*, **sweep** *the handle of a
machine*.

s (?) has become **š** in **šŭ**, **šə** *she*.

s has also remained before **ü** in French words, whereas in
the lit. language it has become **š**: **siuge('r)** *sugar*, **siue('r)**
sure.

2. Medially between voiced sounds we have z: bīzm
lesom, biznes *business*, buzed *butterfly*, dlazn *to glaze*, fezn
pheasant, frozn *frozen*, fuzi *soft, spongy*, mizl *to drizzle* (*of
rain*), rīzd *rancid* (*of bacon*), rizn *risen*, þāzn *thousand*,
uzbn *husband*, wizn *to wither*.

z has also remained before ü in French words, but has
become ž in the lit. language: meze(r) *measure*, pleze'(r)
pleasure, treze(r) *treasure*.

The ð in siðez *scissors* is difficult to explain. It is just
possible that it may have been influenced by saið *scythe*,
just as mud *might* (verb) has probably been influenced by
kud *could*, sud *should*, and be-int *behind* by frunt *front*,
and beed *to bathe* by weed *to wade*.

In combination with voiceless sounds s has been retained:
besk *to bask*, blosm *blossom*, fasn *to fasten*, kist *a chest*,
kēsn *to christen*, musl *muscle*, rasl *to wrestle*, rust (O.Icel.
röst) *rest, repose*, trāst *to trust*, þrosl (OE. þrostle) *thrush*.

3. ās *house*, dlas *glass*, džais (O.Fr. giste) *joist*, gīs *geese*,
kēs *to curse*, kus *kiss*, lās (pl. lais) *louse*, mās (pl. mais)
mouse, muns *months*, oes *horse*, ues(t) *hoarse*, ðis *this*.

anz *hands*, bleez *blaze*, duz *dost, does*, but dus te? *dost
thou?* greez *to graze*, iuz *to use*, loiz (OE. losian) *to lose*,
nuez *nose*, raiz *to rise*, ruez *rose*, temz (ME. temse) *hop-
sieve*, tluez *clothes*.

Final z is very common in originally unstressed forms,
as iz, z *is*, ðaz *thou hast*, ĭz *he has, he is*, ez, uz *us*, never us
even as stressed form, ez *as*.

§ 311. s has disappeared in: pei (ME. pese) *pea*, ridl
(ME. redels) *riddle*, šimi *chemise*, tšeri (O.Fr. cerise)
cherry.

The Gutturals.

C.

§ 312. Germanic **k**, generally written **c** in OE., remained a guttural initially before the guttural vowels a, ā, o, ō, u, ū and their mutations e, ǣ, e, ē (œ̄), y, ȳ, but became a palatal before the palatal vowels æ, ǣ (=OHG. ā), e (= Germanic e) ea, eo, ēa, ēo, i, ī and their mutations e, ie (=i-umlaut of ea, eo), īe (i-umlaut of ēa, ēo).

Medial **c** and cc remained a guttural before a following a, o, u, but became palatal when an i or j originally followed, as sēc(e)an = Goth. sōkjan *to seek*, þecc(e)an from older *þakjan *to cover*, bryce from older *brukiz *breach*. See Sievers, OE. Gr. §§ 206–7.

But already at an early period the palatals became gutturals again in many cases in the Anglian dialects, e. g. sēcan *to seek*, þencan *to think*, cāld *cold*. See Sweet, HES. § 535, Kluge, Grundriss der germanischen Philologie, i. pp. 836–41.

1. Initial **c** before consonants.

c has disappeared before **n**: **neid** *to knead*, **naif** *knife*, **nī** *knee*.

It has remained before **r**: **kraps** *the renderings of lard*, **kreev** *to crave*, **krinž** *to cringe*, **kriuk** *crook*, **kroe** *craw*.

It has become **t** before **l**: **tlād** *cloud*, **tlam** *to famish*, **tlāt** *clout*, **tleg** (Lowland Scot. **clag**) *to clog*, **tlenk** *to flog, box on the ears*, **tlie(r)** *clear*, **tliet** *coltsfoot*, **tlien** *clean*, **tlim** *to climb*, **tliɲ** *to cling*, **tlip** *to clip*, **tliu** *a ball of string or worsted*, **tlīv** *to cleave*, **tloe** *claw*, **tloek** *to scratch with the fingers or claws*, **tlok** *to cluck*, **tlomp** *to tread heavily*, **tluek** *cloak*, **tlueþ** *cloth*, **tlueve(r)** *clover*. **k** has disappeared in **nek-leþ** *neckcloth, handkerchief*.

2. Initially before vowels.

kā *cow*, kaf *chaff*, kaind *kind*, kait *kite*, kanl *candle*, kāt *cart*, kāv *to carve*, keək *bread of every kind*, keə(r) *care*, kei *key*, kek *hemlock*, kemp (ME. kempe *shaggy*) *small coarse white hairs in wool*, kep *to catch (a ball*, etc.), kest (ME. kesten) *to cast*, ketl *kettle*, kēgət *kirkgate* (but tšētš *church*), kēnl *kernel*, kēs *to curse*, kōsməs *Christmas*, kīl *to cool*, kil (OE. cwellan) *to kill*, kiln *kiln*, ə-kin *akin*, kīn *keen*, kindm (OE. cynedōm) *kingdom*, kiŋ-kof (cp. ME. kinken *to pant, gasp*), *whooping cough*, kīp *to keep*, kist *a chest, box*, kit (ME. kitte, cp. Mid. Du. kitte) *a pail*, kitl *to tickle*, kitl *to bring forth kittens*, kitšn *kitchen*, koef *calf*, koəl *to call*, kal *to gossip*, koən *corn*, koit *coat*, koud *cold*, kouk (see NED. sub colk) *coke*, kout *colt*, kubəd *cupboard*, kud (OE. cwidu) *cud*, kuəm *comb*, kūk *cook*, kum *to come*.

tšaid *to chide*, tšap *chap*, tšavl *to nibble at, gnaw, chew*, tšeu *to chew*, tšētš *church*, tšiəp *cheap*, tšīk *cheek*, tšikin *chicken*, tšildə(r) *children*, tšin *chin*, tšerəp *to chirp*, tšīz *cheese*, tšiuz *to choose*, tšoək *chalk*, tšoul (ME. chavel, O. Low Germ. kafal) lit. *jaw*, only used in the phrase tšīk ən tšoul *said of two people walking closely together*, tšuək *to choke*, tšuf *proud, haughty*.

3. Initial sc.

skab *scab*, skaftin *shafting*, skelp (ME. skelpen) *to beat, flog*, skep (O. Icel. skeppa) *a large wicker basket for holding spinning bobbins*, skeəlz *scales*, skēf *scurf*, skai *sky*, skift *to shift, remove*, skil *skill*, skin *skin*, skoup *scoop*, skuft *the nape of the neck*, skuil *school*, skul *skull of the head*, skute(r) *to spill*, skraml *to scramble*, skreəp *to scrape*, skrat (ME. scrattin) *to scratch*, skriəm *to scream*, skrīk (O. Low Germ. scrīcōn) *to shriek*.

šak *to shake*, šait *cacare*, šaiv (ME. schīve, M. Low Germ. schīve) *a slice*, šakl *shackle*, šap *shape*, šel *shell*, šelf *shelf*, šeed *shade*, šeem *shame*, šee(r) *share*, šie(r) *to shear*, šil (ME. schellen, but Prom. Parv. p. 446 has schillin) *to shell peas*, šin *shin*, šip *ship*, šiuk *shook*, šop *shop*, šot *shot*, šut *shut*, šuðe(r) *to shudder*, šuv *to shove*, šreŋk *shrank*, šrimp *shrimp*, šriŋk *to shrink*.

Initial sc has become s in: sal, sl, s *shall*, sud, sed, st *should*.

4. When medial c has not become final in the W. dialect.

esked (cp. ME. aske *lizard*) *newt*, fikl *fickle*, kokl *cockle*, miks (by metathesis from OE. miscian) *to mix*, sikl *sickle*, twiŋkl *to twinkle*.

flike(r) *to flicker*, neekt *naked*, snikit *a small passage*, wokŋ *to waken*.

kitšn *kitchen*.

meed *made*, musl *mussel*, teen *taken*, feseen *forsaken*.

5. When c or its further development is final in the W. dialect.

bek *beck*, beek *to bake*, brek *to break*, briuk *brook*, daik *ditch*, dreek *drake*, fleek *flake (of snow)*, bried-fleik (O. Icel. fleki *hurdle*) *a hurdle on which oat-cakes are dried*, flik *flitch of bacon*, flok *flock*, ik (cp. Low Germ. hicken) *to hitch*, iuk *hook*, kok *cock*, lavrek *lark*, lek *to leak*, leek *to play*, lik *to lick*, liuk *to look*, lok *lock*, mak *to make*, muk *muck*, nek *neck*, niuk *nook*, nok *to knock*, pak *bundle*, pluk *pluck*, prik *to prick*, reek *rake*, reik *to reach*, rik *smoke*, sāk *to suck*, sek *sack*, seek *sake*, slek *small coal*, slek *to extinguish a fire with water*, slumek *a dirty, untidy person*, sneek *snake*, snek (ME. snekke) *latch of a door*, spek *speck*, speik *to speak*, steek *stake*, suek *to soak*, tak *to take*, tik *tick*, tiuk *took*, tlik (OE. clyccan) *to clutch, seize, catch hold*, þak *thatch*, þik *thick*, weik (ME. weke) *the wick of a lamp or candle*, wāk (noun) *work*, wōk *to work*, wik (O. Icel. vik (noun) *stirring, moving*) *quick, alive*.

boek *balk*, **beam**, **toek** *to talk*, **woek** *to walk*.

beɒk *bench*, **driɒk** *to drink*, **eɒk** *hank*, **speɒk** *to hit*, **þiɒk** *to think*.

bāk *bark*, **bēk** *birch*, **foek** *fork*, **māk** *mark*, **moek** *maggot*, **stāk** (OE. **stearc** *strong, severe*) *very, quite*, **wāk** (OE. **wærc**, O. Icel. **verkr**) *ache, pain*.

Palatal nc has become **nš**: **drenš** (OE. **drencan**) *to drench*.

bitš *bitch*, **bleitš** *to bleach*, **breitš** *breach*, **britš** *breech*, **etš** *to hatch*, **fotš** *to fetch*, **krutš** *crutch*, **latš** *latch*. **leitš** *leech*, **meitš** *to measure*, **mitš** *much*, **notš** *a run at the game of cricket*, **pitš** *pitch*, **sitš** *such*, **speitš** *speech*, **stitš** *stitch*, **stretš** *to stretch*, **swetš** (OE. **swæcc** *a taste*) *a sample of cloth*, **tletš** (cp. O. Icel. **klekja** *to hatch*) *a brood of chickens*, **teitš** *to teach*, **witš** *which*, **wotš** *to watch*.

6. Final **sc**.

ask (ME. **harsk**, cp. Dan. **harsk**) *dry, rough, harsh*, **besk** *to bask*, **busk** *to go about from place to place singing and playing for money*.

eš *ash-tree*, **flš** *fish*, **fleš** *flesh*, **freš** *fresh*, **peš** (ME. **paschen**, cp. Swed. **paska**) *to knock about, smash, dash*, **reš** *rash*, **weš** *to wash*, **wiš** *to wish*.

sc has become **s** in **as** (OE. **æsce**) *ash*, **as-midin** *ash-pit*, **as** beside **aks** (OE. **āscian, ācsian**) *to ask*, **mens** (OE. **mennisc** *dignity, honour*) *neatness, tidiness*.

§ 313. **k** has disappeared through assimilation in **kēget** *kirkgate*, **kiɒ-kof** *whooping cough*, beside **kiɒk** (ME. **kinken** *to pant, gasp*) *to cough (of whooping cough)*, **wāte** (lit. *work day*, kd > kt > tt > t) *week day*. ɒks > ɒs in the phrase **þiɒs te?** *thinkest thou?* as **ednt'e out te (e) dunt**, **þiɒs te?** (lit. *hadst not thou ought to have done it, thinkest thou?*) *don't you think you ought to have done it?* Many people pronounce it as if it were **þiɒ ste?**

§ **314.** The relation, if any, of **bleg**, plural **blegz**, to *blackberry* is difficult to explain. It may be that **blakberi** became **blagberi** by assimilation, and that then **beri** was dropped. **blag** would regularly become **bleg** in the W. dial., see § 59.

g.

§ **315.** OE. initial **g** was a voiced spirant before both vowels and consonants. Before guttural vowels and their mutations (cp. § 312) it was a guttural spirant, as also before **æ** (Sievers, OE. Gr. § 212), but before the palatal vowels **e** (=Germanic **e**), **ea**, **eo**, **ēa**, **ēo**, **i**, **ie** it was a palatal spirant. At a later period the guttural spirant became an explosive before consonants, guttural vowels, and **y̆** (=i-umlaut of **ŭ**), **ē** (=i-umlaut of **ō**); but the palatal spirant remained. On forms like Mod. Engl. **give**, **get**, **begin**, etc., see Sweet's New English Grammar §§ 817-8, and Kluge in Paul's Grundriss I. pp. 843-4.

Medially between vowels it was a voiced spirant. After **n** (=ŋ) it was an explosive. And when geminated (written **cg**) it was also a voiced guttural or palatal explosive according as it was originally followed by a guttural or palatal vowel.

During the OE. period final **g** became **h** after long guttural vowels and **r**, **l**, Sievers § 214.

1. Initial **g** before consonants.

It has disappeared before **n**: **neeg** *to gnaw*, **nat** *gnat*.

It has remained before **r**: **gēsl** *gristle*, **gree** *grey*, **grīn** *green*, **grund** *ground*.

Before **l** it has become **d**: **dlad** *glad*, **dlāmi** *sad, downcast*, **dlas** *glass*, **dlium** *gloom*, **dlue(r)** (ME. **glōren**, Swed. **glōra**) *to stare*, **dlumpi** *sulky, morose*.

2. Initially before vowels.

Initially before vowels it has had the same development as in lit. Engl.:

gab (cp. O. Icel. **gabba**) *impudence, cheek,* **ganə(r)** *gander,* **gavlək** (OE. **gafoluc** *spear*) *crowbar,* **geəp** *to gape,* **geət** *gate,* **gəst** *guest,* **gət** *to get,* **gilt** (O. Icel. **gilta**) *a young female pig,* **bə-gin** *to begin,* **giv, gi** *to give,* **goit** *a water channel, mill-stream,* **guət** *goat,* **goud** *gold,* **guid** *good.*

jād *yard,* **jān** *yarn,* **jel** *to yell,* **jelp** *to yelp,* **jəst** *yeast,* **jestədə** *yesterday,* **jīld** *to yield,* **joən** *to yawn,* **jolə** *yellow,* **juək** *yolk.*

3. When **g** or its further development has not become final in the W. dial.

æg has become **eə**: **breən** *brain,* **eel** *hail,* **feən** *fain, gladly,* **feə(r)** *fair,* **meən** *main,* **neəl** *nail,* **peəl** *pail,* **sleən** *slain,* **sneəl** *snail,* **teəl** *tail,* see § 65. But we have **sed** (OE. **sǣdə** beside **sægdə**) *said.*

ag has become **oə**: **doən** *to dawn.*

āg has become **oe** in **oən** *own.*

eg has become **eə** and has thus fallen together with **ee** from **æg**: **breəd** (OE. **bregdan**) *to resemble, act like another person,* **geən** (O. Icel. **gegn**) *near, direct,* **geən** *gain,* **leəd** *laid,* **leən** *lain,* **reəl** *rail,* **reən** *rain,* **seəl** *sail.* See § 84.

ig has become **ī**: **stīl, stī** *stile,* **tīl** *tile,* cp. also **stī** *ladder.* But we have **sail** from **sigelian** *to drain through a sieve,* **saið** from **sigþe** *scythe.* **ig** cannot have become **ī** at a very early period in the North, otherwise it would have become **ai** like old **ī**. Cp. also Easther, A Glossary of the Dialect of Almondbury and Huddersfield, sub **sile** and **stigh**.

og has become **ou**: **floun** *flown.*

ug has become **ā**: **fāl** *fowl,* **kāl** *cowl.*

4. When **g, cg**, or their further development have become final in the W. dialect.

a. g has combined with the preceding vowel along with which it has become a long vowel or a diphthong.

æg: dee *day*, mee (emphatic form) *may*.

ag: droe *to draw*, loe *law*.

ăg: lou *low*, ou *to owe*.

ǣg: gree *grey*, tlee *clay*; kei *key*, nei *to neigh*.

eg: wee *way*, wei *to weigh*.

ēg: dī *to dye*, drī *dreary, gloomy, tedious*, tī *to tie*.

ĭg: stī *sty*, stī *ladder*.

og: bou (OE. boga) *bow*.

ōg: biu *bough*, driu *drew*, iniu (pl.) *enough*, as este inif bried? *hast thou enough bread?* But este iniu poreets? *hast thou enough potatoes?* pliu *plough*, sliu *slew*.

ō̄g: slī *sly*.

ug: să *sough, drain*; but suf-oil *manhole of a drain*, bă *to bow*, să (OE. sugu) *sow*.

ȳg: drai *dry*.

ēag: ī (pl. īn) *eye*.

ēog: flī *to fly*, flī *fly*, lī *to tell a lie*.

b. After l we have e, i: bele *to bellow*, fole *to follow*, gales *gallows*, swole *to swallow*, tale *tallow*, beli *belly*.

After r we have e, i: bore *to borrow*, mare *marrow*, sore *sorrow*, beri *berry*, beri *to bury*, weri *to worry*.

c. Final ig in unaccented syllables has become i: bodi *body*, dizi *dizzy*, evi *heavy*, moni *many*, oni *any*, rudi *ruddy*.

d. We have f in: duef *dough*, duefi *cowardly*, lit. *doughy*, dwăf *dwarf*, inif (sing.) *enough*, sluf *slough*, suf-oil *manhole of a drain*, trof *trough*, uf *displeasure, an offended manner, rage*.

Here may conveniently be placed druft (OE. drūgaþ) *drought*, sterep (OE. stīg-rāp) *stirrup*, băkm (OE. beorg + ham, see N.E.D. sub bargham) *the collar of a horse*.

NOTE.—să *drain*, and iniu (pl.) *enough*, are from the inflected forms.

e. The W. dialect has **g** :

dreeg *to drawl,* **eeg** *the berry of the hawthorn,* **ig** (OE. **hyge** *mind*) *mood, temper,* **meeg** *maw,* **neeg** *to gnaw,* **seeg** *a saw.*

beg *bag,* **big** *big, great,* **breg** *to brag,* **brig** *bridge,* **brigz** *a trivet, in brewing, to put across a tub to support the hop-sieve,* **deg** (cp. Swed. **dagga** *to bedew*) *to besprinkle with water,* **dig** *to dig,* **dog** *dog,* **dreg** *to drag,* **dregz** *drags,* **eg** (ME. **eggen**) *to incite, urge on,* **eg** *egg,* **flig** (ME. **fligge,** cp. OHG. **flukke** *able to fly*) *fledge,* **flog** *to flog,* **fog** (ME. **fogge** *rank grass*) *after-grass,* **frig** *coire,* **frog** *frog,* **geg** (ME. **gaggin**) *to gag,* **ie-wig** *earwig,* **leg** *leg,* **lig** *to lie down,* **lug** (ME. **luggen,** Swed. **lugga** *to lug, drag*) *to pull the hair of the head,* **mig** *midge,* **og** *the wool of a sheep which has been shorn for the first time,* **pig** *pig,* **prog** *wood collected for the fire on the fifth of November,* **reg** *rag,* **rig** *back,* **rigin** *ridge of a house,* **seg** *sedge,* **seg** (ME. **saggin**) *to distend,* **šeg** *shag,* **tug** (ME. **tuggen**) *to tug, plod.* **twig** *twig,* **ug** *to carry,* **weg** *to wag.*

f. The W. dialect has **dž** in : **edž** *hedge,* **edž** *edge,* **sledž-ame(r)** *sledge-hammer,* **wedž** *wedge.*

g. Palatal **ng** has become **nž** : **inž** *hinge,* **krinž** *to cringe,* **sinž** *to singe.*

h. **bai** (OE. **bycgan**) *to buy,* **lee** (OE. **lecgan**) *to lay,* **see** (OE. **secgan**) *to say* are from the forms without gemina-tion.

h,

§ 316. OE. initial **h** was an aspirate like the **h** in Mod. Engl. **hand.** In other positions it was a spirant like the **ch** in German **nach, ich.**

§ 317. *a.* Initial **h** has disappeared in the W. dialect :

ap (ME. happen) *to wrap up*, eft *haft*, *handle*, oil *hole*, uel *whole*, ut *hot*.

loup (O.Icel. hlaupa) *to jump*, luef (OE. hlāf) *loaf*.

nit (OE. hnitu) *nit*, nut (OE. hnutu) *nut*.

riꞃ (OE. hring) *ring*, riuk (OE. hrōc) *rook*.

wie(r) *where*, wiet *wheat*, wāf *wharf*, wen *when*, wot *what*.

§ 318. *b*. Medial and final h have disappeared except in the examples under *c, d* :

eit *eight*, eit *height*, feit *to fight*, reit *right*, streit *straight*, weit *weight*.

brīt *bright*, flīt *flight*, frīt *fright*, līt *light*, līts (ME. lihte) *the lungs of animals*, mīt (noun) *might*, nīt *night*, plīt *plight*, rīt *wright*, sīt *sight*, slīt *slight*, tīt *tight*.

bout *bought*, brout *brought*, doute(r) *daughter*, out *aught*, out *ought*, nout *naught*, rout *wrought*, sout *sought*, tout *taught*, þout *thought*.

ei *high*, but efe(r) (OE. hēahfore) *heifer*, nei *nigh*, but neebe(r) (OE. nāah-gebūr) *neighbour*.

sī *to sigh*, see Mayhew OE. Phonology, § 814, soe *he saw*, þī *thigh*.

fere (OE. furh, ME. furh, furwe) *furrow*, ole (OE. holh, ME. holwe) *hollow*.

§ 319. *c*. h has become f in : draft *draught, draft*, kof *cough*, laf *laugh*, ruf *rough*, tof *tough*, woef (OE. walh *sickly taste*) *insipid*.

lafte(r) *laughter*, slafter *to slaughter*.

Beside þriu (OE. þurh) we have also þrif *through*.

§ 320. *d*. hs has become ks : nekst *next*, oks *ox*, siks *six*, woks *to grow*.

The French Element.

§ 321. The consonants of the French words occurring in the W. dialect have for the most part been already treated along with the other consonants. There therefore only remain to be added a few examples of **k**, **g**, **š**, **tš**, **dž**.

k.

§ 322. **k** has remained : **koul** (O. Fr. **coillir**) *to rake*, **koese** (O. Norm. Fr. **causie**) *causeway*, **keed** *card*, **kees** *case*, **keisn** (lit. *occasion*) *need, necessity*, **kontréeri** *contrary*, **kreek** *to creak*.

skafl *scaffold*, **skaflin** *scaffolding*, **skoud** *to scald*, **skeelit** *scarlet*, **kwaleti** *quality*, **kwari** *stone quarry*, **kwaiet** *quiet*, **kweet** *quart*, **keekes** *body, carcase*, **blenkit** *blanket*, **blenk** *blank*, **ink** *ink*, **renk** *rank*, **avek** *havoc*, **biek** *beak*, **leelek** *lilac*, **paik** *to pick, choose, select*, **puek** *pork*, **fakt** *fact*, but pl. **faks**.

§ 323. **kl** has become **tl** in **tlāk** *clerk*, **tleem** *claim*, **trietl** *treacle*. The change of initial **kl** to **tl** is quite regular in native English words also (§ 312, 1), but **trietl** is the only example I know where medial or rather final **kl** has become **tl**.

§ 324. **kw** has become **tw** in : **twil** *quill, pen*, **twilt** *quilt*, **twilt** *to beat, thrash*.

§ 325. **wišin** *cushion*, seems to be the same as the literary word originally, but I cannot for the present offer a satisfactory explanation of the exact relation in which they stand to each other.

g.

§ 326. g has remained: **gāl** *the matter which gathers in the corner of the eye* (see Florio, s.v. **cispa** *a kind of waterish matter in sore eyes*, called of some **Gowl**. Or it is **cispi** *waterish* or *gowly eyes*), **galək** (O. Fr. **galc**) *left hand*, **garit** *garret*, **geete(r)** *garter*, **gizn** *to choke*, **gol** *goal*, only used in the game of **lits ən gōts** (§ 177), **grant** *grant*, **əgrivéət** *to aggravate, vex*, **əəgifái** *to argue, dispute*.

š.

§ 327. We regularly have š in cases where the lit. language has this sound : **fešn** *fashion*, **pešn** *passion*, **rediš** *radish*.

finiš *finish*, **vāniš** *varnish*, **blemiš** *blemish*.
branš *branch*, **əənšn** *ancient*.

dž.

§ 328. dž has generally remained in words where the lit. language has this sound. In the W. dial. dž also occurs after **n** : **džais** *joist*, **dželəs** *jealous*, **dželi** *jelly*, **džoul** *to knock, strike*, **džoint** *joint*, **džoəm** *the side post of a door* or *chimney piece*, **džoənes** *jaundice*, **eədž** *age*, **damidž** *damage*, **fuedž** *forge*, **indžói** *to enjoy*, **leɲwidž** *language*, **pidžn** *pigeon*, **soudže(r)** *soldier*.

indžn *engine*, **moəndž** *mange*, **moəndži** *mangy, peevish*, **streəndž** *strange*, **tšeəndž** *change*.

§ 329. dž has become d in: **Doəd** *George*, **Dued** *Joe*, **Duez**, **Duezi** *Joshua*, **doi** *joy, darling*, a pet word applied to children. This last word gives a clue to the explanation of

the change, which is no doubt due to the imperfect pronunciation of children being imitated by grown-up persons.
The proper names must originally have been used in
addressing children only, just as doi still is, and then afterwards have become used for grown-up persons.

tš.

§ 330. We regularly have **tš** in the same words in
which the literary language has it: **tšapl** *chapel*, **tšeedž**
to charge, **tšeeme(r)** *chamber*, **tšeri** *cherry*, **tšimli** *chimney*,
tšois *choice*, **tšons** *chance*, **tšont** *chant*.

preitš *to preach*, **poutš** *to poach*.

ACCIDENCE.

—◆—

CHAPTER VII.

NOUNS.

A. Formation of the Plural.

1. Plurals in -əz, -z, -s.

§ 331. Nouns ending in s, š, z, ž add əz to form the plural, as las *lass* lasəz, fees *face* feesəz, but ās *house* has āzəz; diš *dish* dišəz, wotš *watch* wotšəz; nuəz *nose*, nuəzəz, saiz *size* saizəz; edž *hedge* edžəz, džudž *judge* džudžəz.

§ 332. Nouns ending in a vowel or voiced consonant other than z, ž add z, as: lad *lad* ladz, gam *game* gamz, ratn *rat* ratnz, leeð *barn* leeðz, dee *day* deez. But nouns ending in -nd, (-r) lose the -d, (-r) before the plural ending §§ 302, 259, as frend *friend* frenz, faðe(r) *father* faðez.

§ 333. Nouns ending in a voiceless consonant other than s, š add s, as lat *lath* lats, kap *cap* kaps, dieþ *death* dieþs, māþ *mouth* māþs, wāf *wharf* wāfs, ruif *roof* ruifs.

But nouns ending in **f** preceded by a vowel or diphthong (except **ui**) which was long in OE., and nouns originally ending in **-lf** change the **f** into **v** and add **z** in the plural, as **luəf** *loaf* **luəvz**, **naif** *knife* **naivz**, **koəf** *calf* **koəvz**.

2. Plurals in **-n**.

§ **334**. There are only three nouns which have **-n** in the plural: **ī** *eye* **īn**, **oks** *ox* **oksn**, **šū** *shoe* **šuin**.

3. Plural in **-r**.

§ **335**. The only example of this class is **tšildə(r)** *children*. In the singular we use **bān**, the plural of which is **bānz**, and is in more general use than **tšildə(r)**.

4. Plurals with umlaut.

§ **336**. These are: **fuit** *foot* **fīt**, **guis** *goose* **gīs**, **lās** *louse* **lais**, **man** *man* **men**, **mās** *mouse* **mais**, **tuiþ** *tooth* **tīþ**, **wumən** *woman* **wimin**.

5. Singular and Plural alike.

§ **337**. **as** *ash, ashes*, **flš** *fish, fishes*, **šīp** *sheep*.
Nouns expressing time, space, weight, measure, and number, when preceded by a cardinal numeral, as **iz nət bin sīn fə tən jiə(r)** *he has not been seen for ten years*, but **its jiəz sin ə wə sīn** *it's years since he was seen*, and similarly with **munþ** *month*, **wik** *week*. **þrī mail þrə Koəvlə** *three miles from Culverley*, but **mailz þrə ðiə(r)** *miles from there*, and similarly for **inš** *inch*, **fuit** *foot*, **jiəd** *yard*, **eəkə(r)** *acre*, etc. **tən pund ə meit** *ten pounds of meat*, cp. lit. Engl. *a ten-pound note*, but **ðə wə punz ont weəsted** *there were pounds of it wasted*, and similarly with **āns** *ounce*, **stuən** *stone*, **undəd weit** *hundred weight*, etc. **tū kweət ət best** *two quarts of the best (ale)*, **siks galn** *six gallons*, **nain šilin** *nine shillings*, etc. **fouə skuə(r)** *four scores*, but **skuəz on əm** *scores of them*, etc.

6. Miscellaneous.

§ **338.** Some nouns are only used in the plural as: **kruds** *curds*, **laps** *a kind of woollen waste made in spinning*, **līts** *lungs of animals*, **loks** *small pieces of wool which have been detached from the fleece*, **mezlz** *measles*, **noilz** *the short hairs taken out of the wool by the combing machine*, **roidz** *clearings (of a wood)*, now only used in the phrase **West Roidz** *West Royds*, **siðez** *scissors*, **sperinz** *banns of marriage*, **teɒz** *tongs*, **trūzəz** *trousers*. Others have a different meaning in the singular and the plural, as **brig** *bridge* pl. **brigs** *bridges, a trivet to put across a tub to support the hop-sieve*, **green** *grain* **greenz** *malt which has been used in brewing beer*, **grund** *ground* **grunz** *sediment*.

Nouns with double plural endings are rare, but we have them in : **beləsez** *bellows*, **galəsez** *braces*, **stepsez** *steps*.

In speaking of cows the form **bies** is generally used, as **ā moni bies ejə nā?** *how many cows* (lit. *beasts*) *have you now?*

poridž *porridge*, always, and **broþ** *broth*, frequently, require the plural form of the verb as **ðem poridž worent əz guid əz ðe out tə (ə) bīn**, lit. *them porridge were not as good as they ought to have been.*

B. Formation of the Genitive Case.

§ **339.** The sign of the genitive both singular and plural is generally omitted when one noun qualifies another; the two nouns thus forming a kind of compound, as **ðemz mi faðe buits** *those are my father's boots*; but **ðem buits ə mi faðez** *those boots are my father's*, **tlad faðe buits** *the boy's father's boots*, but **tbuits ə tlad faðez** *the boots of the boy's* *father*, ðem bānz (never bānzez) muðe(r) *those children's mother.*

When the genitive is not followed by another noun, the gen. singular and plural have the same form as the nom. plural. The only exceptions are that nouns which end in -vz in the plural have -fs in the gen. singular, waifs *wife's*, and the two umlaut-plurals men, wimin have sing. manz, wumenz, plural menz, wiminz.

CHAPTER VIII.

ADJECTIVES.

1. The Articles.

§ 340. The indefinite article ə *a*, ən *an*, differs from lit. Engl. in so far that ə may be used before both vowels and consonants. It is equally right to say: av etn ə or ən apl *I have eaten an apple*. In nidiət *idiot* and noreišn *row, disturbance*, the initial n has come from the indef. article, ðis nidiət *this idiot*, wots tmiənin ə čis noreišn`? *what is the meaning of this* (lit. *oration*) *row?* Cp. lit. Engl. newt for ewt. Observe the phrase: a wər i sitš ən ə steet *I was in such* (*an*) *a state*.

§ 341. The definite article t *the* is generally attached to the following word, as tman *the man*, tkoilz *the coals*, tak tguid ənz *take the good ones*, tloed ə tmanə(r) *the lord of the manor*, a duənt noe wot tman did wit *I don't know what the man did with it*, a no(ə) uə tman wo(r) *I know who the man was*.

When the word following the definite article begins with t or d, the only trace of the article is that t and d become suspended or popularly expressed lengthened. We make a clear distinction between teebl *table* and t'eebl *the table*, dlium *gloom* and d'lium *the gloom*. ‑

Cp. the similar distinction between ꬴit *eight*, and ꬴit' *eighth*.

We however always use ðə before loꬴd when it means *God*, as ðez nuꬴbdi bꬴd ðə loꬴd ꬴn mī, noꬴz wot iv ꬴd tꬴ baid *there is nobody but the Lord and myself, know what I have had to suffer.* ðə (never t) is also used after uꬴ *who*, wot *what*, in such expressions as : uꬴ ðə divl did ðat ? *who the devil did that ?* wot ðə ꬴꬳment duz ꬴ wont ? *what the hangment does he want ?* a duꬴnt noꬴ wot ðə ꬴꬳment i did wit *I don't know what the hangment he did with it.*

> NOTE.—In order to obtain information on this difference in the use of t and ðə in some other Yorkshire dialect, I wrote to Mr. Bradley, the Joint Editor of the New English Dictionary, who is thoroughly conversant with the Sheffield dialect; and from his kind communication I learn that the distinction in the Sheffield dialect is practically the same as in my own. I venture to quote the following extract from his letter, which will be found interesting and instructive.—'t' lord o' t' manor—(decidedly). When "Lord" means God, the association of liturgical and Bible reading generally cause the full pronunciation (ðə) to be used. But I have, though rarely, heard t' Lord, in rather off-hand, irreverent speech; and "Lord knows" without any article at all is common enough. A don't know what t' man did wi' it—(certainly not ðə man, nor man without article). What the hangment, What the devil, What the plague, etc.— (always ðə, never t or omitted). A know who t' man wor—(certainly not ðə, nor omitted).'

2. Comparison of Adjectives.

§ 342. The comparative is formed by adding -ə(r) and the superlative by adding -ist to the positive. This rule also holds good for familiar adjectives of two or more syllables. But unfamiliar adjectives of more than one syllable sometimes form the comparative and superlative by prefixing muꬴ(r), muꬴst.

fāꬴ(r) *far*, fārꬴ(r), fārist; juꬳ *young*, juꬳꬴ(r), juꬳist or juꬳst; uꬴlsm *wholesome*, uꬴlsm-ꬴ(r), uꬴlsm-ist; biutifl *beautiful*, biutifl-ꬴr, biutifl-ist.

§ **343.** The following adjectives are compared irregularly as in lit. Engl. :

bad *bad* il *ill* }	wāə(r)	wāst
guid *good*	betə(r)	best
lat *late*	latə(r)	latist, last
litl *little*	les	liest
moni *many* mitš *much* }	muə(r)	muest
niə(r) *near*	niərə(r̄)	niərist, nekst

NOTE.—The use of vari before adjectives is the same as in lit. Engl.: vari guid *very good.* But instead of using vari we sometimes repeat the adjective with ez *as* : guid ez guid *very good*, dāk ez dāk *very dark.*

3. Numerals.

§ **344.** *a.* Cardinal and ordinal numerals.

Cardinal.	*Ordinal.*
wun *one*	fēst
tū *two*	seknd
þrī *three*	þēd
fouə(r) *four*	fouet
faiv *five*	fift
siks *six*	sikst
sevm *seven*	sevnt
eit *eight*	eit'
nain *nine*	naint
ten *ten*	tent
(ə)levm *eleven*	(ə)levnt
twelv *twelve*	twelft
þētīn *thirteen*	þētīnt
fouetīn *fourteen*	fouetīnt

I

Cardinal.	Ordinal.
fiftīn *fifteen*	fiftīnt
sikstīn *sixteen*	sikstīnt
sevntīn *seventeen*	sevntīnt
eitīn *eighteen*	eitīnt
naintīn *nineteen*	naintīnt
twenti *twenty*	twentit
twenti wun *twenty-one*	twenti fēst
twenti tū *twenty-two*	twenti seknd
þēti *thirty*	þētit
foti *forty*	fotit
fifti *fifty*	fiftit
siksti *sixty*	sikstit
sevnti *seventy*	sevntit
eiti *eighty*	eitit
nainti *ninety*	naintit
unded *hundred*	undet
þāzn *thousand*	þāznt

§ 345. The old form uən *one* is still retained in the phrase tuen *the one of two*, as tuen on em est, lit. *the one of them has it*, i. e. *one of the two has it*. The unaccented form is ən or rather vocalic n, as it wer ə guidn *it was a good one*. We may also note wun-ā *somehow*, wun-ā er enuðe(r) *somehow or other*.

On the suspended t' in eit' *eighth*, see §§ 341, 306.

m for older n (§ 270) is regularly heard in sevm, (ə)levm; but in sevnt, (ə)levnt, sevntīn, etc., m for older n is seldom, if ever, heard.

All the ordinals, except seknd and þēd, end in t. Most of these are, of course, new formations made after the analogy of fēst, fift, sikst, twelft which had t in OE. See § 309. In a similar manner the lit. Engl. ordinals *fifth*.

sixth, twelfth, and all those ending in *-nth* are new formations made after the analogy of such forms as *fourth*, OE. fēowerða.

§ 346. In playing at games, e. g. *marbles* tooz, boys have the following ordinals, denoting the order in which each is to begin the game. The boy who calls out feri has the first turn. The order is feri *first*, seki *second*, þōdi *third*, lari *last*.

> NOTE.—too is used for a marble of any kind. When made of marble or alabaster it is called e wait ali, if streaked with red veins e bluid ali; when of glass e glas ali; when made of powdered stone e stueni; when made of clay e pot donek.

§ 347. *b.* Fractional numerals: kweete(r) *quarter*, e fouet or wun peet āt e foue(r) *a fourth*, e þōd or wun peet āt e þrī *a third*, and similarly tū þōdz or tū peets āt e þrī *two thirds*, oef *half*, as e oef pund, oef pund, or oef e pund *half a pound*, oepni *halfpenny*, oepeþ *halfpennyworth*.

§ 348. *c.* Multiplicatives: simpl *simple*, dubl *double*, tribl, þribl *threefold*, foue-foud *fourfold*, wuns *once*, twais *twice*, þrī taimz *three times*.

§ 349. *d.* Numerals in composition: e tūþri lit. *a two (or) three, a few*, as ler em ev e tūþri *let them have a few*, tupms *two pence*, fipms *fivepence*, þrepms *three pence*, etc.

CHAPTER IX.

PRONOUNS.

1. Personal.

§ 350.

FIRST PERSON.

Singular.	*Plural.*
Nom. ai, (a, i)	wī, (wi, wə)
Obj. mī, (mə)	uz, (əz, s)

SECOND PERSON.

Nom. ðǟ, tā, (ðǝ, ta, tə)	jī, (ji, jə)
Obj. ðī, (ðə)	jī, (jə)

THIRD PERSON.

Singular.

Masc.	*Neut.*	*Fem.*
Nom. ī, (i, ə)	it, (t)	šū, (šu, šə)
Obj. im	it, (t)	ə(r), (ə(r).

Plural.

Nom. ðēə, (ðe, ðə)	
Obj. ðem, (əm, m).	

The weak forms are in parentheses. They are far more frequently employed than the strong ones; the latter are only used to express special emphasis.

The weak form i *I* is older than a, it arose from the shortening of ī before the latter became ai, whereas a is the regular weak form of ai, cp. the weak forms abəd *yes but*, wol *until*, wa *why*, beside the strong forms aibəd, wail (noun) *while*, wai. Examples of the first person are:

muni guə wi jə? *must I go with you?* sali ət təmoən? *shall I have it to-morrow?* if id nobəd ə bit ə bras, a wodnt (or ad nət) diu sitš wāk *if I had only a little brass (money), I would not do such work*, al kum ən sī jə, wen i gər ə bit ə taim *I will come and see you, when I get a bit of time*, as ə dun inā *I shall have done presently*, a fan əm i tloin *I found them in the lane*, gi m(ə) ə feu *give me a few*, ðə teld mə ða wər iə(r) *they told me (that) thou wast here*. wi or wə bān dān til *we are going down the hill*, sud wə len im it? *should we lend him it?* ðel or ðəl stop wol wə kum *they will stop until (while) we come*. lets as im *let us* or *me ask him*, šə þeŋkt əz fə tpeenz wid teen wit *she thanked us for the pains we had taken with it*. The z in the strong form uz is never voiceless as it is in lit. Engl. The weak form ə is only used when it is attached enclitically to a preceding voiceless consonant.

The strong form tā and the weak forms ta, tə can only be used interrogatively and in subordinate sentences, as wil tá weš it? *wilt thou wash it?* witə len met? *wilt thou lend me it?* wies tə kum þriu? (lit. *where hast thou come through*) *where do you come from?* kan tə diut bi ðisen? *canst thou do it by thyself?* wen tət redi wil send ðət *when thou art ready we will send thee it*. as or asl gi ðə (ə) oepni if tə elps mə, *I shall give thee a halfpenny if thou helpest me*, ðat nuən sə wīl əs tə wo(r) *thou art not so well*

as thou wast, ðal (never tal or tǝl) find im ǝt iz wǎk *thou
wilt find him at his work.*   At first sight one might be
inclined to assume that the forms tǎ, tǝ.have arisen from
assimilation with verbal forms ending in -t, e. g. ǎt (§ 396)
art, out (§ 394) *oughtest*, dǝ̄st (frequently dǝ̄s § 390) *durst*;
but these are the three solitary instances in which the
second person singular ends in -t where assimilation could
take place.   See the personal endings (§ 385).   It is far more
probable that the forms have arisen from their unaccented
position in the sentence.   If this is right then the def. art.
t has a similar origin.   However the t of the article arose,
I certainly do not believe that it is a clipped form of ðat
that, which is regularly used as a demonstrative (§ 354), but
never as a rel. pronoun or conjunction; the latter are
expressed by ǝt (§§ 356, 401).   am bān tǝ tak ðe wi mǝ
I am going to take thee with me.   ji or jǝ sed ǝt im it reɒ
you said that I am in the wrong, wot did jǝ see tul im?
what did you say to him?   wil jǝ sam mǝ ðem tluez up?
will you pick up those clothes for me?   jǝv etn oǝl tmeit suǝ
jǝl e tǝ diu bāt nā wol setǝdǝ *you have eaten all the meat
so you will have to do without until Saturday*, if jǝ (not ji)
sī mi faðe(r), as im tǝ kum uǝm *if you see my father, ask
him to come home*, wi soe jǝ i tmiln *we saw you in the mill.*
The old objective form of the second person plural has
entirely died out; cp. on the other hand the disappearance
in Modern English of the old nom. ye except in liturgical
and the higher literary language.   The pronoun of the
second person singular is still extensively used, but it is
not so general now as it was twenty years ago.   When I
was a lad the following was the rule : ðā was used in every
case except that jī was used (1) in addressing strangers,
especially grown-up people, or as a mark of respect to
masters and old people; (2) children in addressing their

parents ; (3) people who had made each other's acquaintance
after they had grown up usually employed jī in speaking
to each other.

The masc. of the third person singular is the only pronoun
which has not at least two forms for the obj. case. im is no
doubt used as a weak form so as to prevent confusion with
the obj. case of the plural. t is attached to the preceding
word. The nominative of the feminine presents great
difficulties. Dr. Sweet in his New English Grammar
(§ 1068) gives the following explanation for the lit. Engl.
form she : the old demonstrative sēo became shō through
the intermediate stage seŏ(sjoo), then shō became contaminated with the old personal pronoun hēo, which gave
rise to the form shēo which would regularly become she in
Mod. English. This explanation may or may not be right
for the lit. language, but a form shēo could not possibly
become šū, but only šī in the W. dial. as also in the other
dialects round about Windhill; cp. the Dialect Tests in
Ellis, EEPr. v. On the other hand, the uncontaminated
form shō would not become šū but šiu in the modern
dialect, cp. tiu *too*, diu *do*, etc. § 164 c; unless we may
assume, which I do not believe is the case, that the one
solitary example (šū *shoe*, but pl. šuin §§ 163–4 c) containing ū from older ō has not been borrowed from the lit.
language. On the various origins of W. ū see § 40. For
the present the form šū *she* still remains a riddle. The
strong form ðem is from OE. ðǣm (ðām), the dat. plural of
the demonstrative pronoun sē, sēo, ðæt, whereas the weak
forms em, m are from OE. heom, the dat. plural of the
personal pronoun hē, hēo, hit.

Examples of the third person are: iz bīn on trant oel
twik *he has been on the spree all the week,* eze fotšt ðat flik
e beekn ? *has he fetched that flitch of bacon ?* i ied it wen e

wər ət jār ās *he heard it when he was at your house*, tiznt
main *it is not mine*, ezə funt? *has he found it?* gimət *give
me it*, estət? *hast thou it?* wots ə dun wit? *what has he done
with it?* šuz in ə mad ig *she is in a bad temper*, šu or šə
oləs wešez ə tmundə *she always washes (the clothes) on the
Monday*, ešə or es šə sarəd tpigz? *has she served the pigs?*
stop wol šə kumz *stop until she comes*, ðed or ðed ə gīn me
ten šilin fot *they would have given me ten shillings for it*,
wil ðə suin bi iə(r)? *will they soon be here?* ðel suin bi iər if
ðə kum reit uəm *they will soon be here if they come straight
(right) home*, al sel jəm *I will sell you them*, kan jə diu
bāt əm? *can you do without them?*

It is hardly possible to give a very clearly defined and
accurate rule for the use of the weak nominative forms:

> a, wi ; ji ; i ; šu ; ðə beside
> i, wə ; jə ; ə ; šə ; ðə.

The former set is mostly used in making direct assertions,
and the latter in interrogative and subordinate sentences.
i *I* and ə *he* are never used in making direct assertions, but
the other pairs are, and when the one form and when the
other is used, seems to depend upon sentence rhythm.

The obj. case of all persons is often used reflexively, as
al weš mə nā *I will wash myself now*, am džust bān tə don
mə *I am just going to dress myself*, i leed im dān i tfīld
he lay down in the field, kum fored lad ən sit ðe dān ən al
set tketl on *come forward lad and sit (thee) down and I
will set the kettle on (and make some tea)*.

We always use the obj. case where in refined lit. Engl.
the nom. is used:

1. After the substantive verb, as its mī, þī, ð(r), im, uz,
jī, ðem, lit. *it is me, thee, her, him, us, you, them*. Note
ðemz əm ət i want *those are the ones that I want*.

2. When the verb refers to different persons, as **im ən mī wənt** *he and I went*, **Bil ən imz guən dān truəd** *Bill and he have gone down the road*, **uz ən ðəm wə təgeðər oəl d'ee** *we and they were together all the day.*

3. When the subject of the principal sentence is separated from the predicate by a subordinate sentence, as: **im ət did ðat out tə əᴅ** *he who did that ought to be hanged*, **uz əts dun sə mitš for im mə guə tə d'ogz fər out ī keez** *we who have done so much for him may go to the dogs for aught he cares.*

2. Possessive.

§ 351. *a.* Conjoint: **mai, (mi)** *my*; **āə(r), (wə(r))** *our*; **ðai, (ði)** *thy*; **jāə(r), (jə(r))** *your*; **iz, is** *his*; **it** *its*, **ē(r), (ə(r))** *her*, **ðee(r), (ðə(r))** *their*.

The weak forms are in parentheses. As in the personal pronouns so also here the weak forms are far more frequently used than the strong ones. **mi, ði, ðə(r)** are from the Middle English weak forms **mi, ði, ðer**, and not Modern weakenings of the strong forms; otherwise we should have had **ma, ða** for our **mi, ði**, see § 350. **wə(r)** has been formed from **wə** after the analogy of **jə** *ye*, **jə(r)**, thus **jə** : **jə(r)** :: **wə** : **wə(r)**. **iz** is used before vowels and voiced consonants and **is** before voiceless consonants, as **iz ās** *his house*, **iz oən** *his own*, **iz muðə(r)** *his mother*, **is koit** *his coat*, **is faðə(r)** *his father*, **estə sīn it faðə(r)**? *hast thou seen its* (=*the child's*) *father?* **it iəd wāks** *its head aches.*

§ 352. *b.* Absolute: **main** *mine*, **āz** *ours*, **ðain** *thine*, **jāz** *yours*, **iz** *his*, **its** *its*, **ēz** *hers*, **ðeez** *theirs.*

3. Reflexive.

§ 353.

FIRST PERSON.

Singular.	*Plural.*
misen	wesen
misel	wesenz
miseln	wesel
	weseln

SECOND PERSON.

ðisen	jesen
ðisel	jesenz
ðiseln	jesel
	jeseln

THIRD PERSON.

Singular.

Masc.	*Neut.*	*Fem.*
i(s)sen	itsen	esen
i(s)sel	itsel	esel
i(s)seln	itseln	eseln

Plural.

ðesen
ðesenz
ðesel
ðeseln

The stress is always on the second syllable. When these pronouns are used emphatically the stress on the second syllable is of course stronger than when they are used reflexively. All the forms -sel, -seln, -sen are often heard without any distinction in meaning.

Such a variety of forms must be quite modern, and is probably due to importation from neighbouring dialects. The -sen-forms are far more common than either of the other two. In the Eastern North Midland dialects, to which Windhill belongs (Ellis, EEPr. v. pp. 364–408), I find the following forms : -seln at Huddersfield and Halifax ; -sen at Bradford, Leeds, Dewsbury, Rotherham, Sheffield, Wakefield. In this division of dialects no -self-forms seem to be known.

In order to find out the areas of the -sel, -seln, and -sen-forms I have carefully examined all the classified word-lists and comparative dialect specimens in Ellis, EEPr. v, with the following results. -sel is the only form that occurs in all the North Northern, West Northern, and East Northern dialects, except at Holderness (S.E. York-shire) and South Ainsty, where we find -sen. The North North Midland, West North Midland, and South North Midland dialects have only -sel. The Border Midland dialects, which embrace the county of Lincolnshire, have only the -sen-form. The -sen-form does not seem to occur south of Lincolnshire. -self is regularly found without exception in all the Eastern dialects. The Mid Southern dialects have -self, -zelf, except at Much Cowarne (nine miles N.E. of Hereford) we find -sel and in Western Dorset -zel. The North Border Southern, Mid Border Southern, and South Border Southern dialects have only -self. In the East Southern dialects, which embrace almost the whole of Kent, with East Sussex, examples are wanting except that -saaf, pl. -saavz occurs at Faversham (eight miles W.N.W. of Canterbury). The Northern West Southern dialects regularly have -zel. In the Southern West Southern dia-lects all three forms, -sel, -zel, and -self, occur. For the Western West Southern dialects examples are wanting.

The South Western dialects seem to have -self, but more examples are wanting to be certain, as only one example of the reflexive occurs in this division, viz. at Docklow (five miles E. S. E. of Leominster). For the North Western dialects there is only one example given in Ellis, viz. -sel for Pulverbach (seven miles S.W. of Shrewsbury).

wəsen, etc. have been formed from the weak possessive wə(r) *our*, which is itself a .new formation, § 351. There is no difference in meaning or usage between wəsen and wəsenz, ðəsen and dəsenz. jəsen is used for the sing. and plural *yourself, yourselves*, but jəsenz *yourselves* has always a plural meaning.

The simplex self occurs in the dialect, as ə tself seem dee *on the self same day.*

4. Demonstrative.

§ 354.

Sing.	ðis *this*	ðat *that*	jon *yon.*
Plural.	ðiəz *these*	ðem *those*	jon *yon.*

ðis and ðiəz are often followed by iə(r) *here,* and ðat, ðem by ðiə(r), *there,* as ðis iər äs wonts ə lot ə tlienin *this house wants a lot of cleaning,* dus tə laik ðiəz iə(r)? *dost thou like these?* a känt eit ðat ðiə meit *I can't eat that meat,* i ga mə ðat ðiə koit *he gave me that coat,* ðem ðiər aplz kost tupms *those apples cost twopence,* ðemz vari guid bəd ðiəz əz or ə betə(r) *those are very good but these are better.*

ðem is the only word used for *those,* a form ðuəz would be quite foreign to the dialect.

5. Interrogative.

§ 355.

Masc. and Fem.   *Neut.*

Nom., Obj. **uə** *who*   **wot** *what*, **witš** *which.*

Gen. **uəz** *whose.*

uəm *whom* is never used in the W. dialect. Beside **wot** we have also **wor**, on which see § 290.

6. Relative.

§ 356. The relative pronoun is expressed either by **ət** for all genders and numbers, or by **uə** for the masc. and fem., **wot** for the neuter. **ət** is invariably used when the antecedent is expressed; in other cases we always use **uə**, **wot**. Thus: **im ət sed suəz reꞤ** *he who said so is wrong,* **tman ət i soə jestedə** *the man whom I saw yesterday,* **tlas ət i gav ə pund ə aplz tul əz ətn əm oəl** *the lass to whom I gave a pound of apples has eaten them all,* **tkoilz ət tə bout dān i Windil ə vari guid** *the coals which thou boughtest down in Windhill are very good,* **did jə sī ðem ət did it?** *did you see those who did it?* **ðem men ət tə so(ə) i truəd wər on trant** *those men whom thou sawest in the road were on the spree.*

a no(ə) uəz dunt *I know who has done it,* **we no(ə) uəz it iz** *we know whose it is,* **a noə wot tə sez** *I know what thou sayest,* **a ken or kꞤ gəs uə ðaz bīn wi** *I can guess with whom thou hast been,* **a duent belīv wot ə sez** *I don't believe what he says*; but **a duənt belīv ə wĕd (ət) i səz** *I don't believe a word (that) he says.*

The obj. case of **ət**, but never of **uə**, **wot**, is often omitted: **tman i soə** *the man (whom) I saw,* **tkoilz ə bout** *the coals (which) he bought.*

ǝt is of Norse origin and was originally only used as a
conjunction with the meaning of *that*.   But already in Old
Icelandic it came to be used both as a relative pronoun and
conjunction just as it still is in the W. dialect: **a no(ǝ) ǝt
im i tgǝǝt** *I know that I am in the way*.   See Noreen,
Altisländische und altnordische Grammatik, § 402.   ǝt occurs as a rel. pronoun in the Northern English dialects so
early as the thirteenth century, see J. A. H. Murray, The
Dialect of the Southern Counties of Scotland, p. 194.

It may be useful to note here that ðat is never used in
the dialect either as a rel. pronoun or as a conjunction.

7. Indefinite.
§ 357.

sum *some*, **sumdi** *somebody*, **sumǝt** (lit. *somewhat*) *something, anything*.

out *aught*, **nout** *naught, nought*.

inif, pl. **iniu** *enough*: **gim(ǝ) ǝ feu, neǝ ðaz ed iniu** *give
me a few, no thou hast had enough*, **ejǝ briǝd inif?** *have you
enough bread?*

feu *few*, **ivri** *every*, **ǝǝl** *all*, **els** *else*, **sitš** *such*, **uðǝ(r)**
other.

oǝðǝ(r) (OE. āwðer) *either*, **noǝðǝ(r)** (OE. nāwðer) *neither*.
Cp. § 123 and see Sievers, OE. Grammar, §§ 346, 348.

oni (OE. ǣnig) *any*, **onibodi** *anybody*, **moni** (OE. monig,
manig) *many*.   The o in **oni** is due to the influence of the o
in **moni**.   The following question would be quite unintelli-
gible to anyone but a North countryman: **ez or ǝz oni on
jǝ oni on jǝ?** inquired a man of a company of persons, after
asking two or three of them individually for a match, lit.
has any on you any on you? i. e. *has any of you got one?*

tuǝn (lit. *the one*) *one of two or more*: **tuǝn on jez dunt**

one of you has done it. Strong form **wun** (nom.), weak
form **ən** (obj.) *one*, pl. **ənz** *ones*, **wun ənuðə(r)** *one another*,
nuə, weak form **nə** *no*, **nuəbdi** *nobody*; **nuən** *none* has no
weak form. **nuən** is often used in the place of **nət**: **am
nuən bān** *I am not going*, **ðat nuən tfuil ət tə liuks** *you
are not the fool you look to be.*

　　u(ə)-ivə(r) *whoever*, **wotivə(r)** or **tšiuz-wot** (lit. *choose-
what*) *whatever.*

CHAPTER X.

VERBS.

§ 358. The verbs are divided into two great classes :— Strong and Weak—according to the formation of the preterite and past participle. Besides these two great classes of strong and weak verbs, there are a few others which will be treated under the general heading of *Minor Groups*.

§ 359. The strong verbs form their preterite by means of ablaut. In order to facilitate the use of the book for philologists I have sub-divided them into seven classes and have adopted the order given in Sievers' Old English Grammar, §§ 382–97.

A great many verbs which were strong in OE. are now weak in the dialect ; on the other hand a few, which were originally weak, have become strong. The lists contain all the strong verbs in general use. When two forms of the preterite and past participle are in existence, the less usual one is enclosed in brackets. Some verbs, which now usually have a weak preterite, still retain the old strong past participle, e. g. **feseen** *forsaken*, **fretn** beside **frieted** *fretted, mourned*.

There is only one form for the singular and plural of the preterite just as in lit. Engl. The present and

the past participle of all classes have, as a rule, been regularly developed from their corresponding OE. forms.   But
the preterite of some classes, e. g. the whole of the first and
second, are new formations made after the analogy of the
pret. of the fourth and partly the fifth classes.   Some few
verbs have passed over from one class into another.   All
these points will be discussed in their proper places.

§ 360. The preterite and the past participle of weak
verbs end in -ed, -d, -t. See §§ 380-3. Many verbs, originally
weak, have both a strong and a weak past participle.
See §§ 380-3.

A. Strong Verbs.

§ 361.

CLASS I.

Infin.	Pret. Sg.	Pret. Pl.	P. P.
OE. ī	ā	i	i
W. ai	ee		i
aid *hide*	eed		idn
baid *endure*	beed		bidn
bait *bite*	beet		bitn
daiv *dive*	deev		divm
dlaid *glide*	dleed		dlidn
draiv *drive*	dreev		drivm
kontraiv *contrive*	kontreev		kontrivm
raid *ride*	reed		ridn
rait *write*	reet		ritn
raiv *tear*	reev		rivm
raiz *rise*	reez		rizn
slaid *slide*	sleed		slidn
straid *stride*	streed		stridn
straik *strike*	streek		strukɒ
straiv *strive*	streev		strivm

K

Infin.	*Pret. Sg.*	*Pret. Pl.*	*P. P.*
šain *shine*	šeən		šaind
šait *cacare*	šeet		šitn
þraiv *thrive*	þreəv		þrivm

§ 362. The pret. of all verbs of this class is a new formation. The ee can arise neither from the OE. singular nor plural form. From the former we should have had uə (§ 122) and from the latter i (§ 89). The only classes of verbs which regularly have ee in the pret. are the fourth (§ 371) and part of the fifth (§ 372). To merely say that the pret. of Class I has been formed after the analogy of Class IV and part of Class V would be avoiding the real difficulty, which consists in giving a satisfactory reason why they should have had such an influence, seeing that they had no forms in common with Class I in OE. One might perhaps be inclined to think that the identity of the vowel in a pp. like ʒifenn *given* (Ormulum, i. 71) with that in a pp. like risenn *risen* (Ormulum, ii. 47) may have given rise to the new formation. But that would not do. In the dialect the pret. of **gi(v)** is **ga(v)**=Ormulum ʒaff, **gaff**, ii. 16. At present I cannot even suggest a satisfactory explanation.

§ 363. The pp. of šain is always weak, and I have also occasionally heard a weak pret. šaind. For the pret. of **straik** I have often heard **striuk, strak**, the latter of which seems to be a shortening of the Northern ME. form **strāk**; the pp. of this verb corresponds to the early Mod. Engl. lit. form **struken**.

§ 364. **aid** (OE. **hȳdan**) and **daiv** (OE. **dȳfan**) were weak in OE. **raiv** (O. Icel. **rīfa**) and **þraiv** (O. Icel. **þrīfa**) are of Norse origin. **straiv** (O. Fr. **estriver**) was already strong in ME. **kontraiv** must be a late borrowing from

lit. Engl., the ME. form **controuen** (u = v) from O. Fr.
controver would not have become **kontraiv** in the W.
dialect.

CLASS II.

§ 365.

	Infin.	Pret. Sg.	Pret. Pl.	P.P.
OE.	ēo	ēa	u	o
W.	ī		ee	o
	iu (§ 187)		ee	o
	ī		eu	ou
	frīz *freeze*		freez	frozn
	tlīv *cleave, split*		tleev	tlovm
	tšiuz *choose*		tšeez	tšozn
	flī *fly*		fleu	floun

§ 366. All the other verbs, which formerly belonged
to this class, have become weak.

OE. **cēosan** would regularly have become *tšiz (§ 187) in
the dialect. **tšiuz** seems to be an early borrowing of the
ME. West Midland form **chüsen**, which would regularly
become **tšiuz** in the dialect.

The **ee** in the pret. is not regularly developed from OE.
ēa, which has become **ie** (§ 179), but is due to the analogy
of such verbs as **weev** *wove*, **need** *kneaded*. Just as we
have the pp. **wovm**, **nodn**, pret. **weev**, **need**, so to the pp.
frozn, **tlovm**, **tšozn** there has been formed a new preterite
freez, **tleev**, **tšeez**.

CLASS III.

§ 367. This class had in OE. four sub-divisions:

1. Verbs having a medial nasal + a consonant.

2.	,,	,,	l +	,,
3.	,,	,,	r or h +	,,

K 2

4. When the stem vowel was followed by two consonants other than a nasal, l, r, or h + a consonant. Sievers,
OE. Gr. §§ 386–9.

All verbs originally belonging to 2. have become weak.
The same also applies to sub-divisions 3. and 4. with the
exception of **feit** *fight*, and **brust** *burst*.

Infin.	*Pret. Sg.*	*Pret. Pl.*	*P.P.*
1. OE. i	o (a)	u ·	u
W. i	a		u
i	e (§ 59) ·		u
begin *begin*	**began**		**begun**
spin *spin*	**span**		**spun**
swim *swim*	**swom** § 58 (**swam**)		**swum**
win *win*	**wan** (**won**)		**wun**
bind *bind*	**ban**		**bun**
find *find*	**fan**		**fun**
wind *wind*	**wan** (**won**)		**wun**
run *run*	**ran**		**run**
2. **briŋ** *bring*	**breŋ**		**bruŋ**
diŋ *reproach, revile*	**deŋ**		**duŋ**
fliŋ *throw*	**fleŋ**		**fluŋ**
iŋ *hang*	**eŋ**		**uŋ**
riŋ *wring*	**reŋ**		**ruŋ**
riŋ *ring*	**reŋ**		**ruŋ**
siŋ *sing*	**seŋ**		**suŋ**
sliŋ *sling*	**sleŋ**		**sluŋ**
spriŋ *spring*	**spreŋ**		**spruŋ**
stiŋ *sting*	**steŋ**		**stuŋ**
striŋ *string*	**streŋ**		**struŋ**
swiŋ *swing*	**sweŋ**		**swuŋ**
tliŋ *cling*	**tleŋ**		**tluŋ**
driŋk *drink*	**dreŋk**		**druŋk**

Infin.	Pret. Sg.		P.P.
siŋk *sink*	seŋk		sukŋ
sliŋk *slink*	sleŋk		slukŋ
stiŋk *stink*	steŋk		stukŋ
šriŋk *shrink*	šreŋk		šrukŋ

Infin.	Pret.	Pret. Pl.	P.P.
3. W. Sax. eo	ea	u	o
O. North. e	æ	u	o
W. ei (§ 87)		ee	o
feit *fight*		feet	fotn

Infin.	Pret. Sg.	Pret. Pl.	P.P.
4. OE. e	æ	u	o
W. u		a	u
brust *burst*		brast	brusn
þrust *thrust*		þrast	þrusn

§ 368. On the present form run, see Sweet NE. Gr.
§ 1382. The pret. and pp. ban, fan, wan and bun, fun,
wun are very widely spread in the Midland and Northern
dialects, see the Word-lists in Ellis, EEPr. v. The pret.
breŋ and pp. bruŋ are no doubt new formations after the
analogy of forms like seŋ, suŋ; the weak pret. and pp.
brout is also much used, but is not so common as the
strong forms. iŋ (ME. hengen, O. Icel. hengja) and riŋ (OE.
(h)ringan) were originally weak verbs. diŋ (O. Icel. dengja),
fliŋ (O. Icel. flengja), sliŋ (O. Icel. slöngva) are of Norse origin.
striŋ seems to be quite a modern formation from the noun.

The pp. of verbs whose stem ends in ŋk regularly lose
the medial guttural ŋ in the W. dialect. I have assumed
in the Phonology (§ 274) that ŋ has disappeared through assimilation before the following kŋ in the pp. of these verbs.
This is possible and not at all improbable; but we must
not exclude the possibility that some of these pp. may be

of Norse origin, e.g. drukɒ (O. Icel. drukkenn), sukɒ
(O. Icel. sokkenn), and that the remaining ɒk-verbs may
have followed the analogy of these. This is a point well
worth investigating, but of the five verbs ending in -ɒk in
the present and preterite, Ellis has unfortunately only the
pp. of driɒk, and I have accordingly read through all his
Word-lists, Dialect tests, and Comparative Specimens to see
how far the form without medial ɒ in the pp. extends.
The following is the result: The medial ɒ is retained in
all the Eastern, Western, and Southern dialects, with
the exception of South Devon (Ellis, p. 163), which is
probably a mistake on the part of Dr. Ellis' informant.
All the Border Midland, Southern, North Midland, Western
Mid Midland, Eastern Mid Midland, East Mid Midland,
Western South Midland, Eastern South Midland, Northern
North Midland, and Western North Midland dialects have
medial ɒ except at Colne Valley and at Burnley, where
double forms—without and with medial ɒ—seem to occur
(pp. 334 and 351). In the Eastern North Midland division
to which my own dialect belongs the form without medial
ɒ is found at Huddersfield, Halifax, Dewsbury which have
drufen, at Keighley, Bradford, Leeds, Rotherham, Elland,
and Calverley where the nasal has disappeared before the
following k; but medial ɒ occurs at Barnsley, Sheffield, and
Marsden (seven miles S. W. of Huddersfield). In the East
Northern division, Mid Yorkshire, North Mid Yorkshire,
New Malton, Lower Nidderdale, Washam River district,
South Cleveland, North East Coast, Danby and Skelton
in Cleveland, and Whitby, all have the form without medial
ɒ, but Market Weighton, Holderness, Malton, Pickering,
and The Moors, Sutton and Goole retain the medial
guttural nasal. All the West Northern dialects—for which
there are a great number of examples in Ellis—lose the

medial ɒ except at Upper Swaledale. The same is also the
case for the North Northern dialects, except that at New-
castle-on-Tyne the medial ɒ seems to exist (Ellis, p. 647).
For the Lowland division of English dialect districts in
Scotland only forms without medial ɒ are registered. It
is however important to note that Dr. Murray, The Dialect
of the Southern Counties of Scotland, has pp. **drunk** beside
drukken, and only **slunk, stunk, sunk, schrunk (scrynkit).**
This would certainly seem to favour the idea that our
drukɒ is of Norse origin, and that the pp. of the four other
verbs have been formed after the analogy of it.

In **feet** *fought* the vowel of the singular seems to have
been carried over to the plural at an early period. The
latter form then became generalized. The short o in the
pp. is quite regular (§ 100).

On the forms **brust, brast, brusn** see Sweet, NE. Gr.
§ 1354, and on þrust (ME. þrusten, þrusten, O. Icel. þrȳsta)
see loc. cit. § 1348.

CLASS IV.

§ 369.

	Infin.	*Pret. Sg.*	*Pret. Pl.*	*P.P.*
W. Sax.	e	æ	ǣ	o
O. North.	e	æ	ē	o
1. W.	ei (§ 87)	ee (§ 70)	ou (§ 103)
	steil *steal*	steel	stoun
2. W.	ie (§ 75)	ee	oe (§ 104a)
	bie(r) *bear*	bee(r)	boen
	swie(r) *swear*	swee(r)	swoen
	šie(r) *shear*	šee(r)	šoen
	wie(r) *wear*	wee(r)	woen
3. W.	e (§ 88)	a	o
	brek *break*	brak	brokɒ

§ 370. To this class also belongs **kum** (OE. **cuman**) *come*, **kom** (**kam**), **kum** (**kumd**).

§ 371. **wie(r)** (OE. **werian**) was originally a weak verb, but has become strong after the analogy of **bie(r)**, **šie(r)**. Similarly **swie(r)** (OE. **swerian**, pret. sing. **swōr**) has passed over from the sixth class into this.

The **ee** in the preterite is due to levelling. The vowel of the pret. singular of strong verbs was often extended to the plural already in ME. Then this a being in an open syllable became lengthened and was afterwards levelled out into the singular; so that the preterites with **ee** in this and the fifth class are really generalized plural stem-forms. The old pret. pl. form with **ǣ** (**ē**) would have become **ī** in the dialect, § 130. On the other hand, **brak** is the old sing. form. The same is also the case with the **a** in the pret. of verbs of Class V.

CLASS V.

§ 372.

	Infin.	*Pret. Sg.*	*Pret. Pl.*	*P.P.*
W. Sax.	e	æ	ǣ	e
O. North.	e	æ	ē	e
1. W.	ei (§ 87)	ee (§ 371)		o
	neid *knead*	need		nodn
	speik *speak*	speek (spak)		spoknᴅ
	spreid *spread*	spreed		sprodn
	treid *tread*	treed		trodn
	weiv *weave*	weev		wovmᴅ
2. W.	ei (§ 87)	ee		e (§ 73)
	eit *eat*	eet		etn
3. W.	e (§ 88)	a (§ 371)		e (§ 73)
	get *get*	gat		getn
4. W.	i (§ 77)	a (§ 371)		ī
	gi(v)	ga(v)		gīn (§ 79)

1. **spreid** was a weak verb in OE. (sprǣdan, pret. sprǣdde). The pp. of this sub-division have been formed after the analogy of verbs of the fourth class. The pret. **spak** is very often heard.

2. The pret. **eet** is a new formation made after the analogy of **weiv**, etc. The OE. form sing. ǣt, pl. ǣton would have become *īt (§ 130).

4. Instead of **gīn** I have very often heard **gen**, which is no doubt due to the influence of **etn, getn**.

§ 373.

	Infin.	Pret. Sg.	Pret. Pl.	P.P.
W. Sax.	i	ǣ	ǣ̄	e
O. North.	i	ǣ	ē	e
1. W.	i	a (§ 371)		i
	bid *invite to a funeral*	bad		bidn
	it *hit*	at		itn
	nit *knit*	nat		nitn
	sit *sit*	sat		sitn
	slit *slit*	slat		slitn
	spit *spit*	spat		spitn
	split *split*	splat		splitn
2. W.	i	e (§ 59)		u
	dig *dig*	deg		dug
3. W.	i	a		u
	stik *stick*	stak		stuk

1. **it** (O. Icel. **hitta** *find*), **nit, slit, spit, split** were originally weak verbs. I have also often heard the weak pret. and pp. **nited**; **bidn** (OE. **beden**, but already ME. **bidden** with i from the present), **sitn** (OE. **seten**, but already ME. **siten**).

2. **dig** was formerly weak (ME. **diggen, diggede**). The pp. **dug** is difficult to explain. According to Sweet, NE.

Gr. § 1370, the lit. form **dug** does not occur until towards the end of the Early Modern English period (1500–1650). The pp. **dugɴ** is also sometimes heard.

3. **stik** (OE. **stician**) was originally a weak verb. The pp. **stuk** may owe its u to the influence of **stuɴ**, Sweet, NE. Gr. § 1376.

§ 374. To this class also belongs **sī** (OE. **sēon**) *see*, pret. **soe** (§ 63), pp. **sīn** = Old North. **gesēn**.

CLASS VI.

§ 375.

	Infin.	*Pret.*	*P. P.*
OE.	a	ō	a
1. W.	a (§ 71)	iu (§ 164)	ee (§ 312, 4) .
	tak *take*	**tiuk**	**teen**
2. W.	oe (§ 63)	iu (§ 164 c)	oe
	droe *draw*	**driu**	**droen**
3. W.	a	ui (§ 163)	ui
	stand *stand*	**stuid**	**stuidn**

stuidn has its vowel from the preterite. A weak pret. and pp. **standed** is not uncommon. I have also heard a pp. **studn**, the vowel of which seems to be due to the influence of the literary form **stood**.

§ 376.

	Infin.	*Pret.*	*P.P.*
OE.	ēa	ō	a(æ)
W.	ee	iu (§ 164 c)	ee (§ 65)
	slee *slay*	**sliu**	**sleen**

The **ee** of the present is from the past participle. **šak** *shake* generally has the weak pret. and pp. **šakt**; but pret. **šiuk** (§ 164) and pp. **šakɴ** are not uncommon. The pp. of **fesak** *forsake* is **feseen** (§ 312, 4).

Class VII.

§ 377.

Infin.	Pret.	P. P.
OE. ā	ēo	ā
W. oe (§ 123)	iu (§ 190)	oe
bloe *blow*	bliu	bloen
kroe *crow*	kriu	kroen
moe *mow*	miu	moen
noe *know*	niu	noen
snoe *snow*	sniu	snoen
sóe *sow*	siu	soen
þoe *thaw*	þiu	þoen
þroe *throw*	þriu	þroen

þoe was a weak verb in OE. (þāwian or þāwan); snoe (OE. snāw) is the noun used as a verb, which has formed its pret. and pp. after the analogy of the other verbs of this class.

§ 378.

Infin.	Pret.	P. P.
OE. ō	ēo	ō
W. ou (§ 166)	iu (§ 190)	ou
grou *grow*	griu	groun

§ 379.

Infin.	Pret.	P. P.
OE. ea(a)	ēo	ea(a)
W. oe (§ 62)	e (§ 192 a)	oe
foel *full*	fel	foeln

B. Weak Verbs.

§ 380. The weak verbs are best classified according to their formation of the preterite and past participle. We thus distinguish three classes :—1. -ed, 2. -d, 3. -t.

Paragraphs 381-3 contain a fairly complete list of verbs which either differ from literary English in the preterite and past participle, or are interesting from other points of view. When the pret. or pp. has two forms, the less usual one is enclosed in brackets.

CLASS I.

§ 381. The preterite and past participle generally take -ed when the present ends in -t or -d. But a few verbs with short stem-vowels, whose present ends in -t, have the same form in the pret. and past participle; and a few others with a long stem vowel in the present have a short vowel in the pret. and pp.

Infin.	*Pret.*	*P.P.*
bend *bend*	bended (bent)	bended (bent)
bīld *build*	belt (bīlded)	belt (bīlded)
blīd *bleed*	blīded (bled)	blīded (bled)
bluid *bleed*	bluided	bluided
brīd *breed*	brīded (bred)	brīded (bred)
ōt *hurt*	ōt (ōted)	ōt (ōtn)
fīd *feed*	fīded (fed)	fīded (fedn)
grund *grind*	grunded	grunded
. kest *cast*	kest (kested)	kested (kesn)
lied *lead*	lieded (led)	lieded (ledn)
melt *melt*	melted	melted
od *hold*	oded (eld)	odn (oded)
send *send*	sended (sent)	sended (sent)
skrat *scratch*	skrated	skrated (skratn)
spend *spend*	spended (spent)	spended (spent)
šuit *shoot*	šuited	šuited (šotn)
kost *cost*	kost (kosted)	kost (kosted)
kut *cut*	kut	kut ‚kutn)

Infin.	*Pret.*	*P. P.*
let *let*	let	let (letn)
put *put*	put	put (putn)
set *set*	set	set (setn)
šut *shut*	šut	šut (šutn)
wed *marry*	wed	wed (wedn)
wet *wet*	wet (weted)	wet (weted, wetn)
līt *light*	let (līted)	let (letn, līted)
mīt *meet*	met	met (metn)
rīd *read*	red	red
tīm *pour out*	tem (temd)	tem (temd)
biet *beat*	bet	bet (betn)
friet *fret*	frieted (fret)	frieted (fretn)
swiet *sweat*	swieted (swet)	swieted (swetn)
tšiet *cheat*	tšieted (tšet)	tšieted (tšetn)
triet *treat*	tret (trieted)	tretn (trieted)

When I was a boy pret. and pp. forms like **bent, bled, led, spent,** etc., were hardly ever heard, but through the spread of elementary education they are now much used, especially among the younger generation, and will no doubt in the course of time entirely supplant the other forms. In like manner the strong pp. **kesn, putn, fretn,** etc., were far more common twenty years ago than they are now.

Forms like **let** *lit, lighted,* **belt** have been formed after the analogy of such pret. as **met, red,** etc., where the vowel was shortened before the double consonants (e. g. pret. **mette**) already in ME.

CLASS II.

§ 382. The preterite and past participle generally take -d when the present ends in a voiced sound other than -d.

Infin.	*Pret.*	*P.P.*
bə̄n *burn*	bə̄nd	bə̄nd
briu *brew*	briud	briud (briun)
diəl *deal*	diəld (dəlt)	diəld (dəlt)
driəm *dream*	driəmd (dremt)	driəmd (dremt)
eꞃ *hang*	eꞃd	eꞃd
eu *hew*	eud	eud (eun)
fīl *feel*	fīld (felt)	fīld (felt)
iə(ʹr) *hear*	iəd	iəd
leə *lay*	leəd	leəd (leən)
ləin *lean*	ləind	ləind
len *lend*	lend	lend
liən *learn*	liənd	liənd
liəv *leave*	liəvd (left)	liəvd (left)
lig *lie down*	ligd	ligd
loiz *lose*	loizd (lost)	loizd (lost)
miən *mean*	miənd (ment)	miənd (ment)
nīl *kneel*	nīld (nelt)	nīld (nelt)
riu *rue*	riud	riud (riun)
seə *say*	sed	sed
sel *sell*	seld	seld
seu *sew*	seud	seud (seun)
siəz *seize*	siəzd (seəz)ʹ	siəzd
smel *smell*	smeld	smeld
spel *spell*	speld	speld
spil *spill*	spild	spild
spoil *spoil*	spoild	spoild
streu *strew*	streud	streud (streun)
swel *swell*	sweld	sweld
šeəv *shave*	šeəvd	šeəvd
šeu *show*	šeud	šeud (šeun)
šū *shoe*	šūd	šūd
tel *tell*	teld	teld

Infin.	Pret.	P. P.
tlueŏ *clothe*	tlueŏd	tlueŏd
tšeu *chew*	tšeud	tšeud (tšeun)
wokɒ *wake, awake*	wokɒd	wokɒd
gue *go*	went	guen
bai *buy*	bout	bout

The forms delt, felt, left, lost, ment, nelt, and in Class III krept, slept, swept, are the literary forms which are now very commonly used among the younger people.

We regularly use leə, leəd, leəd (leən) in speaking of a hen, pigeon, etc.; but in other cases leə and lig are equally used transitively or intransitively without any distinction in meaning: al lig i bed wol brekfəs(t) taim *I will lie in bed until breakfast time*, al lig mə dān *I will lie (me) down*, al lig it ə tflue(r) *I will lay it on the floor*, ŏə leəd or ligd wol ŏə wə tə lat fə ŏə wäk *they lay until they were too late for their work*, wi ligd or leəd əz dān *we lay down*, ŏəv leəd (ligd or leən) oəl tbleəm ə mī *they laid all the blame on me.*

Class III.

§ 383. The preterite and past participle generally take t when the present ends in a voiceless consonant other than t.

Infin.	Pret.	P. P.
elp *help*	elpt	elpt
katš *catch*	katšt	katšt
krīp *creep*	krīpt (krept)	krīpt (krepm, krept)
kus *kiss*	kust	kust (kusn)
reik *reach*	reikt	reikt
slīp *sleep*	slīpt (slept)	slīpt (slept)
swīp *sweep*	swīpt (swept)	swīpt swept

Infin.	*Pret.*	*P. P.*
šap *shape*	šapt	šapt
teitš *teach*	teitšt (tout)	teitšt (tout)
weš *wash*	wešt	wešt
pīp *peep*	pept (pīpt)	pept (pīpt)
sīk *seek*	sīkt (sout)	sīkt (sout)
þiɒk *think*	þout	þout
wēk *work*	wēkt (rout)	wēkt (rout)
mak *make*	meed	meed

Verbal Endings.

§ 384.

Present : The first person singular and the whole of the plural generally have no special endings, except when the subject of the sentence is a relative pronoun. See § 395, p. 156. The second and third persons singular end in -ez, -z, -s. -ez is used after the spirants s, z, š, ž, as misez *missest, misses*, raizez *risest, rises*, wišez *wishest, wishes*, sinžez *singest, singes*; -z after voiced sounds, as weivz *weavest, weaves*, lenz *lendest, lends*, duz *dost, does*; -s after other voiceless sounds, as elps *helpest, helps*, wēks *workest, works*, eits *eatest, eats*.

On the personal endings of the verbs *have* and *be*, see §§ 395, 6.

Preterite : The singular and plural of strong verbs have no special endings. The singular and plural of weak verbs end in -ed, -d, -t for all persons. See §§ 380, 385.

Participles : The present participle ends in -in (§§ 276, 385). The past participle of strong verbs ends in vocalic -n after dentals (§ 269), -ɒ after gutturals (§ 271), and -m after labials (§ 270). The past participle of weak verbs ends in -ed, -d, -t. See §§ 381–3.

Infinitive : The infinitive has no special ending just as in lit. Engl.

Paradigms.

§ 385. The conjugation of eŋ *hang* and brek *break* will serve as models.

		eŋ	brek
Indic. Pres. Sing.	1.	eŋ	brek
	2.	eŋz	breks
	3.	eŋzˇ	breks
Plur.		eŋ	brek
Indic. Pret. Sing.		eŋd	brak
Plur.		eŋd	brak
Imper. Sing. and Plur.		eŋ	brek
Infin.		eŋ	brek
Pres. Part.		eŋin	brekin
Past Part.		eŋd	brokŋ

§ 386. The future, the perfect tenses, and the passive voice are formed the same as in lit. Engl. The subjunctive mood has entirely gone out of use.

§ 387. TABLE OF TENSES.

Tense.	Indefinite.	Imperfect and Continuous.	Perfect.	Perfect and Continuous.
Present	ᴀ brek *I break*	ᴀm brekin *I am breaking*	ᴀv brokn *I have broken*	ᴀv bĭn brekin *I have been breaking*
Preterite	ᴀ brek *I broke*	ᴀ we brekin *I was breaking*	ad brokn *I had broken*	ad bĭn brekin *I had been breaking*
Future	ᴀs brek *I shall break*	ᴀs bĭ brekin *I shall be breaking*	ᴀs e brokn *I shall have broken*	ᴀs e bĭn brekin *I shall have been breaking*

NOTE.—The full conjugation of the auxiliary verbs will be found : *shall* (§ 391), *will* (§ 397), *be* (§ 396), *have* (§ 395).

C. Minor Groups.

a. Preterite-Presents.

§ **388.** In tenses where it has been thought advisable I have added the affirmative and interrogative forms with and without negation. On the various forms assumed by the personal pronouns, see § 350.

1. *can.*

§ **389.** Pres. strong form **kan**, weak forms **ken, kɲ**. Pret. strong form **kud**, weak **ked**. The weak form **kɲ** is mostly used in combination with the personal pronouns.

AFFIRMATIVELY.

Present.

Sing.		*Plur.*	
ai, a, i kan or kɲ		wĭ, we kan or kɲ	
ðă, tă, te ,, ,,		jĭ, je ,, ,,	
ĭ, e ⎱ ,, ,,		ðee, ðe, ðe ,, :,	
šŭ, še ⎰ ,, ,,			

Pret.

ai, a, i kud or ked		wĭ, we kud or ked	
ðă, tă, te ,, ,,		jĭ, je ,, ,,	
ĭ, e ⎱ ,, ,,		ðee, ðe, ðe ,,	
šŭ, še ⎰ ,, ,,			

Affirmatively with *not.*

Pres.	Pret.
ai, a, i, kanet or kănt	ai, a, i kudnt or kednet
etc.	etc.

L 2

INTERROGATIVELY.
Present.

Sing.	*Plur.*
kan ai, a, i ?	kan wĭ, we ?
„ ŏă, tă, te ?	„ jĭ, je ?
„ ĭ, e ? }	„ ŏee, ŏe, ŏe ?
„ šŭ, še ? }	

Pret.

kud ai, a, i ?	kud wĭ, we ?
etc.	etc.

Interrogatively with *not*.

Pres	Pret.
kanet or kănt ai, a, i ?	kudnt ai, a, i ?
etc.	etc.

kud, ked are used both as an infin. and past part.,
unless, as is more probable, the use of kud, ked, in such
cases, is due to the contamination of two constructions, as a
ius te kud or ked diut *I used to be able to do it*, ad e dunt
if id kud (never ked) *I would have done it if I had been
able.*

2. *dare.*

§ 390. This verb presents no special peculiarities. I shall
therefore only give the first person singular of each tense in
use. The final t regularly disappears in the pret. before
the following negative. A weak form de only occurs in the
phrase a de see *I dare say.*

Present.	Pret.
ai, a, i dāe(r)	ai, a, i dĕst
ai, a, i dārent	ai. a, i, dĕsnt
dāer ai, i ?	dĕst ai, i ?
dārent ai, i ?	dĕsnt ai, i ?

3. *shall.*

§ 391. Present strong form **sal**, weak **sl**, **s**.   Pret. strong form **sud**, weak **sed**, **st**.

AFFIRMATIVELY.

Present.

Sing.	*Plur.*
ai, a sal	wĭ sal
aisl, asl	wĭsl, wesl
ais, as	wĭs, wes
ŏă̆ sal	jĭ, je sal
ŏă̆sl	jĭsl, jesl
ŏă̆s	jĭs, jes
ĭ sal	
ĭsl	
ĭs	ŏee, ŏe, ŏe sal
sŭ, še sal	ŏeesl, ŏesl, ŏesl
šŭsl, šesl	ŏees, ŏes, ŏes
šŭs, šes	

Pret.

ai, a, i sud or sed	wĭ, we sud or sed
aist, ast	wĭst, west
ŏă̆, tă̆, te sud or sed	jĭ, je sud or sed
ŏă̆st	jĭst, jest
ĭ, e sud or sed	
ĭst	
šŭ, še sud or sed	ŏee, ŏe, ŏe sud or sed
šŭst, šest	ŏeest, ŏest, ŏest

Affirmatively with *not*.

Present.

<table>
<tr><td>*Sing.*</td><td>*Plur.*</td></tr>
<tr><td>ai, a salnt</td><td>wĭ, we, salnt</td></tr>
<tr><td>ai, a sänt</td><td>wĭ, we sänt</td></tr>
<tr><td>aisl, asl net</td><td>wĭsl, wesl net</td></tr>
<tr><td>ais, as net</td><td>wĭs, wes net</td></tr>
</table>

ŏă salnt or sänt
ŏăsl, ŏăs net

jĭ, je salnt or sänt
jĭsl, jesl net
jĭs, jes net

ĭ salnt, sänt
ĭsl, ĭs net

šŭ, še salnt or sänt
šŭsl, šesl net
šŭs, šes net

ŏee, ŏe, ŏe salnt or sänt
„ „ „ slnet
ŏees, ŏes, ŏes net

Pret.

<table>
<tr><td>ai, a sudnt</td><td>wĭ, we sudnt</td></tr>
<tr><td>ai, a sed net</td><td>wĭ, we sed net</td></tr>
<tr><td>aist, ast net</td><td>wĭst, west net</td></tr>
<tr><td>etc.</td><td>etc.</td></tr>
</table>

INTERROGATIVELY.

Present.

sal ai, a, i ?
„ ŏă, tă, te ?
„ ĭ, e ?
„ šŭ, še ?

sal wĭ, we ?
„ jĭ, je ?
„ ŏee, ŏe, ŏe ?

Pret.

sud ai, a, i ?
„ ŏă, tă, te ?
„ ĭ, e ?
„ šŭ, še ?

sud wĭ, we ?
„ jĭ, je ?
„ ŏee, ŏe, ŏe ?

Interrogatively with *not*.

Pres.   Pret.

salnt, sänt ai, a, i ?   sudnt ai, a, i ?

etc.   etc.

There is no difference in meaning between the weak
forms s, st and sl, sed, but only in usage. The former are
never used except in combination with the personal pronouns, as aset bi te-moen *I shall have it by to-morrow*,
ðest e guen if ðed kud *they should have gone if they had
been able*, tmen sl (never s) et *the men shall have it*, ði faðe
sed gim(e) e feu *thy father should give me a few*. But the
difference in use between s and sl, st and sed in combination with pronouns seems to be due to sentence rhythm.

4. *must*.

§ **392.** To express lit. Engl. *must*, we have two words
which are never confounded in use:

1. Strong form mun, weak men which expresses a necessity dependent upon the will of a person, as a men get mi
wāk duin bi te-nīt *I must get my work done by to-night*,
je men tel im wen e kumz et as bi bak inā *you must tell
him when he comes that I shall be back presently*, mun i
gue wi je ? *must I go with you?*

mun, men is sometimes used to express *may, can*, as ða
men þiŋk wot te laiks bed ðal e te diut *you may think
what you like but you will have to do it*, mun ðe stop ?
may mean either *must they stop?* or *may they stop?*

The weak form med (§ 393), which generally means
might, is also used as a preterite of mun, as šu sed ðe med
oeðer eit ðat e diu bāt out *she said they must either eat
that or do without anything*.

mun is of Norse origin, O. Icel. inf. mono, later munu

shall, will, pres. sing. mon, later **mun**, pl. **monom**, later
munum, pret. **munda**. The verb presents no peculiarities,
so that only the first person is given here.

Sing.	*Plur.*
ai, a, i **mun** or **men**	wĭ, we **mun** or **men**
„ „ „ **munet** or **muent**	„ „ **munet** or **muent**
mun ai, a, i ?	**mun** wĭ, we ?
munet or **muent** ai, a, i ?	**munet** or **muent** wĭ, we ?

2. For *must* we use **must**, which has no weak form, when
it implies a logical or natural necessity, as **ðа must bi e
fuil if te þiɲks im bān te diut** *you must be (surely you are) a
fool if you think I am going to do it,* **ðem et sed ðat must
bi reɲ i ðer ied** *those who said that must be wrong in their
heads.* In these and similar cases **mun, men** is never used.
Cp. **ðe múst kum ðis wee** = Lowland Scotch *thay byd cum
thys way* with **ðe men kum ðis wee** = Lowland Scotch *thay
mæn cum this way*; the former implying that there is no
other road, the latter that they are under personal restraint
to take this road. On the Scotch verbs **byd, mæn** see The
Dialect of the Southern Counties of Scotland, by Dr.
Murray, pp. 217-8.

5. *may.*

§ 393. Present strong form **mee**, weak **me**. Preterite
strong form **mud**, weak **med**. **mud** is a new formation
made after the analogy of **sud** *should,* **kud** *could.*

AFFIRMATIVELY.

Present.

Sing.	*Plur.*
ai, a, i **mee** or **me**	wĭ, we **mee** or **me**
etc.	etc.

Pret.

Sing.	Plur.
ai, a, i mud or med	wĭ, we mud or med
etc.	etc.

Affirmatively with *not*.

Pres.	Pret.
ai, a, i meent	ai a, i mudnt
„ „ „ menet	„ „ „ mudnet
etc.	etc.

INTERROGATIVELY.

Present.

Sing.	Plur.
me ai, a, i ?	mee wĭ, we ?
mee dă, tă, te ?	etc.
etc.	

The e of mee regularly disappears before a following vowel (§ 193). After the analogy of me i? *may I?* me e? *may he?* I have often heard me we? *may we?* etc.

Pret.

mud ai, a, i ?	mud wĭ, we ?
etc.	etc.

Interrogatively with *not*.

Pres.	Pret.
meent ai, a, i ?	mudnt ai, a, i ?
etc.	etc.

6. *ought.*

§ 394. out remains uninflected for all persons, so that it will be sufficient to give the first person only: ai, a, i out, outnt or outnet. out ai, a, i? outnt ai, a, i?

b. *have.*

§ 395. Pres. strong forms ev, e, weak ev, e.   Pret. strong form ed, weak ed.

The present forms e, e are regular only before consonants: as e dun inā *I shall have done presently,* a sed e guen bed fe ðī *I should have gone but for thee*; but we always say, ai ev em *I have them,* as et or ev it *I shall have it.*   In combination with the pronouns we now use the v form before consonants, as a or av dun *I have done.*

The vowel disappears in the weak forms ev, ed when preceded by the nom. of the personal pronouns, av *I have,* wǐv *we have,* etc.   ad sīn im *I had seen him,* but tmen ed sīn im *the men had seen him.*   And sometimes the verb disappears altogether, as a faiv on em *I have five of them,* ðe guen uem *they have gone home,* ðe stoun em *they have stolen them,* wi or we funt *we have found it*; but wi or we fant *we found it.*   See § 249.

The final -z in the second and third persons singular becomes -s before voiceless consonants, as este ? *hast thou?* if tes te diut *if thou hast to do it.*

AFFIRMATIVELY.

Present.

Sing.	*Plur.*
ai, a, i ev or e ⎫ aiv, av, iv ⎭	⎰ wǐ we ev or e ⎱ wǐv wev
ðǎ, tǎ, te ez ⎫ ðǎz, tǎz, tez ⎭	⎰ jǐ, je ev or e ⎱ jǐv, jev
ǐ, e, ez ⎫ ǐz, ez ⎭ ⎫	
šǔ, še ez ⎫ ⎬ šǔz, šez ⎭ ⎭	⎰ ðe, ðe ev or e ⎱ ðeev, ðev, ðev

Pret.

Sing.	Plur.
ai, a, i, ed ⎱	⎰ wĭ, we əd
aid, ad, id ⎰	⎱ wĭd, wed
ðă, tă te ed ⎱	⎰ jĭ, je ed
ðăd, tăd, ted ⎰	⎱ jĭd, jed
ĭ, ə, ed ⎱	
ĭd, ed ⎰	⎰ ðe, ðe ed
šŭ, še ed ⎱	⎱ ðeed, ðed, ðed
šŭd, šed ⎰	

Infin. ev, e ⎱
　　　　　ev, e ⎰

Present Part. evin
Past　　　,,　　ed, ed, d.

Affirmatively with *not*.

Pres.	Pret.
ai, a, i evnt ⎱	⎰ ai, a, i ednt
aiv, av, iv net ⎰	⎱ aid, ad, id net
etc.	etc.

INTERROGATIVELY.

Present.

Sing.	Plur.
ev ai, a, i ?	e wĭ or we ?
ez ðă, es tă or te ?	e jĭ or je ?
ez ĭ or e ?	
es šŭ, es še ? ⎱	e ðee, ðe or ðe ?
ešе ? ⎰	

Pret.

ed ai, a, i ?	ed wĭ, we ?
etc.	etc.

Interrogatively with *not*.

Pres.   Prct.

evnt ai, a, i ?   ednt ai, a, i ?

etc.   etc.

The plural forms of the present, given above, are only
used in combination with the personal pronouns, in other
cases we use **ez, ez, z, s** (after voiceless consonants) just as
in the second and third person singular, as **ðem menz bĭn
vari guid tə me** *those men have been very good to me*, **tladz
ez gən me sumet** *the boys have given me something*, **uz əts
dun sə mĭtš for im** *we who have done so much for him*, **ez ðem
men sīn ðe ?** *have those men seen thee?* **es taplz guen bad ?**
have the apples gone bad? The same also applies to the
first person, as **its mī əts dunt** *it is I who have done it*, **mī
əts ed sə mĭtš tə baid** *I who have had so much to endure*.

The endings -z, -s for the whole of the singular and
plural are now chiefly confined to the verbs *have* and *be*
(except the second person singular).

With other verbs we now generally only use these
endings in combination with the relative pronoun **et**, as
ðem men diu ðe wāk vari wīl *those men do their work very
well*; but **ðemz tmen et duz ðe wāk tbest** *those are the men
who do their work the best*. Although this is the normal
usage, I have often heard the -z, -s forms used under the
same circumstances as they are for the verb *have*. In the
older stage of the dialect the endings -z, -s must have been
used for all verbs in the manner they are still used for
have. Already in OE. the Northern dialects had the plural
ending -as beside -að, e. g. **bindas** beside **bindað**.

As it may possibly interest some readers to learn how
far the plural endings -z and -s extend, I have examined the
Comparative dialect specimens in Ellis, EEPr. v. The

second and sixth sentences contain the point in question.
The sentences are : (2) 'Few men die because they are
laughed at.' In the dialect specimens this is often rendered
as if it were : 'there are few men who die because they are
laughed at.' In the statistics given below, this sentence
will be referred to as without relative and ending, without
relative with ending, with relative and no ending, with
relative and ending. The sixth sentence is : (6) 'And the
old woman herself will tell any of you that laugh now.'

Western Mid Southern division : at Tedbury with rel. and
ending -z ; at Ledbury and Much Cowarne without rel. and
ending, but (6) with rel. and endings -s -z ; at Eggleton rel.
with ending -z. Eastern Mid Southern: at Hamstead
Norris without rel. and ending, but (6) rel. without ending ;
Southampton to Winchester without rel. with ending -z
and (6) with rel. and ending -s. Northern Border Southern :
at Banbury without rel. with ending -z, and (6) with rel.
and ending -s. Mid Border Southern : at Handborough rel.
and endings -z, -s. Southern Border Southern : no examples.
East Southern : at Faversham without rel. and ending, and
(6) with rel. and no ending. Northern West Southern : at
Wellington (West Somerset) (6) with rel. and no ending.
South West Southern : at Iddesleigh without rel. and
ending, and (6) with rel. and no ending, the same also in
South Devon. Western West Southern : no examples.
South and North Western divisions : no examples. West
Eastern : at Aylesbury (p. 190) *father and mother v* (=*are*)
lame. Mid Eastern : at Ware without rel. and ending, and
(6) with rel. and no ending, the same also for Mid Bedford-
shire and East Haddon. South and North Eastern
divisions : no examples. East Eastern : in South Norfolk,
East and West Suffolk without rel. and ending, and (6)
with rel. and no ending. Border Midland (the county of

Lincolnshire): no examples. Southern North Midland: at
Stalybridge without rel. with ending -n, and (6) with rel.
and ending -s; at Glossop with rel. and ending -n, and (6)
with rel. and ər along with the pres. part.; at Chapel-en-le-
Frith (2 and 6) with rel. and ending -n. Western North
Midland: at Skelmersdale (2 and 6) rel. and endings -z, -s;
at Westhoughton without rel. with ending -z, and (6) with
rel. and iz along with the pres. part.; at Leyland without
rel. with ending -n; at Burnley without rel. with ending -z,
and (6) with rel. and -s along with the pres. part. Northern
North Midland: at Poulton without rel. and ending, but (6)
with rel. and -s; at Goosnargh without rel. and ending, but
(6) with rel. and iz along with the pres. part. Eastern
North Midland: at Huddersfield, Halifax, Keighley, Bradford, Leeds, Dewsbury, Rotherham, both in (2) and (6) with
rel. and endings -z, -s; but at Sheffield without rel. and
ending, and (6) with rel. and no ending. Western Mid
Midland: at Middlewich both (2) and (6) with rel. and
ending -n; the same at Shrigley; at Tarporley (6) with rel.
and ending -n; at Burslem (6) with rel. and ending -s.
Eastern Mid Midland: at Taddington rel. with ending -n,
and (6) rel. with ending -s; at Ashford rel. with ending -z,
and (6) rel. with iz along with the pres. part.; at Winster
(2) and (6) with rel. and endings -z, -s; at Ashbourne rel.
with ending -z, also without rel. with ending -z, and (6)
with rel. and ending -s; at Brampton (2) and (6) with rel.
and ending -n; at Repton (2) and (6) with rel. and endings
-z and -s. East and Western South Midland divisions: no
examples. Eastern South Midland: at Cannock Chase
without rel. and ending -n, but (6) with rel. and ending
-n; at Dudley without rel. with ending -z; at Ather-
stone (2) and (6) with rel. and no ending, at Waltham
without rel. and ending; and (6) with rel. and no

ending. East Northern: at South Ainsty and Holderness
without rel. with ending, -z, and (6) with rel. and ending
-s. Mid Yorkshire, North Mid Yorkshire, New Malton,
Lower Nidderdale, Washburn River, South Cleveland,
North East Coast, and Market Weighton, all have (2) and
(6) with rel. and endings -z, -s. West Northern: at Upper
Swaledale, the Upper Mining Dales, Upper Craven with
Upper Nidderdale, Skipton, and Mid Craven, we have for
(6) rel. with ending -s; at Hawes, Kirkby, Lonsdale, Dent,
Sedburg, Kendal, Orton, Kirkby Stephen, Crosby Ravens-
worth, Langwathby, and Keswick, we have the form without rel. with ending -z; but at Lower-Holker-in-Cartmel,
Coniston, Long Sleddale, Temple Sowerby, Clifton, Holme
Cultram, Carlisle, and Knaresdale without rel. and ending;
at Milburn, Ellonby, and Upper Swaledale with rel. and
ending -z. All the dialects in this division have for (6) rel.
with ending -s except at Coniston, where we have with rel.
and no ending. North Northern: at South Shields (6) with
rel. and ending -s; at Newcastle and Berwick-upon-Tweed
without rel. and ending, and (6) with rel. and no ending.
The Lowland division: at Bewcastle, Hawick, Edinburgh,
Arbroath, Keith, and Dunrossness without rel. and with
ending -z, but (6) with rel. and ending -s; at Stranraer and
Wick without rel. and ending, but for (6) with rel. and no
ending. The above are the only comparative specimens of
the Lowland division given in Ellis. But Dr. Murray, The
Dialect of the Southern Counties of Scotland, pp. 211–2,
states that the plural and first pers. singular without -s are
only used when the verb is accompanied by its proper
pronoun; when the subject is a noun, adjective, interrogative or relative pronoun, or when the verb and subject are
separated by a clause, the verb takes the termination -s in
all persons. Dr. Murray informs me that the persons who

supplied Dr. Ellis with the comparative specimens for Stranraer and Wick have given inaccurate versions with regard to the verbal endings. The probability is that Dr. Ellis has misunderstood the versions, because in a note (p. 683) he distinctly says that he took down the two versions hurriedly, and was afraid that some of the finer shades might have escaped him.

c. be.

§ 396. The vowel disappears in the weak forms of the present, and when followed by a consonant the verb disappears altogether in the plural, as **wil guə wen tət redi** *we will go when thou art ready,* **ðer at it əgiən** *they are at it again*; but **ðə bān uəm** *they are going home,* **we selin əm ət oepni ə kweet** *we are selling them at a halfpenny a quart.* The -z in the third person becomes -s before and after voiceless consonants, as **tbried ət .te bouts nuən guid** *the bread which thou boughtest is not good,* ** šes þiɒkin ə gu(ə)in** *she is thinking of going.*

AFFIRMATIVELY.

Present.

Sing.	Plur.
ai, a, i am }	{ wĭ, we āe(r)
aim, am, im }	{ wĭ(r), we(r)
ðắ āt, te āt }	{ jĭ, je āe(r)
ðắt, tắt, tet }	{ jĭ(r), je(r)
ĭ iz, ə iz }	
ĭz, əz } }	
šŭ iz, še iz } }	{ ðee, ðe, ðo āe(r)
šŭz, šez } }	{ ðee(r), ðe(r), ðe(r)

Pret.

Sing.	Plur.
ai, a, i wo(r) or we(r)	wĭ, we wo(r) or we(r)
etc.	etc.

Infin.	bĭ, be
Pres. Part.	bĭ-in
Past „	bĭn

AFFIRMATIVELY WITH *not*.

Present.

Sing.	Plur.
ai, a, i amet }	{ wĭ, we ānt
aim, am, im net }	{ wĭ, we net
ðă, tă, te ātnt }	{ jĭ, je ānt
ðăt, tăt, tet net }	{ jĭ, je net
ĭ, e iznt }	
ĭz, ez net } }	{ ðee, ðe, ðe ānt
šŭ, še iznt } }	{ ðee, ðe, ðe net
šŭz, šez net }	

Pret.

ai, a, i wornt	wĭ, we wornt
ai, a, i we-net	wĭ, we we-net
etc.	etc.

INTERROGATIVELY.

Present.

am ai, a, i?	ăwĭ, ăwe?
ăðă, ătă, ăte?	ăjĭ, ăje?
izĭ, ize?	
iz šŭ, še? }	ăðee, ăðe, ăðe?
išŭ, iše? }	

M

Pret.

Sing.	*Plur.*
wor ai, a, i ?	wowĭ, wowe ?
woŏắ, wotă, wote ?	wojĭ, woje ?
wor, ĭ, e ?	
wošŭ, woše ?	woŏee, woŏe, woŏe ?

INTERROGATIVELY WITH *not.*

Present.

amet ai, a, i ?	ānt wĭ, we ?
ătnŏắ, ătntă ?	
ătnte ?	ānt jĭ, je ?
iznt ĭ, e ?	
iznt šŭ, še ?	ānt ŏee, ŏe, ŏe ?

Pret.

wornt ai, a, i ?	wornt wĭ, we ?
etc.	etc.

In forms like **ātnt** *art not,* **wornt** *was, were not,* the n is
vocalic.

The above forms of the present are mostly used in combination with the pronouns, in other cases we generally
use **iz, ez, z, s,** cp. § 395, as **tkoilz iznt dun jet** *the coals
are not done yet,* **ŏez lots on em dān trued** *there are lots of
them down the road,* **ŏemz** or **ŏem e vari guidnz** *those are
very good ones,* **tladz ez** or **e bān wi je** *the lads are going
with you,* **ŏez fouks ets** or **et er oles grumlin** *there are
people who are always grumbling,* **mĭ ets se pueli** *I who
am so poorly,* **ŏĭ ets nout te diu med elp me e bit** *thou,
who hast nothing to do, mightest help me a bit.*

d. *will.*

§ 397. Present, strong form **wil,** weak **el** which loses
its vowel in combination with the pronouns.

Preterite, strong form **wod**, weak forms **wəd, ed**, the latter loses its vowel in combination with the pronouns, as **ad lən ðet, bəd a kānt diu bāt it dʒust nā** *I would lend thee it, but I cannot do without it just now*, **tladz wəd** or **ed fotš it, if jə ast əm** *the lads would fetch it, if you asked them.*

wod, wəd is used as an infin. in the phrase: **ius tə wod** *to be formerly wont* or *willing to do a thing*, as **ðe ius tə wəd elp mə nā ən ðen** *they were formerly wont* or *willing to help me now and then.* **wod** is also in common use as a past participle, **a kud** or **ked ə dunt if id wod** *I could have done it if I had wished.* But see the end of § 389.

AFFIRMATIVELY.

Present.

Sing.	*Plur.*
ai, a wil ⎱ ail, al ⎰	⎰ wĭ, wə wil ⎱ wĭl, wəl
ðǎ, tǎ, tə wil ⎱ ðǎl, tǎl, təl ⎰	⎰ jĭ, jə wil ⎱ jĭl, jəl
ĭ, ə wil ⎱ ĭl, əl ⎰	⎰ ðee, ðe, ðə wil
šǔ, šə wil ⎱ šǔl, šəl ⎰	⎱ ðeel, ðel, ðəl

Pret.

ai, a, i wod or wəd ⎱ aid, ad, id ⎰	⎰ wĭ, we wod or wəd ⎱ wĭd, wəd
ðǎ, tǎ, tə wod or wəd ⎱ ðǎd, tǎd, ted ⎰	⎰ jĭ, jə wod or wəd ⎱ jĭd, jed
ĭ, ə wod or wəd ⎱ ĭd, ed ⎰	⎰ ðee, ðe, ðə wod or wəd
šǔ, šə wod or wəd ⎱ šǔd, šed ⎰	⎱ ðeed, ðed, ðəd

M 2

AFFIRMATIVELY WITH *not*.
Present.

Sing.	*Plur.*
ai, a wilnt or wient	wĭ, we wilnt or wient
etc.	etc.

Pret.

ai, a, i wodnt ⎫	wĭ, we wodnt ⎫
aid, ad, id net ⎭	ˎwĭd, wed net ⎭
etc.	etc.

INTERROGATIVELY.
Present.

wil ai, a, i ?	wil wĭ, we ?
wil ð̆ă, tă, te ? ⎫	
wită, wite ? ⎭	wil jĭ, je ?
wil ĭ, e ? ⎫	
wil š̆ŭ, še ? ⎭	wil ð̆ee, ð̆e, ð̆e ?

Pret.

wod ai, a, i ?	wod wĭ, we ?
etc.	etc.

INTERROGATIVELY WITH *not*.
Present.

wilnt, wient ai, a i ?	wilnt, wient wĭ, we ?
etc.	etc.

Pret.

wodnt ai, a, i ?	wodnt wĭ, we ?
etc.	etc.

e. *do*.

§ 398. As an independent verb diu has its full conjugation like any other verb. The pret. did is used for all persons singular and plural. Present part. diu-in, which has been reformed from the inf., otherwise we should have had *du(i)in (§ 163); past part. duin, dun. Present wit *not* is duent, dunet, pret. didnt.

When used interrogatively as an auxiliary verb we have diu for the first person singular and for tho plural strong form diu, weak forms de, di. When *do* is used affirmatively as an auxiliary verb it has, of course, no weak forms.

PRESENT.

Affirmatively.

Sing.	*Plur.*
ai, a, i diu	wĭ, we diu
ðă, tă, te duz	jĭ, je diu
ĭ, e duz ⎞	
šŭ, še duz ⎠	ðee, ðe, ðe diu

Interrogatively.

diu ai, a, i ?	de or di wĭ, we ?
duz ðă, dustă, duste ?	de or di jĭ, je ?
duz ĭ, e ? ⎞	
duz šŭ, duše ? ⎠	de or di ðee, ðe, ðe ?

The verb *do* is not used so frequently in asking questions as in lit. Engl.: wot þinste, sal we gue? lit. *what thinkest thou, shall we go?* wod e diut, þink je? *would he do it, do you think?* See § 249.

APPENDIX.

CHAPTER XI.

Adverbs, Prepositions, and Conjunctions.

I. ADVERBS.

§ 399. 1. Adverbs of manner and degree: The adverbs of manner mostly end in -li, as ādli *hardly*, oekedli *awkwardly*; but we have the stress on the suffix in siueli̯ *surely*, ekuedinlái *accordingly*.

ā *how*, ā-ive(r) old people say āmive(r) *however* which seems to have been contaminated with āsemive(r) *howsoever*, with the particle sem = the O. Dan. sum, O. Icel. sem; apm (lit. *happen*), me bi *perhaps*, nobed lit. *not but*, *only*, oles *always*, omest *almost*, tiu *too, also* (instead of tiu we very often use en oel lit. *and all*, it wer e vari guidn en oel *it was a very good one too*, aim bān en oel *I am going too*), vari *very*, wīl *well*. But when *well* begins the sentence we use wel just as in lit. Engl., as wel, a niver ied sitš en e þin i oel mi boen deez *well, I never heard such (an) a thing in all my born days*; but its oel vari wīl *it is all very well*, šuz nuen se wīl te-dee *she is not very well to-day*.

sue, weak form se *so*. Instead of sue we often use ðat, as i we ðat mad *he was so angry*, še we ðat week wol še kudnt stand *she was so weak that* (lit. *while*) *she could not stand*.

The adverbs *also*, *thus*, *why* are not used. To express

also we use **tiu, ən oəl,** *thus* is **i ðis weə,** and *why,* **wot fo(r), wots ə guən fo(r)?** *why has he gone?,* **a duənt noə wot əz dun ðat fo(r)** *I don't know why he has done that.*

Adverbs of place : **oniwiə(r)** *anywhere,* **iə(r)** *here,* **iðə(r),** *hither,* **jondə(r)** *yonder,* **sumwiə(r)** *somewhere,* **ðiə(r)** (weak forms **ðe(r), ðə(r))** *there,* **wiə(r)** *where.*

Adverbs of time : **inā** *bye-and-bye, presently,* **binā** *by this time,* **ivə(r)** *ever,* **jəstədə** *yesterday,* **jəstənīt** *last night,* **jət** *yet,* **nā** *now,* **nivə(r)** *never,* **oft** *often,* **sin** *since,* **suin** *soon,* **tə-deə** *to-day,* **tə-moən** *to-morrow,* **tə-moən-tnīt** *to-morrow (the) night,* **tə-nīt** *to-night,* **ðen** *then,* **wen** *when.*

Affirmative and negative particles : **ai** *yes* (**jəs** is also used but it is not so common as **ai**), **neə** *no* (**nou** *no* has been borrowed from the literary language), **nət** *not* (instead of **nət** we often use **nuən**); cp. § 357.

2. PREPOSITIONS.

§ 400. **aftə(r)** *after,* **bə-fuə(r), ə-fuə(r), fuə(r)** *before,* **bə-twin, twīn** *between,* **bi,** weak **bə** *by,* **bə-int** *behind,* **bin** *within,* **dān** *down,* **ə, əv** (before vowels) *of,* **ə-bāt, bāt** *about, without,* **ə-būn, būn** *above,* **ə-giən, giən** *against,* **ə-leŋ ə** *along of, on account of,* **ə-meŋ** *among,* **ə-nent** *opposite,* **ə-said, bə-said** *besides,* **ə-stied ə, stied ə** *instead of,* **fo(r)** *for,* **frə, fre** *from,* **in, i** *in* (**i** is very common before both vowels and consonants), **intə, intəv** (before vowels), **intul** *into,* **nie(r)** *near,* **nobəd** *except,* **on** (weak form **ə**) *on, of,* **ouə(r), ovə(r)** *over,* **sin** *since,* **tə, təv** (before vowels), **tul** *to,* **þriu, þrə** *through, from,* **undə(r)** *under,* **up** *up,* **wi** *with,* **wiðāt** *without.*

3. CONJUNCTIONS.

§ 401. The following are the chief conjunctions in addition to those prepositions and adverbs which may be

used as conjunctions: **bed** *but,* **be-kos, kos** *because,* **en** *and,*
et *that* (ðat is never used as a conjunction in the dialect), **if**
if, **noeðe(r)** *neither,* **oeðe(r)** *either,* **ne(r)** *nor* (after compara-
tives *than,* **bete ner i þout** *better than I thought*), **o(r), e(r)**
or, **ðoe** *although,* **wol** *until, that* (**stop wol e kumz** *stop
until he comes,* **še we ðat badli wol ðe þout šeđl nive mend**
she was so ill that they thought she would never get better).

SPECIMENS.

—·•·—

It was originally my intention not to give any specimens of the dialect in this volume, but to reserve them for
a second which was to contain a complete glossary of
such dialect words as are not in use in the Modern literary
language, together with extensive specimens of the dialect.
With this end in view I have been collecting materials for
a great number of years; but various circumstances prevent me from entertaining the hope of being able to
publish them for some years to come. I have therefore
decided to give a few specimens in the present volume,
trusting that they may be found useful to those readers
who may wish to make themselves familiar with the
dialect. To anyone who takes the trouble to read them
I venture to say that they will be found both amusing and
instructive.

There is a great quantity of stories and poems printed
in the dialect, but as they stand they are practically
worthless for the purposes of this book. The transcription is neither accurate nor consistent. All the specimens
given here are from printed sources. To number III.
I have added the original in order to show the kind of
transcription usually employed in such books.

The sources are:—III. (The Yorkshireman's Comic An-
nual, 1884, pp. 37–38), IV. (ditto, 1885, pp. 14–17), V.
(ditto, 1882, pp. 24–26), VI. (Yorkshire Sketches, by Wil-
liam Cudworth, pp. 11–17), VII., VIII., IX. (Dialect and
other Poems, by Ben Preston, pp. 31–33, 11–12, 1–10).

I.

Comparative Specimen.

See Ellis, EEPr. vol. v. p. 7*. In this and the Dialect Test I have inserted the forms in parentheses in the literary English Specimens in order to facilitate the reading of the dialect versions.

1. 'wel, neəbə(r), jī ən im mə buəþ laf ət ðis niuz ə main. uə keəz ? ðats noəðər iə nə ðiə(r).

2. feu men dī kos ðə laft at, wī noə, duənt wə ? wot səd mak əm ? its nət vari laikli, iz it ?

3. āsəm·ivə ðiəz ə tfaks ə tkeəs, suə džust od jə din, frend, ən bi kwaiət wol iv dun. ākɯ !

4. ·aim siuər a iəd əm seə—sum ə ðem fouks ət went þriu tuəl þiɯ frə tʃēst ðəsenz,—þat a did, [seəf] siuər i·nif,—

5. ət tjuɯist sun isen, ə gēt lad ə nain, niu is faðə voiz ət wuns, ðo(ə) it ·wo sə kwiər ən skwiəkin, ən ad trāst ·im tə speik t'riuþ oni deə, ai, a ·wod ðat.

6. ən toud wumən əsen l tel oni on jə ət laf nā, ən tel jə streit of, tiu, bāt mitš boðə(r), if jəl nobəd as ə(r), oə ! wiənt šə ?—

7. ət oni reət šu teld it ·mī wen i ast ə(r), tū ə þrī taimz ouə(r), šu did, ən ·šū outnt tə bi reɯ i sitš [ən] ə point əz ðis, wot þiɯk jə ?

I.

Comparative Specimen.

1. Well, neighbour, you and he may both laugh at this news of mine. Who cares? That is neither here nor there.

2. Few men die because they are laughed at, we know, don't we? what should make them? It is not very likely, is it?

3. Howsoever these are the facts of the case, so just hold your [din] noise, friend, and be quiet till I have done. Hearken!

4. *I* am [sure] certain I heard them say—some of [them] those folks who went through the whole thing from the first themselves,—that did I, [sure] safe enough,—

5. That the youngest son himself, a great [lad] boy of nine, knew his father's voice at once, though it *was* so queer and squeaking, and I would trust *him* to speak the truth any day, aye, I *would* [that].

6. And the old woman herself will tell any of you that laugh now, and tell you straight off, too, without much bother, if you will only ask her, oh! won't she?—

7. [at any rate] leastways she told it *me* when I asked her, two or three times over, did she, and *she* ought not to be wrong on such a point as this, what do you think?

8. wel əz a wə se(ə)-in, ˈšūd tel jə, ā, wiər ɔn wen šə fan
d'rukṇ ānd ət šə koəlz ər uzbn.

9. šu sweə šə so(ə) im wi ər oən īn, ligin rɔit ət ful lenþ,
ə tgrund, in iz guid sundə koit, tlois bi d'uər ə tās, dān ət
tkoənər ə jon loin.

10. i wə ruərin ə·weə, sez šū, fər oəl twēld laik ə puəli
bān, ər ə litl las in ə friət.

11. ən ðat apṃd, əz ər ən ə doutər-i-loə kom þriu tbak
jād frə iṃin twet tluəz āt tə drai ə twešin deə.

12. wol tketl wə boilin fə t'iə, wun fain brīt sumər
aftənuin, nobəd ə wik sin kum tnekst þēzdə.

13. ən, di jə noə? a nivə liənd nə muə nə ðis ə ðat
biznəs up tə tə·deə, əs siuər əz mi neəm z džon šepəd, ən a
duənt wọnt tiu oəðə(r), ðiə nā!

14. ən su(ə) am bān uəm tə mi supə(r). guid nīt, ən
duənt bi sə redi tə kro(ə) ouər ə bodi ə·giən, wen ə toəks ə
ðis ðat ə tuðə(r).

15. its ə weək fuil ət preəts bāt riəzn. ən ðats mai last
wēd. guid bai.

8. Well as I was saying, *she* would tell you, how, where, and when she found the drunken [hound] that she calls her husband.

9. She swore she saw him with her own eyes, lying [right] stretched at full length, on the ground, in his good Sunday coat, close by the door of the house, down at the corner of yon lane.

10. He was [roaring] whining away, says she, for all the world like a [poorly barn] sick child, or a little [lass] girl in a fret.

11. And that happened, as she and her daughter-in-law came through the back yard from hanging out the wet clothes on [the] a washing day.

12. While the kettle was boiling for [the] tea, one fine bright summer afternoon, only a week [since] ago come next Thursday.

13. And, do you know? I never learned [no] any more [nor] than this of that business up to to-day, as sure as my name is John Shepherd, and I don't want to either, there now !

14. And so I am going home to [my supper] sup. Good night, and don't be so [ready] quick to crow over a body again, when he talks of this that or t' other.

15. It is a weak fool that prates without reason. And that is my last word. Good bye.

II.

Dialect Test.

See Ellis, p. 8*, and compare the version given below with the one in Ellis (p. 389), which contains several strange mistakes both in the version and the notes to it. If his rendering of the dialect test of other dialect speakers is as inaccurate as that of the Windhill dialect, the value of these tests for phonetic and philological purposes is not very great. The classified word-list (pp. 391-4) also contains many mistakes. The only way in which I can account for these inaccuracies is partly through the hurried manner in which the dial. test and classified word-list were taken down and partly through their not having been revised.

1. su(ə) a seə meəts, jə sī nā ət im reit ə·bāt ðat litl las kumin frə tskuil jondə(r).

2. šuz gu(ə)-in dān truəd ðiə þriu tred geət ə tleft and said ə tweə.

3. siuər i·nif, tbān z guən streit up tə d'uər ə treꝛ ās,

4. wiə šl tšons tə find ðat drukꝛ diəf wiznd felə (more commonly tšap) ə tneəm ə toməs.

5. wi oəl no(ə) im vari wīl.

6. wiənt toud tšap suin teitš ə nət tə diu it ə·giən, puə þiꝛ !

7. liuk! iznt it triu?

II.

Dialect Test.

1. So I say, mates, you see now that I am right about that little [lass] girl coming from the school yonder.

2. She is going down the road there through the red gate on the left hand side of the way.

3. Sure enough, the [barn] child has gone straight up to the door of the wrong house,

4. where she will chance to find that drunken deaf [wizzened] shrivelled fellow of the name of Thomas.

5. We all know him very well.

6. Won't the old chap soon teach her not to do it again, poor thing!

7. Look! Isn't it true?

III.

TBATL Ǝ T'LUƷZ LAINZ.

ai, Greǝs, las, it wǝr oǝl ouǝr ǝ bit ǝv ǝ tluǝs kuǝd. am
nǝt wun ǝ tsuǝt tǝ guǝ peilin up ǝn dān dinin fouk ouǝ(r),
ǝz ǝ riul; ða noǝz ðat. wot ·ai wont is piǝs ǝn kwaiǝtnǝs,
bǝd if fouk wiǝnt let mǝ ev it [or et], al mak ǝm sit up fot,
5 ǝz oni wumǝn ·wod ǝt ǝd ǝr oǝn weǝ tǝ mak i twēld, ǝn ǝ lot
ǝ bānz tǝ mak ǝn mend fo(r), nivǝ neǝm ǝ uzbn ǝt nivǝ
blakliǝdǝd ǝ greǝt ǝ wešt ǝ windǝ sin wed wǝ wo(r). ða
noǝz ǝz wīl ǝz ·ai noǝ wot ǝ gǝt wešin ai ev ivri wik—ǝ lot
ǝ muki smoks ǝn skǝ̄ts, ǝt jǝ mǝ boil ǝn betǝ boil, ǝn ðen bi
10 niǝli ǝz bad ǝz wen jǝ bǝ·gan. ðe duǝnt koǝl it tgriǝzi miln
fǝ nout. tiuzdǝ z olǝs bīn mai wešin deǝ fǝ ðiǝz siks jiǝ bak
ǝ muǝ(r). a olǝs put t'luǝs tǝ stīp tnīt ǝ·fuǝ(r), ǝn get up ǝt
faiv ǝ·tlok i tmoǝnin, ǝ·fuǝ Ben ǝn tbānz guǝz tǝ ðǝ wāk,
ǝn gets tsetpan ǝ·geǝt, ǝn z ivri tlāt āt suin aftǝ brekfǝs
15 taim, if ðǝz ǝ guid druft, fǝr if ðǝz wun þin muǝ nǝr ǝ·nuðǝr
ǝt maks Ben liuk blak its ǝ lot ǝ tluǝz inin ǝ·bāt.

ðats bin mai we(ǝ) ǝ gu(ǝ)in on, ǝn šuz noǝn it ǝz wīl ǝz
iv noǝn it misen. wol ðis apmd wi wǝr ǝz guid neǝbǝz ǝz
nīd bī. wi mud fratš ǝ bit nā ǝn ðen ouǝ tbānz—fǝ ðat
20 Siuzi ǝ ǝz iz ǝ rcit ·teǝstril ǝv ǝ las, ǝn giz āǝ Džoni sum reǝ
slaps sumtaimz—bǝd wiv nivǝr ed nǝ boðǝ tǝ miǝn out wol
nā. ǝn if tǝl bǝ·līv mǝ, las, av dun muǝ fǝ ðat ðiǝ wumǝn
nǝr if šǝd bīn mi oǝn sistǝ(r). a neg·lektǝd mi oǝn uǝm tǝ

III.

Ay, Grace, lass, it wor all ovver a bit of a tloaze cord. I'm nut one o' t'soart to go peylin' up an' dahn dingin' fowk ovver, as a rule; thah knaws that. What I want is peace an' quietness, but if fowk weant let me hev it, I'll mak' 'em sit up for it, as onny woman wod 'at hed her awn way to mak' i' t'world, an' a lot o' barns to mak' an' mend for, nivver name a husband 'at nivver blackleeaded a grate or weshed a winda sin' wed we wor. Thah knaws as weel as I knaw what a gurt weshin' I hev ivvery week—a lot o' mucky smocks an' skirts, 'at ye may boil an' better boil, an' then be nearly as bad as when yo began. They don't call it t'greasy miln for nowt. Tuesday's awlus been my weshin' day for these six year back or more. I awlus put t'tloaze to steep t'neet afore, an' get up at five o'clock i' t'mornin', afore Ben an' t'barns goes to ther wark, an' gets t'set-pan agate, an' hez ivvery claht aht sooin after brekfast time, if ther's a gooid druft, for if ther's one thing more nor another 'at mak's Ben lewk black it's a lot o' tloaze hingin' abaht.

That's been my way o' goin' on, an' shoo's knawn it as weel as I've knawn it mysen. Whol this happen'd we wor as gooid nabors as need be. We mud fratch a bit nah an' then ovver t'barns—for that Susey o' hers is a reyt tay-strill of a lass, an' gives ahr Johnny some rare slaps some-times—bud we've nivver hed no bother to mean owt whol nah. An' if ta'll believe me, lass, I've done more for that theer woman nor if shoo'd been my awn sister. I ne-

N

weət on ə wen šə wə ligin in ə tlast bān ; av swild tpasidž
25 duznz ə taimz wen its bīn ō tōn ; ən a wə nivər ə·giən takin
kɛər ə tās for ə wen šəz wontəd tə guə tə tmītin. šūz ə
grand ən tə guə tə tmītin, šū iz ðat ; bəd a oləs sed, ən al
se(ə) ə·giən, ət ðem ət prə·fesəz tə bi sə piuər ən guid əz oləs
twāst wen ðə kum tə bi reit reknd up. a wuns niu ə pāsnz
30 doutər ət didnt no(ə) ā tə freəm tə weš ə pot up, ən šə kəd
fešn tə guə tə t'šapil ivri sundə i twik. bəd jə duənt no(ə)
u(ə) is sānd wol jəv bodmd əm reit ; ən if onibodi kəd ə
teld mə þrī wik sin ət Meəri Džeglz əd ə dun əs šu ez dun tə
mə, ast ə þroən d'ištlāt i ðə feəs ən teld əm ðə wə nuən
35 wot ðə out tə bī. bəd ðəz nout tə bi sed fot. ðes sum
fouk əd disiəv ə maiklskoup, ðe sə dīp.

wel, əz a wə telin ðə, av oləs wešt ə t'iuzdə ðis moni ə
jiə(r), fər a laik tə gu(ə) āt ə bit əv ə mundə, wen iv getn
əm ðə sundə tluəz brušt ən saidəd ə·weə, ən a mak nout ə
40 wešin ən beəkin tə-geðər ət tbak end ə twik, wen
jə səd bi tliənin. suə tiuzdə . z mai deə, ən šu noəz it.
wel, ə fotnit sin kum jəstədə, a gat up ət faiv ə·tlok, əz
iuzl, ən went at it laik ə oəs wol ə·bāt brekfəs taim. ðen
a tiuk t'luəs kuəd ən þout ad bi getin ə tūþri þinz āt. bəd,
45 wod tə bə·līv it ? Meəri əd guən ən putn ər oən kuəd āt
ən getn it ful ə tluəz. a kəd ādli bə·līv mi oən īn. a nivə
niu ə weš wol wednzdə ə·fuər i oəl mi laif, su(ə) a guəz up
tul ər, ən a sez, 'wots tmiənin ə ðis laik?' 'tmiənin ə
wot?' šu sez, əz inisnt əz ə stuft miul. 'didnt tə no(ə) it
50 wə mai wešin moənin?' a sez. 'apm a did,' šu sez, 'ən
apm a didnt, bəd a spuəz av əz mitš reit tə iɯ mai tluəz āt
əz ðā ez tə iɯ ðain.' ðis netld mə ; su(ə) a sez, ' ða noəz

glected my awn hoam to wait on her when shoo wor liggin'
in o' t'last barn; I've swilled t'passidge dozens o' times
when it's been her turn; an' I wor nivver ageean takkin' 30
care o' t'hahse for her when shoo's wanted to go to t'meetin'.
Shoo's a grand un to go to t'meetin', shoo is that; bud I
awlus said, an' I'll say ageean, 'at them 'at professes to be
so pure an' gooid is awlus t'warst when they come to be
reyt reckoned up. I once knew a parson's dowter 'at 35
didn't knaw hah to frame to wesh a pot up, an' shoo could
feshan to go to t'chapel ivvery Sunday i' t'week. Bud ye
doan't knaw who is sahnd whol ye've bottom'd 'em reyt;
an' if onnybody could ha' teld me three week sin' 'at Mary
Jaggles wod ha' done as shoo hez done to me, I sud ha' 40
thrawn t'dishclaht i' ther face an' teld 'em they wor noan
what they owt to be. But ther's nowt to be said for it.
Ther's some fowk 'ud deceive a michaelscowp, they're so
deep.

Well, as I wor tellin' tha, I've awlus weshd o' t'Tuesday 45
this monny a year, for I like to go aht a bit of a Monday,
when I've gotten 'em ther Sunda' tloaze brushed an' sided
away, an' I mak' nowt o' weshin an' bakin' together at
t'back end o' t'week, when ye sud be tleanin'. So Tuesday's my day, an' shoo knaws it. Well, a fortnit sin' come 50
yesterday, I gat up at five o'clock, as ushal, an' went at it
like a horse whol abaht brekfast time. Then I tewk
t'tloaze cord an' thowt I'd be gettin' a toathree things aht.
Bud, wod ta believe it? Mary hed goan an' putten her
awn cord aht an' gotten it full o' tloaze. I could hardly 55
believe my awn een. I nivver knew her wesh whol Weddinsday afore i' all my life, so I goes up tul her, an' I says,
'What's t'meanin' o' this like?' 'T'meanin' o' what?'
shoo says, as innocent as a stuffed mule. 'Didn't ta knaw
it wor my weshing mornin'?' I says. 'Happen I did,' 60
shoo says, 'an' happen I didn't, bud I suppose I've as mitch
reyt ta hing my tloaze aht as tha hez ta hing thine.' This
nettled me; so I says, 'Thah knaws varry weel 'at Tues-

vari wīl ət tiuzdə z mai deə, ən su(ə) al þeŋk ðə tə get ðem

tlāts ə ðain āt ə truəd əs suin əs tə kan.' 'uə tə toəkin

55 tul?' šu sez. 'ða noəz vari wīl u(ə) im toəkin tul,' a sez,

'suə let s e nə boðə(r).' ðen šu tōnz rānd ən šu sez, 'av əz

mitš reit tə ðis grund ən tə ðat tluəspuəst əz ðā ez, ən al sī

ðə fat ə·fuər al tak əm dān, suə nā ða noəz.' 'al pūl əm

dān if tə duznt,' a sez. 'if tə duz ðal get ði topin pūld,' šu

60 sez. 'ən uəl pūl it?' a sez; 'uəl pūl it, Meəri Džeglz?'

ən a went up tul ə tə šeu ər a wə nuən fleəd on ə(r), nər oni

sitš laik. 'ðal sī uə,' šu sez, 'suə get intə tās wi ðə.' a wə

sum ən mad, ða mə bi siuə(r), su(ə) a sez, 'get intə tās

ðisen, jə oud þiŋ; uə stāvd tkat?' 'uə kudnt þoil tə kīp

65 wun?' šu sez. 'uə boild d'ištlāt up wi tbroþ?' sez ai.

'uə senz ðə bānz āt i regz?' sez šū. 'uə z reŋ i ðər iəd?'

sez ai. 'ðā āt, ən oəl bə·leŋin ðə,' šu sez.

a wornt bān tə stand sitš leŋwidž əz ðat oni loŋə(r),

su(ə) a þriu mi kuəd dān ən ran intə tās ən gat tkāvin

70 naif. ðen a fliu ət ə kuəd wi it in ə džifi. bəd ad nə suinə

bə·gun ə seəgin wi it nə šə rušəz at mə wi tloŋ bruš ən

ramz it intə mi feəs, fər oəl it wə kuvəd wi wet ən muk.

ad sitš ən ə muki feəs əz ða nivə soə sin tə wə boən. bəd

a wə nuən bān tə bi bet, su(ə) a fotšt mi oən loŋ bruš, ən

75 aftə rubin it i tsludž i tmidl ə truəd a went ən peəntəd ivri

reg ət šəd iŋin āt wi it. Meəri ðen fotšt ə peəlful ə sudz ən

þriu əm ouər āə duəstnz, bəd a gat ə pigin ful ə tseəm suət

ə stuf ən let ər ev it feər i tfeəs. ə reglə krād əd getn rānd

bi ðis taim, ən tladž kept siŋin āt oəl suəts ə lou stuf, ən

80 wot əd ə bīn tupšot on it oəl a duənt no(ə) if āə Ben ednt

apmd tə kum uəm təv iz brekfəs džust ðen.

day is my day, an so I'll thenk tha to get them clahts o'
thine aht o' t'road as sooin as ta can.' 'Who're ta talkin' 65
tul?' shoo says. 'Thah knaws varry weel who I'm talkin'
tul,' I says, 'so let's hev no bother.' Then shoo turns
rahnd an' shoo says, 'I've as mitch reyt to this grund an'
to that tloaze-post as thah hez, an' I'll see tha fat afore I'll
tak' 'em dahn, so nah thah knaws.' 'I'll pool 'em dahn if 70
ta doesn't,' I says. 'If ta does thah'll get thy toppin'
pooled,' shoo says. 'An' who'll pool it?' I says; 'who'll
pool it, Mary Jaggles?' an' I went up tul her to show her
I wor noan flayed on her, nor onny sitch like. 'Thah'll
see who,' shoo says, 'so get into t'hahse wi' tha.' I wor 75
some an' mad, thah may be suar, so I says, 'Get into
t'hahse thysen, ye owd thing; who starved t'cat?' 'Who
couldn't thoil ta keep one?' shoo says. 'Who boiled
t'dishclaht up wi' t'broth?' says I. 'Who sends ther barns
aht i regs?' says shoo. 'Who's reng i' ther heead?' says I.
'Thah art, an' all belengin' tha,' shoo says.

I worrant bahn to stand sitch langwidge as that onny
longer, so I threw my cord dahn an' ran into t'hahse an'
gat t'carvin' knife. Then I flew at her cord wi' it in a
jiffy. Bud I'd no sooiner begun o' sawin' wi' it nor shoo 85
rushes at me wi' t'long brush an' rams it into my face, for
all it wor covered wi' wet an' muck. I'd sitch a mucky
face as thah nivver saw sin' ta wor born. Bud I wor noan
bahn to be bet, so I fotched my awn long brush, an' after
rubbin' it i' t'sludge i' t'middle o' t'road I went an' painted 90
ivvery reg 'at shoo hed hingin' aht wi' it. Mary then
fotched a pailful o' suds an' threw 'em over ahr doorstuns,
bud I gat a piggin' full o' t'same soart o' stuff an' let her
hev' it fair i' t'face. A reggalar crahd hed gotten rahnd
by this time, an' t'lads kept singin' aht all soarts o' low 95
stuff, an' what 'ad ha' been t'upshot on it all I don't knaw
if ahr Ben heddant happened to come hoam to his brekfast
just then.

'What's up nah?' says Ben; so I at it an' tell'd him,

'wots up nā ?' sez Ben ; su(ə) a at it ən teld im, ol·ðoə še
wər ektərin ə·weə laik mad ivri bit ə t'aim.   fə wuns Ben
tiuk mai said, ən i tiuk ə tluəz, ən tkuəd, ən ivriþiŋ džust
85 əz it wo(r), ən beŋd əm slap on təv ər oən duəstnz.   ðe
wər ə bit ə kwaiətnəs ðen fər ə bit, ən a gat mi oən kuəd
ful ə tluəz āt ə·fuə Ben went bak ə·giən təv iz wāk.   in ə
wail ət aftə(r), ā-ivə(r), a iəd ə lafin noiz, su(ə) a popt mi iəd
āt ə d'uə(r), ən ðiər if toud bīzm ednt guən ən kut mi lain
90 dān, ən oəl mi tluəz wə ligin ə tfluə(r).   a faiəd up ən a
went təv ər ās, bəd šu slamd d'uər i mi feəs ən put tlatš
dān su(ə) əz i kudnt get in.   'al mak ðə peə fə ðis, jə
treš !' a šātəd þriu tkei-oil.   'mak on !' šu šātəd bak, ən ad
tə gu(ə) ən sam mi tluəz up ən weš əm ouər ə·giən.   wot əd
95 ə kum tə pas if it ednt tānd āt tə bi ə wet deə a kānt tel ;
bəd it kom dān laik kats ən dogz, ən wi buəþ ed tə drai wo
tluəz i tās.

wen nīt kom a wə fleəd ðəd bī ə boni rumpəs, fə Ben wo
boilin wi reədž.   if oni ə Meəri bānz kom niər āəz šu fotšt
100 əm in wi ə tlatə(r), ən þriətnd tə kil əm if ivə ðə leəkt wi
ðem þiŋz oni muə(r).   ʻwir əz guid əz jī !' sez āə Dik.
' bəd jāə muðəz ə bad ən ; šuz bān tə bi teən tə tlokup,' sez
Meəriz juŋist las.   þiŋz gat tə sitš ən ə pitš, indīd, wol āə
Ben went ən ofəd tuəl famli, big ən litl, āt tə feit.   ā-ivə(r),
105 Meəri uzbn z ə nais kwaiət suət əv ə tšap, ən av nout tə
sc(ə) ə·giən ʻim, ən i wodnt oəðə mel nə mak.   ən ðats wot
wiv getn tul, ən ā wis kum on tnekst tiuzdə ðə loəd uənli
noəz.   bəd as nivə fə·giv ə(r) ; nivə wol i liv ; tnasti guid-
fə-nout !   aftər oəl ət iv dun for ər ən oəl, ən nivə tšeədžd
110 ər ə oəpni pīs.

wornt ðat ə nok ət d'uə(r) ?   a þout it wo(r).   kum in.
wel, if it iznt Meəri !   ða sez ða þout it wə wednzdə ?   ən

although shoo wor hectorin' away like mad ivvery bit o' 100 t'time. For once Ben tewk my side, an' he tewk her tloaze, an' t'cord, an' ivverything just as it wor, an' beng'd 'em slap on to her awn doorstuns. Theer wor a bit o' quietness then for a bit, an' I gat my awn cord full o' tloaze aht afore Ben went back agean to his wark. In a 105 while at after, hahivver, I heeard a laughin' noise, so I popt my heead aht o' t'door, an' theer if t'owd besom heddant goan an' cut my line dahn, an' all my tloaze wor liggin' o' t'floor. I fired up an' I went to her hahse, but shoo slammed t'door i' my face an' put t'latch dahn so as I 110 couldn't get in. 'I'll mak tha pay for this, ye tresh!' I sharted threw t'keyhoil. 'Mak' on!' shoo sharted back, an' I hed to go an' sam my tloaze up an' wesh 'em ovver agean. What 'ud hev come to pass if it heddant turned aht to be a wet day I can't tell; bud it com' dahn like 115 cats an' dogs, an' we both hed to dry wer tloaze i' t'hahse.

When neet com' I wor flay'd there'd be a bonny rumpus, for Ben wor boilin' wi' rage. If onny o' Mary's barns com' near ahrs shoo fotched 'em in wi' a clatter, an' threaten'd to kill 'em if ivver they laikt wi' *them things* onny more. 120 'We're as gooid as ye!' says ahr Dick. 'Bud yahr mother's a bad un; shoo's bahn to be ta'en to t'lockup,' says Mary's youngest lass. Things gat ta sitch a pitch, indeed, whol ahr Ben went an' offered t'whoal family, big an' little, aht to feyt. Hahivver, Mary's husband's a nice, 125 quiet sort of a chap, an' I've nowt to say agean *him*, an' he woddant awther mel nor mak'. An' that's what we've getten tul, an' hah we sal com' on t'next Tuesday the Lord oanly knaws. Bud I'se nivver forgive her; nivver whol I live; t'nasty gooid-for-nowt! After all 'at I've done for 130 her an' all, an' nivver charged her a hawpney piece.

Worrant that a knock ot t'door? I thowt it wor. Come in. Well, if it isn't Mary! Thah says thah thowt it wor Weddinsday? An' thah wants to be reyt? So dew I. I don't knaw what we've hed to fall aht abaht; an' I've 135

ða wonts tə bi reit? suə diu ai. a duənt noə wot wəv ed
tə foəl āt ə·bāt; ən av džust bin sɛ(ə)in ət if ivə ðə wər ə
115 wumən ət i þout out ə·bāt it wə ðī. kum in wi ðə. av
bin evin ə bit ə frendli tšat wi Greəs iə(r). tketl z on,
ən av ə fati keək i tuvm, ən a dāə seə ðez ə drop ə
Džəmeəkə sumwiə(r). sit ðə dān, las.

just been sayin' 'at if ivver theer wor a woman 'at I thowt
owt abaht it wor thee. Come in wi' tha. I've been
hevin' a bit ov a friendly chat wi' Grace here. T'kettle's
on, an' I've a fatty cake i' t'oven, an' I dar' say theer's a
drop o' Jamaica somewheer. Sit tha dahn, lass.   140

IV.

TKUKŪ TLOK.

a wə dān ət Līdz tuðə wik, ən bi-in reəðə drai aftə
liukin rānd t'ān, a apmd tə pop intəv ə eələs nət fāə frə
tsteišn, wiə ðə wə bān tə bī ə rafl fər ə kukū tlok. a də
seə jəl noə wot ə kukū tlok iz; ā-ivə(r), its ə tlok əts getn
5 ə oil i tfeəs ont wiər ə bēd pops āt ivri āər ən šāts 'kukū'
ə·stiəd ə straikin, ən šāts wuns ivri oəf āər əz wīl. nā it
wə tseəm ət ðis rafl əz it iz ət ivri uðə(r)—ðe wər oəl
wontin tə bi twinə(r). ðe wə niəli oəl juɯ tšaps ət wər in,
ən ət ə·bāt sevm ə·tlok ðe bə-gan ə mustɹin tə·geðə(r). wol
10 ðə wə weətin ðiə fər əm oəl tēnin up, ðe kəd toək ə nout
nobəd ðis kukū tlok. 'am siuər ai sl win it,' sed Ned ə ·
oud Bilz. 'ðal nət win ðis,' sed Krakə(r). 'av nət bīn in
ə ɹafl jət bəd wot iv wun.' 'ðat tlok l bi ·main tə·nīt, ər els
am tšet,' sed Džim Tanə(r). 'ə diəl on jəl find jəsenz
15 mis·teən,' sed juɯ Stroəbəɹi, kos av kum þrī mail ə pāpəs
tə fotš it.' t'aim kom ət last for əm tə šak, ən if jəd nobəd
sīn əm eɯin on t'eəbl tə sī wot numəz wə tēnd up, jəd aktli
ə þout ðə wə bān tə swol·ə tbeəsin. trafl wər ouər ət last,
ən Bili Mušrəm wə di·kleəd tə bi twinə(r). wen (ə)levm
20 ə·tlok kom, tlanloəd teld əm it wə taim tə bi skiftin, suə
Bili gat is tlok ən went uəm. nā Bili didn't no(ə) ət it wər
ə kukū tlok, ən id niə sīn wun ə·fuə(r), su(ə) it koəzd im ə
diəl ə trubl, əz al tel jə in ə bit 'so ðə, Džini wot iv brout
ðə,' i sed tə twaif, əz i tlapt t'lok on t'eəbl wen ə gat uəm.
25 'wiər es tə getn ðat þriu, Bili?' šu sed. 'av wun it,' sed
Bili. 'ai, its ə boni ən. av niə sīn wun laik ðat ə·fuə(r).
bəd let s bi šapin fə bed, Bili, fər its getin lat.' 'al iɯ t'lok

up ə·fuər i guə,' sed Bili, əz ə wɛnt fər ə nɛəl ɔn tamə(r).
aftər əd uꞃ it up ə·giən twoəl, ən sɛt tpɛndləm wɛgin, ðɛ
wɛnt tə bed ; bəd ðɛd nuən bīn in moni minits ə·fuə ðə iəd 30
sumət šāt 'kukū!' 'wot ðə crɔment s ðat?' sed Bili.
'neə, ai kānt tɛl,' sɛd Džini. 'am siuər a iəd ɛumdi šāt
kukū,' sɛd Bili. 'suə did ai, Bili,' sɛd twaif. Bili gat up,
strak ə līt, ðen wɛnt dān-tstɛəz. i liukt oəl up ən dān,
bə·int d'uəz, intə tkubəd ən tkoil oil, bəd kəd find nout, 35
su(ə) i wɛnt ən gat intə bed ə·giən. in ə bit i iəd 'kukū'
twɛlv taimz. 'iə ðɔ, Džini,' i sɛd, 'ðats plɛən i·nif, bi
gum!' ən džumpt āt ə bed, strak ə līt, ran dān-tstɛəz, gat
od ə tpuəkər ən bə·gan tə unt up ən dān ə·giən. 'a kꞃ sī
nout dān iə(r), Džini,' i sɛd, aftə liukin up ən dān fər ə·bāt 40
ten minits, 'džust fīl if ðəz onibodi undə tbɛd.' 'neə, bi
gum, Bili ; briꞃ tlīt ən kum ən liuk fə ðisen.' 'ðat nuən
fleəd, ā tə?' sed Bili, bə·ginin tə bi frītnd isɛn, ən diðərin
wol ə kəd ādli od tkanl i tstik. 'neə, am nət ə bit fleəd,'
šu sɛd, 'bəd av iəd fouk se(ə) ət twɛlv ɔ·tlok ət nīt s t'aim 45
ət bogədz bə·gin tə nok ə·bāt, ən its džust ə·bāt twɛlv nā.'
ðat wər i·nif fə Bili. tkanl flopt āt ə tstik, ən i rušt upstɛəz
ən tumld intə bed əz if sumdi wər aftər im. 'oə, mɔ̄ðə(r)!'
skriəmd Džini, þiꞃkin Bili əd sīn sumət. Bili kuvəd iseln
ouə tiəd wi t'luəz ən krept dān tə tbodm ə tbɛd. id gɛtn 50
sə fāə dān ət wun əv is fīt uꞃ ə bit ouə tbodm, ən tkitlin
bi-in upstɛəz ən wontin sumət tə leək wi, gat od ə Bili tuəz
wi it tloəz. 'mɔ̄ðə(r)!' Bili šātəd, əz i drɛgd iz lɛg up.
'þīvz!' skriəmd Džini, əs šu kuvəd ə·seɛ̇ ouə tiəd. noəðər
on əm dɔ̄st stɔ̄ fər ə·bāt ten minits. ət last Džini sɛd, 55
'Bili! Bili!' 'od ði din las.' 'dus tə þiꞃk ðis ās əz ˏ
oəntəd, Bili?' 'am siuər it iz,' sɛd Bili, 'ən al flit tfɛ̄st þiꞃ
ə mundə moənin. a niə bə·līvd i bogədz ə·fuə(r), bəd a kꞃ
bə·līv it nā, bə·kos av fɛlt wun.'˝ 'fɛlt wun?' sed Džini.
'ai e fə siuə(r), las.' 'ən wot wor·it laik?' šu sɛd. 'a kānt 60
tel. it kom ən gat od ə mi tu(ə) ə bit sin.' Džini flopt ouə
tiəd ə·giən, ən Bili þiꞃkin šəd sīn sumət, flopt ouə tiəd tiu.
in ə bit, ivriþiꞃ bi-in kwaiət, Džini popt ər iəd āt ə bed

ə·giən. 'Bili, a wiš it wə moənin,' šu sed. 'suə diu ai,'
65 sed Bili, əz ə flopt iz iəd āt. 'am feən ðā iəd it əz wīl əz
mī, ər els ða məd apm ə þout ad bin driəmin.' 'it wə nuə
driəmin, Bili, fə noəðər on əz əd bīn ə·slīp.' ðe buəþ leəd
lisnin, ən ivriþiŋ wə sə kwaiət ðe kəd iə t'lok tikin dān-
tsteəz. 'kukū!' wə šātəd ə·giən. 'jonz tseəm din ə·giən,'
70 šu sed ; 'am siuər its dān-tsteəz. gu(ə) ən ev ə·nuðə liuk.'
'a duənt noə wiə tkanl iz,' i sed ; 'it tumld āt ə tstik
sumwiə(r).' 'wel, itl nuən bi fāər of; get up ən liuk fot.'
Bili gat up, went on iz anz ən nīz, ən bə·gan gruəpin ə·bāt
tfluə fə tkanl. nā Džini əd uŋ ə frok ən skēts on ə neəl ət
75 t'op ə tsteəz, ən Bili apmd tə tutš əm wen i wər untin
fə tkanl, ən ðe kom tumlin on im. i džumpt intə bed
wi sitš fuəs ət i nokt iz waif āt ə tuðə said. 'mēðə(r)!
þīvz!' skriəmd Džini, ən šu opmd twində ən šāted 'elp!'
ə plīsmən ət wə džust pasin, þiŋkin sumət wə reŋ i tās,
80 brast d'uər opm ən went in. 'wot s tə diu iə(r)?' i sed.
'kan jə sī onibodi ðiə(r)?' Džini šātəd. 'ā kan i sī i d'āk?'
i sed, əz i šut d'uə tə kīp onibodi frə gu-in āt. 'stop ðiə
wol Bili gets ə līt,' šu sed, 'kos ðəz oəðə þīvz ə bogədz i
tās.' Bili gat ə līt, ən im ən tplīsmən siətšt buəþ upsteəz
85 ən dān, bəd kəd find nout. 'jə fə·gat tə liuk undə tbed,'
sed Bili. ə·weə tplīsmən went upsteəz, ən Bili ən twaif
krept aftər im. nout wə fun undə tbed, suə tplīsmən sed ət
ðə must ə bin mis·teən. wol ðə wər upsteəz tbēd šātəd
'kukū' ə·gien. dān kom tplīsmən, tū steps ət wuns, ən
90 Bili ən twaif krept aftər im. ə siətš wə ðen meəd i ivri
niuk ən koənə(r), īvm undə t'iəpot ən tsoltselə(r), bəd
nout wə fun. 'ðes sumət kwiər ə·bāt ðis,' sed tplīsmən.
'ðes sumət vari kwiə(r),' Džini sed. 'e jə ivər iəd
sitš dinz əz ðem i tās ə·fuə(r)?' tplīsmən ast. 'nivər ə·fuə
95 tə-nīt,' Džini sed. 'wel,' sed tplīsmən, bə·ginin tə bi əs
fleəd əz oəðə Bili ə twaif, ən gu-in əz wait əz ə šīt, 'as bi
rānd ə·giən in ə·bāt ən āə(r), ən al liuk in,' həd i wə feən tə
get āt, ən ðev nət sīn im sin. Bili ən twaif krept upsteəz
ə·giən, ən džust əz ðed getn intə bed ðe iəd 'kukū' wuns

muə(r). 'wel, ðis kaps oəl ət i ivər iəd tel on,' sed Bili. 100
'its tlast nīt i ðis ās fə mī,' sed Džini. 'a wodnt stop iər
if ðəd let mə liv rent-frī.' 'its nu(ə) ius gu-in dān-tsteəz
ə·giən, iz it, las, wi krɔ find nout ?' ' neə, wi məd džust əz
wīl stop wiə wə āər ən kīp wokrɔ wol moənin.' ðe wispəd
tə wun ən·uðə wol tū ə·tlok, ən ðen ðe iəd 'kukū' twais. 105
' bi gum, its jondər ə·giən !' Bili sed, ən it oləs sānz i tseəm
pleəs. av ə guid maind tə sit dān-tsteəs ə bit ən sī if i krɔ
find it āt.' 'diu, Bili,' šu sed. Bili let tkanl, krept pratli
dān-tsteəz, ən piəkt isen i trokin tšeə(r), bəd i suin fel
ə·slīp. i didnt iə tbəd šāt wen it wər oəf past tū, nə Džini 110
noəðə(r), fə šəd guən tə slīp tiu. Bili wokrɔd džust ə·fuə
þrī ə·tlok, ən findin id bīn ə·slīp, i dlanst rānd tās, bəd i soə
nout. in ə bit tbəd kom āt ən šātəd 'kukū' þrī taimz.
Bili kest iz īn up ət t'lok wen ə iəd it fəst taim, ən ðen i
gat up tul it wen it šātəd tseknd taim, ən wen it šātəd 115
tþəd taim id ə guid liuk at it wol it popt in ən wə šut up.
'oə, av fun ðə āt ət last, ev i ?' i sed. 'Džini! Džini! av
fun tbogəd āt; kum dān ən liuk at it.' 'wot iz it, Bili?'
šu sed. 'its ə bəd getn intə t'lok,' sed Bili. Džini kom
dān-tsteəz, ən ðen Bili went tə t'lok·ən traid tə opm d'uə 120
wiə tbəd wo(r), bəd i kudnt manidž it. 'ā ðə ɛrɔments ez
it getn ðiə(r)?' Džini sed. 'neə, a kan nət tel,' sed Bili.
ðe buəþ traid tə get ət tbəd wol oəf past þrī, wen it popt āt
ən šātəd 'kukū,' ən ðen went in ə·giən. Bili traid to get
od ont, bəd it wə tə šāp for im. 'ðat ən oud fešnd raskl, 125
bi gum !' sed Bili, 'bəd ðal apm nət bi sə fleəd wen təz bīn
iər ə de(ə) ə tū.' ' wel, Bili,' sed twaif, 'a nivə niu sitš ən
ə þirɔ i mi laif. av oməst ə guid maind tə nok it nek āt fə
frītnin əz ən kīpin əz wokrɔ niəli oəl tnīt. kil it fəst þirɔ,
ən let s e nə muə boðə wi it.' tlast ət i iəd ə·bāt Bili ən is 130
kukū tlok, i wə fiksin ə fāntn for it tə drirɔk āt on, ən ə
boks for it tə eit āt on, ə·said ə toil wiər it kept popin it iəd
āt.

V.

ðis əz ə kwešn ət oft kumz up fə dis·kušn, ən wen ə niuli
wed kupl es tə di·said it ðe sumtaimz a loŋ wail ə·bāt it. i
mi juŋ deəz, wen a wə wōkin ət tmiln, niuz wə brout intə
tməkanik šop ət Sam Wilmən ən An Aris wə bān tə bi wed əs
5 tnekst sundə. ðis niuz wə brout in džust ə·fuə tindžn stopt
ət brəkfəs taim, ən suə wen wəd getn naisli set dān tə wə
moənin miəl oud Dik Tšəri seŋ āt tə Sam—' wot, a ges ðat
bān tə bi wed tnekst sundə.' ' wa,' sed Sam, ' am þiŋkin ə
sumət ə tsuət.' ' wel, nā,' sez oud Dik, ' if tə miənz tə gu(ə)
10 on smui·ðli ən bī ə api man, duənt spoil ði waif wi pamprin
ə(r), əz if šə wər ə sik bān, bəd bə·gin əs tə miənz tə kari
on ; if tə duznt, ðal e tə riu. ət tvari taim ət oud Dik wə
givin ðis əd·vais tə Sam, ə lot ə wed wimin əd geðəd rānd
An Aris i tweivin šeəd, ən ðe sed təv ə(r), ' nā, An, las,
15 wotivə tə duz, sī ət tə stanz up fə ði reits ; duạnt gi weə
tul im ən inš. if tə wuns bə·ginz tə nukl undər il mak ə
kum·pliət sleəv ən drudž on ðə ; its oləs tbest weə tə bə·gin
əz wə in·tend tə kari on.' its oft bin sed ət fouk rekŋz
nout ə əd·vais unles ðə guə təv ə loəjər ən peə siks ən
20 eitpms fot ; bəd buəþ Sam ən An þout təd·vais ðed getn wə
wōþ aktin on. rent deəz ən wedin deəz ·wil kum ət last,
ðoə lanloədz ən braidgriumz þiŋks ðe kum on ət ə sneəl
galəp, ən wen tnekst mundə moənin kom rānd Sam ən An
wə man ən waif. ' its siks ə·tlok bi ðis wotš ə ðain,' sed
25 Sam, ' a þiŋk its ə·bāt taim tə gat up ən let tfaiə(r).' ' a
wə džust þiŋkin,' sed An, ' ət ·tād leəd reəðə tə loŋ, get up
wi ðə, ðal find sum kinlin i tuvm. ' a mən e ðī tə get up,'
sed Sam ; ' es tə fə·getn wot tə sed jəstədə—didnt tə promis

tə luv, onər ən ɔˑbeə ?' 'am prəˑpeəd tə diu oəl i promist,'
sed An, 'bəd ə bodi kānt diu ivriþiɳ ət wuns, al luv ən ³⁰
onə ðə nā, if tl get up ən līt tfaiə(r), ən wen tketl boilz ðə
mən koəl mə dān-tsteəz ən al əˑbeə ðə.' 'kum, kum,' sed
Sam, 'if tə þiɳks tə kɳ traifl wi mə i ðis weə ðal find āt ði
misˑtak. a as ðə tə diu nout ət i kānt bak up wi skriptə(r),
fə sant Pītə sez—"waivz, nukl undə tə jər uzbnz."' 'duz ³⁵
ə ?' sed An. 'al bəˑlīv it wen i sī it.' 'ðen ða sl suin sī it,'
sed Sam, ən i bānst āt ə bed ən ran dān-tsteəz in is šāt.
wol ə wə rumidžin əˑbāt fə t'estiment, wot duz An diu bəd
nip intə t'lozit, sam up oəl iz wātə tluəz, fliɳ əm dān tə
tbodm ə tsteps, bout t'šeəmə duər i tinsaid, ən ðen krīp bak ⁴⁰
əˑgiən intə bed. in ə bit, Sam in iz əri tə get bak, gat wun
əv is fīt feltəd in iz dudz, ən fel forəd, bumpin iz nuəz
əˑgiən tšāp edž ə wun ə tsteps. ðis put im intəv ə bit əv ə
pešn, ən wen ə gat tə tsteəz iəd, ən fan d'uə fest, i sweər ə
gāt uəþ, ðoə id bīn ət t'šapil tnīt əˑfuə(r). 'ðiə lad,' sed ⁴⁵
An, 'if təs swoən wi t'estiment i ði and, a wodnt bi ðī fər
oəl tbras i tbeɳk, ðez nuəbdi sə ādnd əs tə diu ðat nobəd
trif-raf ət gets intə tkuot-ās.' 'a tə bān tə opm d'uə ən
liuk ət ðis tekst ?' sed Sam. 'al liuk at it, wen tə lets mə
no(ə) ət tketl z boilin, its nu(ə) ius getin up əˑfuə(r),' ən An ⁵⁰
kuvəd ər iəd up i tbed tluəz ən feə kiɳkt əˑgiən wi lafin, tə
þiɳk ā šəd bafld im ; bəd wen šə iəd tās duə guə tul wi
ə gāt beɳ, it put ə bit əv ə dampər on ə məriment.
'wiərivə kan tmadlin bi of tul ?' sed šū, 'a oməst wiš id
getn up misen ən let tfaiə(r), its nuə gāt džob, ən if id jīldəd ⁵⁵
ðe wod ə bīn piəs bəˑtwīn əz. wišt! a þiɳk a iər is
fuit kumin up tsteps. if ə pīps þriu tlok-oil il bi eəbl
tə sī mə. al rekɳ tə bi əˑslīp'. suə šu leəd wi ə feəs tə d'uər
on stātəd ə snuərin laik ə peər ə blaksmiþ beləsəz ət əd getn
ə bad koud. in ə bit šu stātəd up ən leind on ər elbou ən ⁶⁰
ākɳd. šu iəd ə soft, pərin noiz ən nā ən ðen ə sānd əz if
sumət wə skratin wud. 'oo diə(r),' šu sed, 'its nuən im, its
nobəd tkat ət s mīdləs fər ə drop ə milk.' it wə nu(ə) ius
An trai-in tə foəl əˑslīp, šu kudnt, suə šə dond əˑsen ən krept

65 reit pratli dān tsteəz. oəl wər əs koud ən sailnt əz ə tšə̄tš
əv ə wikdeə. Saɯ wə nuəwiə tə bi sīn, bəd iz wātə dudz
wə guən, suə šə niu id set of sumwiə(r)—bəd wiə(r)? šu
samd up tfaiə šūl, þiɯkin šud guə tə tbodm ə tjād tə tkoil-
oil ən fotš ə šūlfl ə koilz, nət ət šə þout ə lītin tfaiə(r), oə,
70 nou, šud eit it suinə(r), bəd šud get oəl redi fər im, su(ə) əz
ə kəd ev ə bleəz in ə minit. bəd, bə-oud! wen šə wontəd
tə gu(ə) āt šu fan ət d'uə wə fest, ən šu kudnt opm it. šu
wər ə priznə lokt up i tās. wen šə boutəd ə bed-rām duər
ən bafld ər uzbn, šu laft reəli, þiɯkin it wər ə vaɹi guid
75 džuək; bəd wen šə wə bafld ən bestəd ə·sen šu kudnt laf.
uðə fouk məd apm ə sīn tfun ont, bəd An didnt—šu brast
āt ə ruərin. if šəd ed oni wāk tə guə tul šud ə guən tə
tmiln, if šə kəd ə getn āt ə tās; bəd šu ed nə wāk, šud gīn
up ə liumz, fə Sam əd sed, 'ðasl nivə guə tə tmiln ə·giən,
80 las, əz loɯ əz a kɯ kīp ðə. wen šə bə·þout ər ə ðem wēdz
šu ruəd ādə nər ivər ən pūld sum eər of ər iəd ən fleɯ it on
tfluə(r), əz if ðat, sumā, kəd mend matəz. oəl ət wuns šə
bə·þout ər ət tnekst duə neəbər əd ə kei ət əd opm ðeə
duə(r), suə wen šəd baþt ər īn wi koud wotə(r), šu stātəd ə
85 pundin tfaiə bak wi tpuəkə(r). In ə bit tneəbə wumən kom
āt ən steəd in ət twində tə sī wot wər up. 'am lokt in,'
sed An, 'a wont jə tə opm d'uə wi jāɔ kei.' tneəbə ran uəm
fə tkei ən opmd d'uər in ə krak. 'wotivə did jəɹ uzbn lok
jə in fo(r)?' sed tneəbə(r). 'wa,' sed An, trai-in tə laf, it
90 sīmz id fəgetn mə, it iznt twenti fouər āəz jət sin wi wə tīd
tə·geðə(r), ən ə man kānt get intə niu weəz oəl ət wuns. a
də se(ə) it əd tliən slipt iz maind ət i ed ə waif, su(ə) iz lokt
d'uər ən teən tkei in is pokit əz iuzl. Samz ə tšap ət boðəz
iz iəd ə guid bit wi tpə·petiuəl muəšn. ən av īvm noən im
95 set of tə tpump wi tfaiə šūl in iz and ən ðen kum sliɯkin
bak fə twotə kit. puər An sed oəl ðis in ə məɹi of-and weə
ət əd ə di·siəvd tvaɹi oud lad isen, bəd it didnt blind
twumən ət livd tnekst duə(r). əs šə went bak təv ər oən ās
šu sed, lou dān, 'ðat wumən z bin ruərin, ðez ə fratš on bi
100 nā.' wel, a diu þiɯk ət ðat deə wə tloɯist, drī-ist, ən muəst

mizrəbl deə ət ivər An əd past sin šə wə boən. wot əd
bəˑkum ə Sam šu kudnt imˑadžn. i didnt kum niə fər ə
bait ə dinə(r), ət givin ouə taim i nivə tɛ̄nd up, ən ət ten
əˑtlok ət nīt šəd nivə sīn is feəs. if šə went wuns tə tentri
end, šu went ə undəd taimz i tāə tə ākɲ fər is fuit, bəd it 105
wər oəl i veən. Sam wə noəðə tə bi iəd nə sīn. twāst ont
wo(r), šu kudnt fešn tə guə sīk for im, šu felt əz if šəd
reəðə dī nər oni ə tmiln lasəz səd ṅo(ə) ət Sam əd left ə
tvari de(ə) aftə twedin deə. oəl þouts ə koɲkrin ər uzbn ən
setin up fə tmeəstə wə skatəd tə twind; it wə fāə betə tə 110
bi oni suət əv ə drudž ən sleəv nə liv ðat weə; su(ə) ət aftə
ten əˑtlok ət nīt, šu kinld tfaiər ən meəd əz nais ə supər əz
anz kəd mak, nət fər əˑseln, bəd fə Sam. əs fər ə šu ednt etn
ə māþfl oəl ðat blesid deə, nə kudnt; ðe wər ə lump in ə
þroit sə big ət šə kudnt swolə ət oəl. əs fə Sam, wiər edˑī 115
bīn ən wot ed ˑī bin diu-in? aftə liəvin uəm i went streit
təv iz wāk, gat iz brekfəs ən iz dinər ət ə kofi-šop, ən ət oəf
past faiv ət nīt wondəd up ən dān tstrīts əz dezələt ən
mizrəbl əz oni man wīl kan bī. əz ə wə moəndrin up ən
dān i ðis weə i gat mikst up wi ə krād ə fouk oəl gu-in i 120
wun diˑrekšn. i went wi tstriəm, fər i didnt keə mitš wiər
ə went, ən ət last fan isen in ə tšapil. in ə wail ən oud
man, wi ə feəs laik ən eəndžilz, stuid up ən preitšt laik ən
eəndžil, preitšt piəs bəˑtwīn kuntri ən kuntri, piəs bəˑtwīn
man ən man, ən last əv oəl, piəs bəˑtwīn man ən waif. it 125
sīmd tə Sam əz if, sumweə, toud man əd getn tə noə wot
wər up bəˑtwīn im ən twaif, fər i liukt streit ət im ən teld
im ðe səd bi nə strugl fə tmeəstəšip bəˑtwīn man ən waif, bəd
ət in oəl þiɲz, big ə litl, luv səd bi tmeəstə(r). wen Sam
gat āt ə ðat tšapil iz āt bəˑgan tə sofn tād iz juɲ waif, tə 130
mak eksˑkiusəz fər ə kondukt, ən aftər ə desprət batl wi is
praid ət lastəd wol əˑlevm p.m. i þout id gu(ə) uəm ən trai
tə fəˑget ən fəˑgiv. wen ə gat niə tentri end, i tutšt o duə
step wi is fuit, ən wə vari niə foəlin. An so(ə) im ən ran
intə tās riɲin ər anz ən krai-in ' oə diə(r), iz drukɲ, iz 135
drukɲ.' tpuə las dəsnt feəs im i likə(r), suə šə id əˑsen

ə·bak ə tkitšin duə(r). in ə bit Sam kom in, bəd nət drukŋ,
i wə soubər i·nif ən sorafl i·nif. i sat im dān i tām tšeər ən
liukt rānd. tfaiəsaid wə wām ən brīt ən taidi, ə nais supə
140 wə redi, is slipəz leən bi tfendə(r), ivriþiŋ dun fər is
kumfət ət wumən kud diu. i leind bak in is tšeər ən šu
kəd sī t'iəz wun aftər ə·nuðə run sloəli dān is feəs. in ə bit
An ventəd tə kum āt ən sed pitifli, 'Sam!' i tānd iz iəd, iz
legz peətəd, ən i eld āt iz āmz. i les nər ə tik-tak šə wə
145 siətəd on iz nī, wi ər āmz rānd iz nek, sobin əz if ər āt əd
brek. aftə ðat ðe wə nivə nout sed əs tə 'uə z tə bi
tmeəstə(r)'; buəþ sed 'luv sl bi tmeəstə(r),' ən ðat satld it.

VI.

ƎN OUD BOIZ REKƎLEKŠNZ.

'tēnd fifti!' bi tmegz, bəd its taim tə bi liukin rānd
tkoənəz nā, ən nuə mis·tak. džust ə bit loŋər ən as bi wun
ə ðem leŋki tšaps bāt šuin, ən stokinz ivə sə mitš tə big, ət
Wiliəm toəks ə·bat i tpleə. bəd a nuən laik it, ən ðat s
flat. wen ə tšap kumz tə ðat, wot kumz təv im? wa, īz 5
nokt ə·bat þriu pilə tə puəst, ən tmuəst ət fouk se(ə) on im
iz—' ai, puər oud tšap, īs sīn iz best deəz.' its tšiəfl, kum-
fətin toək iz ðat fər ə tšap ət s muild ən broild, ən duin iz
best tə kīp bodi ən soul tə·geðə(r), ən apm riəd ə lot ə juŋ
ənz tə elp tə kari on twēligig biznəs ə twēld. after oəl its 10
laik stopin ət ə guid beətin šop wen ə tšap s reikt iz oəf
sentri, əz it giz im·ə tšons ə samin isen tə·geðə laik, ən
makin ə dženrəl baləns up ə oəl iz dun ən left undun. a
wundər ā moni on əz l bi eəbl tə stand it ən kum of wi ə
baləns ə treit said! am fit tə þiŋk ðəz nobəd iər ən ðiə wun. 15
əs fə misen, al tak tult ən mak nə buənz ə·bāt it—av bīn ə
reglə raskl þriu tfēst wik a wə boən. mi muðə s sed suə
moni ə taim, su(ə) it mun bi triu. ā-ivər a kəd fešn tə liuk
ər it feəs aftə t'aimz šəs teld mə ðat, a kanət imadžin, ən
am nuən bān tə dis·piut it, nət ai. ðez moni þāzn muə bīn 20
teld tseəm teəl. su(ə) as nuən bi bāt kumpni. bəd liəvin
džuəkin ə·said, a riəli ən onistli bə·līv a wər ə raskl i mi juŋ
deəz. tnumər ə kitlinz iv þrotld, duks iv traid tə mak
piək, doŋkiz teəlz iv prikt, prə·sāvz iv stoun, tluəs-kuədz iv
snikt, windəz iv brokŋ, fati-keəks iv etn, ən misdə·miənəz 25
bāt numər ət əd ə bīn ə eŋin džob i toud fešnd taimz wen
eŋin wə fešnəbl. oəl ðiəz kraimz ən moni muə raiz up

laik guəsts kundžəd bi ðem tū wēdz—'tēnd fifti.' a meə

bi þout ə braznt ānd, bəd ðes sum ə mi triks al bi ɛɒd if

30 im sori fo nā! a wodnt giv ə tos fər ə juɒstər ət eznt ə spāk

ə divlri ə·bāt im. wot if ə duz galəp þriu ə siut ə tū ə tluəz

ə jiə(r). ad reəðə peə fər ə siut ə kuədiroi nər ə wudn ən

oni taim. ðe wər ə trik a wuns pleəd toud skuil misis, oud

Mali Begstə wī koəld ə(r). ə reər oud las wə Mali i d'eəz

35 bə·fuə skuil buədz ən buəd skuilz wə þout on. šu wər ə·bat

tšap əv ə beəl ə botni, wi ə feəs laik ə raizin sun stikin āt

ə t'op; litl fat āmz, ən anz əz big əz ə šūldər ə mutn. šu

kəd noəðə rīd nə rait, bəd ðat didnt matər i ðem deəz. šu

·wor eəbl tə beək avə-keək, ā-ivə(r), ən ðat wər ə muə

40 konsikwens tə Mali. wel, wot bə·twīn beəkin avə-keək ən

liukin aftər ə·bāt twenti bānz, Mali əd ə wāk set. a duənt

no(ə) ā šəd ə getn on, if šə ednt ə ed tə iuz ə þibl i tavə-

keək biznəs. it kom in sə andi tə wokɒ uz juɒ ənz up wi,

ən kīp əs þriu fratšin. it wər ə bit oəkəd sumtaimz wen

45 Mali əd bin stərin tþin uət-meil, ən sudnli snigd tþibl āt tə

gi sum on əz ə swiləkər on tsaid ə tfeəs. toud las wə reəðə

fond ə wopin mī, bəd a di·tāmind tə ə mi ri·vendž, ən wun

de(ə) ad ə fain tšons. Mali wə dān ə wun fuit, ət reəðə

spoild ə woəkin. ðe wər ə peər ə kats ət toud las wə vari

50 fond on, suə wot did i diu bəd tī buəþ ðə teəlz tə·geðər ən

iɒ əm ouə tband wiə Mali uɒ ər avə-keək. a niu šəd fleər

up di·rektli šə soə tkats i ðə kwiə pə·zišn. a niu tiu ət šəd

mak streit fə mī wi ·tþibl, suə di·rektli a so(ə) ə kumin a

wopt ə soft avə-keək on tə tfluə reit i toud las weə, ən dān

55 šə kom əs flat əz ə flāndə(r). bai gou, wornt ðər ə meələk

i tmiul-oil oəl in ə minit. toud wumən fiumd ən rould

ə·bāt, wi ə šoət leg stikin up i teə(r); tkats splutəd ən feət;

tladz ən lasəz ran skampərin āt intə tstrīt; ən ai wər ə·bāt

tfəst on əm, fər a niu wot əd apm if i didnt kut mi stiks.

60 eə diə(r), ðem oud fešnd taimz! ðez nuə sitš meələkin i

ðiəz deəz! ast laik tə sī tlad wi tpluk tə sāv sitš ən ə trik

on ə skuil buəd misis! wa, id bi wəþ iz weit i Džiudi Barit

umbugz. wel, aftər id ed ə fəst-reət skuilin, sitš əz ladz

gat i ðem deəz, a wə put prentis təv ə gruəsə(r). nã, a duənt
no(ə) ə muə trai-in sitiweəšn fər ə lad wi ə weəknəs fə swīt 65
stuf nər evin trun əv ə gruəsə šop—ðat iz, wol ə gets ə
reglə siknər ən ðen il wiš isen ət tnoəþ poul, ə sum sitš spot
wiə ðə sāk ais-šaklz fə ðə foənuin driŋkin. litl Nati Belšə
wə mi meəstə(r), ən a wə wot ðə koəl ə induə prentis, witš
ment nout bəd wăk, de(ə) in ən de(ə) āt, ən sleəvin ə·weə tū 70
ə þrī nīts bə·said, wen ðə wər out tə diu i wei-in punz ə
siugər ən penəþs ə suəp, ən sitš laik. a didnt sə mitš keə fə
ðat ət fēst, kos ad ə fain tšons ə pitšin intə figz ən reəzinz,
ən siugə kandi, ən traiflz ə ðat suət, bəd, bi gou, ðat suət ə
þiŋ duznt last fər ivə(r). its kapin ā suin swīt stuf gets əz 75
bitər əz goəl wen ə tšap əz is ful swiŋ at it. ai imadžin its
ə·bāt tseəm wi wot ðə koəl tplezəz ə ðis wāld i dženrəl.
ã-ivər it tiuk ə bit ə taim tə briŋ mə tə tstoəleisn point,
apm ə bit loŋə nər it əd ə dun sum ladz, ən bə·fuər it did
ad reəðər ə kwiər əd·ventə(r). mi misis wər ə bit əv ə 80
skriu, ən kəd ādli þoil mə i·nif tə eit, su(ə) a tiuk it āt i
siugə kandi ər out ət i laikt i tšop, ən nout bəd reit,
noəðə(r). ā iz ə grou-in lad tə þraiv bāt džok? wel, it wə
apmd wun sundə tmoənin ət i felt oəfl pekiš aftə mi
brekfəs, ən ad etn ivri moəsl up ət toud las put āt. a 85
dēsnt as fə nə muər ər els ast ə getn ə flī i mi iər-oil. ad
getn dond redi fə t'šapil, fə toud las wə vari pə·tiklər ə·bāt
mə bi-in reit brout up, šu sed, if šə did pinš mə i vitlz. i
ðem deəz ladz laik mī weə beləs-kaps wi taslz on, ən rānd
krimpt koləz, ən al stand it a wər əs fain əz onibodi mi saiz, 90
bəd wot s ðat wen ə tšap s pinšt in iz džok. wel, it wə
getin vari niə tšapil taim, ən a niu a səd e tə meətš i tfrunt
ə Nati ən twaif, bəd if jəl bə·līv mə, ad ðat kreəvin i mi
insaid a kəd əv etn ə bit ə rainosərəs, aid ən oəl. suə wot
did i diu bəd nip intə tšop tə get sumət tə lain mi stumək 95
wol dinə taim. a niu ad nə biznəs ðiər ə sundəz, bəd
uŋə(r), ðə seə, iz ə šāp þoən, ən bi gou its triu. wel, a ednt
bin i tšop ə minit wen i iəd tmisis siŋin āt—'Džosiuə!
Džosiuə!' ðat wə mi neəm, ən toud las wə sīkin mə. bəd

100 a wə nuən bān tə liəv bāt sumət, su(ə) a seəz od əv ə šaiv ə
unikeək ət toud las ius tə mak up tə sel—reit swīt stuf it
wo(r)—slapt it intə mi beləs-kap āt ə tsīt, ən gat tə d'uə
džust əs tmisis wə bə·ginin tə bel āt ' Džosiuə '! ə·giən. su(ə)
of wi set tə t'šapil. eə, diə(r)! it wə twāst diu ivər i ed,
105 wə ðat. it wə reəðər ə wāɪn moənin ən a wə swiətin laik ə
brok fə fiə toud las səd sə·spekt sumət. a dəsnt tak mi kap
of, kos a wə woəkin džust i tfrunt ə buəþ tmeəstər ən
tmisis, bəd it wər ə roki ruəd tə Džoədn, wə ðat woək! əz
a wāmd up a kəd fīl tunikeək stərin ə mi iəd əz if it wə
110 wik, bəd on a məd guə. ət last wi gat tə tprimitiv šop, ən
əf kuəs a ed tə dof mi beləs-kap. wel, wot wi twām
moənin ən mī swiətin, tunikeək wə stuk fest on t'op ə mi
iəd, ən wə bə·ginin tə swiəl dān tsaidz ə mi feəs tə ðat
də·grī wol ad ə unikeək wig ən nuə mistak. a wiənt tel
115 oəl id tə undəguə þriu ðat džob, bəd a bleəm tmisis fər it
oəl i nət findin mə džok i·nif. av stoun moni ə anfl ə figz,
ən reəzinz, ən þiɲz ə ðat suət, if ðə koəl it steilin, bəd ai
duənt wen ə grou-in lad eznt i·nif grub gīn im, aftər iz adld
it əz ai did wi Nati Belšə(r). eə wel; ā ðiəz ladiš teəlz kum
120 təv ə bodiz maind; ən a nobəd menšn əm tə šeu ət ladz—
rasklz əz ðə āə(r)—ānt suə wiðāt koəz sumtaimz. ðez nuə
tū weəz ə·bāt it; moni on əm əd bi vari difrnt if ðə wə reit
duin tul. am þiɲkin ðes sum əv uz oud boiz ev ə lot tə
ansə for i ðat biznəs. bəd a dārənt gu(ə) on ə bit loɲə(r),
125 ðoə its kapin wot ə lot ə þiɲz duz kum intəv ə tšaps iəd
wol is smūkin ə paip ən þiɲkin ə·bat bi-in tēnd fifti.

VII.

TOUD SĀM TIUN.

sum kouks wāmd mi nīz wi ðə dul red iət
wen id swoləd mi milk ən pobz,
suə tlois up tə tfendər a pūld mi siət
ən a plantəd mi fīt ə tobz.

ðen lītin mi šoət blak paip, a swuɒ   5
reit bak i mi oud ām tšeə(r),
ən a sat wotšin trik əz it reəz ən uɒ
laik ə spərit i tmidnīt eə(r).

sistə Mali ən tbānz wər ə·slīp upsteəz—
ðə wə piəs wi ðat bleətin kriu—   10
su(ə) a smūkt ən a þout ə mi weəstəd jiəz,
ən ə twāk ət wə jət tə diu.

əz a liukt ət ðis laif ən ət tlaif tə bī,
a sed tə misen, " ðā as !
wi kumfət ða noəðə kən liv nə dī,   15
fə ðas seəvd noəðə soul nə bras."

ðen spai-in oud Seətn ə·straid ə t'lād
ət wər uɒ undə t'šeəmə fluə(r),
a dubld mi neiv ən sed, "āk ðə, lad,
al bi didld wi ðī nə muə(r);   20

if mi sinz bi laik liəd, ən laik koək mi pəs,
wa ðəz nuəbdi bəd ðī tə þeɒk ;
bəd wen twēldz ə wik oudə(r), ðā gēnin kās,
as e bīn buəþ tə t'šətš ən tə tbeɒk."

ðen sum minits past ouə mə, sad ən drī,   25
ən mi þouts griu əz dāk əs tnīt,
wen sum druknɒ oud alz ət əd bīn on tsprī
kom siɴin laik mad up tstrīt.

wi ðər anz ən ðə fīt ðe kept biətin t'aim
əz ðər āmz intə teə wə fluɴ,   30
eə! ən twēdz əv ə godləs ən sili raim
təv ən oud sām tiun ðe suɴ.

ai! t'aimz ət iv džoind i ðat grand oud eə(r),
wen oud frenz ət mi said wə sīn,
wen mi laif wər ə sunšaini alidə,   35
ən ðis wiznd oud wēld wə grīn.

i tlīt əv ə sun əts loɴ sin set
a sī t'sapil ə P(r)imruəz Brā,
ən wot frenz on ə sabəþ deə ðiər əz met
ət fər ivər əs peətəd nā.   40

ðe kum ən ðe smail ən ə'weə ðe pas,
bəd ðe oləs liəv wun i viu—
ə puə litl faðələs kuntri las,
ət wuns sat i tsiɴəz piu.

wun kām sumə nīt əz wə seɴ tlast im   45
šu liukt i mi feəs reit ād;
ən ə lips wə wait ən ər īn wə dim
wen i džoind ər i t'šapil jād.

ən šu sed tə mə, "Ben, a fīl feənt ən il,
ða mən gi mə ði ām, oud lad;"   50
ən šu wispəd sum wēdz ət i þiɴk on stil,
fə ðe meəd mə reit prād ən dlad.

su(ə) a əlpt ə wi keər ouə reəl ən stail,
wol wə gat təv ə geədin duə(r),
ðen šu əld mə bi tand sitš ə loɴ, loɴ wail—   55
ən a so(ə) ər ə'laiv nə muə(r).

wel, ðis wēld gets əs koud ən əz ād əs stīl,
ən ət taimz a fīl feən šəz diəd,
fə šəd ād tə sleəv ət ə lium ən wīl
fər ə moəsil ə onist briəd.   60

muə nə twenti jiə šuz bin diəd ən guən,
bəd wiərivə mi lot mə bī,
wen tās əz oəl wišt ən im left ə·luən,
šu oləs kumz bak tə mī.

av wišt ət id teld ə bi tgeədin duə(r)   65
ā dīp wə mi luv ən triu,
fər ə frenz, puə las, ðe wə feu ən puə(r)—
bəd nuə matə(r), a þiŋk šə niu.

ā! if ivər i get tə jond pleəs əbūn,
wiər i leŋ i mi āt tə bī,   70
džust tə iər ə wuns muə siŋ ðat oud sām tiun
əl bi evm əv itseln tə mī.

VIII.

tšoɛt taimɛ(r).

it wə misti ən frosti ən dāk əz ə buit,
ən sə koud jəd ə pitid ə tuəd,
wen i iəd tə mi þiŋkin ə līt litl fuit
pit-patin bə-int mə ə truəd.

nā, ət faiv ər oəf·past, əv ə koud wintə moən,   5
ad nuə þouts əv ə kumreəd ət oəl,
su(ə) a stuid wol ðə kom up ə bit əv ə bān,
laik ə pegi-stik eərin ə šoəl.

'olou, las,' a sed, əz a tapt ər ə tkrān,
'ðal bi duin for i trivər ə tkiln;   10
wot ātə, jə muŋki, ən wiər ātə bān?'
sez šū, 'ə šoət taimə tə tmiln.'

'if ðat meəstər ə ðain z oni tšildə(r)' a sed,
'a səd laik əm tə meətš ət ði bak;
bəd, a gəs, if təd leəd ən āə loɯər i bed   15
ət treəd əd bə·gin tə bi slak.'

'ai! meəstə,' šu sed, 'av iəd tguvnə swiər
ət iz meəd nout bi t'reəd fə ðis eədž,
ən iz oəsəz ən karidžəz nips im sə beə
wol ə ādli kən þoil tə gi weədž.   20

'ðen iz bout ən i·steət, ən iz bīldin ə ās,
eə! ən tkost ont nə moətl noəz jət;
if wə pinš wol wə kubədz wiənt peəstər ə mās
i kən nobəd džust stand on is fīt.

'i sez fərinəz latli əz meəd ə gēt spriŋ,   25
ən ðe liv on tšopt kabidž ən seəm ;
su(ə) it uinz im, jə sī, tə šut bras laik ə kiŋ,
ən ðen sel i tseəm meəkits wi ðem.

'if wə duənt wēk fə litl, wi muənt wēk ət oəl,
ən mi granfaðə sed jəstənīt   30
if it woɪnt fə tšoət taiməz ət tsistm əd foəl,
ən tpliušeə kum bak intə tstrīt.'

a liukt of tī end ət ðat wiznd oud bān,
ən a sed, 'it ə·piəz laik tə mī
ət tfaktri ən tmanšn ən tmeən ə tkonsān   35
əz upodn bi midžez laik ðī.

iər a peətəd wi tbān, ən a kudnt bəd laf,
ðo(ə) a felt nuən sə mitš ət mi iəz,
fər a þout tə miseln—its ə boni kum of
if wə propt bi sitš piləz əz ðiəz.   40

IX.

NATƏRIN NAN.

nuə dāt jəl oəl əv iəd ə·bāt
təpolə Belvədiə(r),
ə stati þout bi sum tə bī
frə ivri feəlin tliə(r).

oəl reit ən streit i mak ən šap,   5
ə moud fə treəs ə men :
ə dānreit, upreit, bemup tšap,
nət mitš unlaik misen.

nā, ðoə jə no(ə) iz nout bəd stuən,
i liuks sə grand ən big,   10
ət litl dəst jə pūl iz nuəz,
ə lug is twistəd wig.

pratli, reit pratli ouə tfluə(r)
ə tip-ə-tuəz jə woək,
ən od jə briəþ fə vari oə,   15
ən wispə wen jə toək.

ðiəz ðat ə·bāt im—bəd a noənt
nət reitli ā tə seə t—
ət maks jə fīl əz smoəl əs þivz
ə·nent ə madžistreət.   20

jəv sīn ðat dolt ə muki tleə
ə tfeəs ə Pudsə Duəz ;
toud madlin z woən it oəl iz laif,
ən fansid it ə nuəz.

jond props əz laik ə peər ə tenz   25
ə Saiksəz, jət, bi tmegz,
wen i wə soubər əz ə džudž
av iəd im koəl əm legs.

su(ə) evm bi preəzd fə self konseət;
wiðāt it, a səd seə,   30
wist eət wəsen wi oəl wə mīt
fər ivər ən ə deə.

wen weəstəz liuks ət tmābl god,
īgoi! ā waid ðe geəp,
ən wundə witš ðe feəvə tmuəst—   35
ə bogəd ər ən eəp.

ən sum wi envi ən wi spait
get fild tə ðat də·grī
ðəd nok iz nuəz of, if ðə dēst,
ə giv im ə blak ī.   40

ī sumā kests ə līt ə þinz
ət fouk nuən wonts tə sī;
ðez feu laiks telin wot ðə āə(r),
ə wot ðə out tə bī.

wa, wa, pə·fekšn nivə did   45
tə Admz bānz bə·len;
ən liuk ət moətlz wen wə wil,
wis find ə sumət ren.

oud Adm gat sə mešt wi tfoəl
ət oəl ə tiumən reəs   50
grouz sadli āt ə šap i tmaind,
i tkeəkəs, ən i tfeəs.

ðez nuən sə blind bəd ðeə kn sī
ə fout i uðə men;
av sumtaimz met wi fouk ət þout   55
ðə soə wun i ðəsen.

ən tbest ə tšaps l find ðəsen
ət taimz i tfouti tlas ;
av dubld neiv ə·fuə tə-deə
ət tfuil i tsīmin dlas.   60

bəd twãst ə fouts ət aiv sīn jət,
i wumən ər i man,
is twiəri, neəgin, neɯin tẽn
ət pleəgd puə natərin Nan.

a went wun sumər aftənuin   65
tə sī ə puər oud man.
ən ādli ed i dākɱd d'uə(r),
wen twərit ðus bə·gan:

'eə! wa! did ivə(r)! wot ə triət
tə sī ði faðəz sun ;   70
kum forəd, lad, ən sit ðə dān,
ən al set tketl on.'

'neə, neə,' a sez, 'am nuən ə ðem
ət koəlz ət t'aim bi t'lok,
ən bumps əm dān i tkoənə tšeə(r),   75
ən dluəz reit ād ət tdžok.'

· ðā nuənkeət, wi tə od ði tuɯ?
il suin bi iər a þiɱk,
suə, if tə l sit ən līt ði paip,
al fotš ə suəp ə driɱk.   80

'oud las,' sez ai, 'ðat ei i buən,
ən reəðə lou i bīf.'
'ai, bān,' sez šū, 'ðis jiər ə tū
av ed ə diəl ə grīf.

'am nət ə wumən ət oft speiks,   85
ə siɱz fouk duəlfl senɱz,
bəd ai kɱ tel mi maind tə ðī,
ða noəz wot þiɱz bə·leɱz.

'ðaz nuətist ai nuən liukt sə stāt,
. ən ai kɲ triuli seə,   90
frə tlast bak end ə tjiə tə nā
av nət bīn wīl ə doə.

'ən wot wi siknəs, wot wi grīf,
am duin ða meə di·pend—
its bīn ə wiəri muild ən teu,   95
bəd nā it gets niə tend.

'av bout oəl tsistər ət i ev
ə blak mərainə gān;
fouks þiɲks am reəli of, bəd, lad,
am þeɲkfl ət im bān.   100

wi twɔ̄ld, ən ivriþiɲ ət s int,
am krost tə ðat də·grī
ət moni ə taim i d'eə av preəd
tə lig mə dān ən dī.

'wot aiv tə tak frə tliəst i tās   105
əz muə nə fleš kən biə(r);
it iznt džust ə taim bi tšons,
bəd ivri de(ə) i tjiə(r).

nuə livin soul ətop ə tiəþ
wə traid əz aiv bin traid;   110
ðez nuəbdi bəd ðə Loəd ən mī
ət noəz wot iv ed tə baid.

frə twind i tstumək, triumətizm,
ən temin peənz i tgium,
frə kofs ən kouds ən tspain i tbak,   115
av sufəd mātədium.

bəd nuəbdi pitiz mə ə þiɲks
am eəlin out ət oəl;
tpuə sleəv mən tug ən teu wi twāk
wol ivə šū kən kroəl.   120

'ən Džoni z tmuəst unfilin briut
ət ivə weər ə iəd:
i wodnt weg ə and ə fuit
if ai wər oəl bəd diəd.

'i tmidst ə oəl iv ed tə diu   125
ðat ruəg wə nivə tman
tə fotž ə koil, ə skāər ə fleg,
ə weš ə pot ə pan.

'fouk sez āə Sal l suin bi wed,
bəd tþouts ont tēnz mə sik;   130
ad reəðər iɳ ər up bi tnek,
ə sī ə bərid wik.

'ən if i þout ə bān ə main
wə boən tə liəd mai laif,
a sudnt þiɳk it wor ə sin   135
tə stik ə wi mi naif.

'av ast āə Džoni twenti taimz
tə briɳ ə swīp tə d'uə(r);
bəd nā ə·fuər il speik ə·giən
al sit i tās ən smuə(r):   140

'ən ðen—guid greišəs, wot ə wind
kumz wiuwin þriu d'uə snek;
a felt it oəl tlast wintə(r), laik
ə witl ət mi nek.

'ðat siɳk paip, tiu, gat stopt wi muk   145
ə·būn ə fotnit sin,
su(ə) ivri āər i d'eə wi tslops
ɑm trešin āt ən in.

'oəl! wen i þiɳk ā aiv bin tret,
ən ā i teu ən straiv—   150
tə tel ðə tonist triuþ, ɑm kapt
tə find miseln ə·laiv.

'wen īz bin reəkin āt ə tnīt,
ət tɯeəkit ər ət tʃeə(r),
sitš þouts əs kum intə mi iəd   155
əz liftəd up mi eə(r).

'av þout, "ai, lad, wen tā kumz uəm,
ðal find mə uɲ bi tnek;"
ən ðen av me bi þout ə·giən
ət kuəd əd apɯ brek.   160

'ər els av mutəd, "if it wornt
sə dāk, ən koud, ən wet,
ad guə tə tnavi ə tə d'am
ən drānd miseln tə-nīt."

'its grīf, lad, nout ət oəl bəd grīf, 165
ət weəsts mə deə bi deə;
suə Seətn temps mə, kos im weək,
tə put miseln ə·weə.'

toud tšap iəd peət ə wot šə sed
əz i kom tlompin in,   170
ən šātəd in ə red feəst reədž,
'od, rot it! od ði din.'

ðen Nan bə-gan tə froþ ən fium,
ən fiz laik botld driɲk;
'wot, ðen, ðaz entəd tās ə·giən,   175
ða ofid liukin sliɲk!

'ða nivə kumz ðiəz duəz wiðin
bəd ðā mən kəs ən swiə(r),
ən straiv tə briɲ mə tə mi greəv
wi brīdin əriz iə(r).   180

'frə ðī ən ðain sin wed wə wo(r)
av teən nu(ə) end ə grīf,
ən nā ða stamps mə undə tfuit,
ðā məðərin ruəg ən þīf.

P

'ðā viln, gi mə wot i brout   185
ðat de(ə) ət wī wə wod,
ən nivə muə wi wun laik ðī
wil ai set fuit i bed.'

iə d'oudi liftəd təv ər īn
ə jiəd ə linin tšek,   190
ən sobd ən ruəd ən rokt əsen,
əz if ər āt əd brek.

ən ðen šu reəv reit up bi truits
ə anfl əv ər eə(r),
ən fitəd laik ə dī in duk,   ·195
ən šutəd āt ə t'šeə(r).

'aə! Džoni, run fə d'oktə(r), lad,
a fil a kānt tel ā;'
sez Džoni, 'līt ði paip ə·giən
šul kum ə·bāt i-nā.'   2co

bəd betər ed it bīn fər im
if īd niə stād ə peg;
mai geətəz! wot ə poəz i gat
frə Nanz riumatik leg.

suin, vari suin, šu kom ə·bāt   205
ən fluŋ ən teər ən reəv,
i sitš ə we(ə) əs feu kəd diu
wi wun fuit i ðə greəv.

ðen at it went ə tuŋ ə·giən
ðat minit šu gat iəz,   210
'ðā viln, ða, ða noəz ði weəz
briŋz on sitš gēdz əz ðiəz.

'aə! if təd straik mə stif ət wuns,
ə stab mə tə mi āt,
a ðen kəd dī kontent, fə fouk   215
wəd noɔ reit wot tə āt.

'unfīlin briut! unfīlin briut!
a niə wə wīl ən stroɳ;
ðez nobəd wun þiɳ tšiəz mə nā—
a kan nət last sə long.   220

'tə stand up fər ə þiɳ ət s reit
it iznt i mi neətə(r);
ðez fouk ət noəz i oləs wo(r)
ə puə(r), soft, kwaiət kriətə(r).

'wun þiɳ ai kɳ seə, if tə-nīt   225
mi laif səd end it liəs,
av duin mi diuti ən ða noəz
av oləs strivm fə piəs.

'a no(ə), a no(ə), ət im i tgeət—
ðaz uðər uəts tə þreš,   230
suə, wen im duin fo(r), ðā mə wed
jond guid fə nout juɳ treš.'

ðen Nan pūld sumət āt ə d'roə(r),
wait əz ə sumə tlād,
sez ai tə Džoni, 'wot s ðat ðiə(r)?'   235
sez Džoni, 'its ə šrād.

'ən kofin kom tiu, bəd a sweə(r)
a wodnt et i tās;
suə wen šəz miuld šə seuz ət ðat,
əs kwaiət əz ə mās.'   240

puə Nan liukt at mə wi ə liuk
sə jondəli ən sad:
'ðal kum tə tbərin?' 'jəs,' a sed,
'a sal bi vari dlad.'

'ðen bid ði muðə(r), Džoni kraid,   245
'ən as ði uɳkl Ben;
ən oəl ə prcəz fə sudn diəþ
sl c mibest "eəmen."'

P 2

NOTES.

The (˙) denotes that the following syllable has the strong stress, thus asem·ive (I. 3), ·aim (I. 4). Before beginning the Specimens the reader is advised to read over §§ 249, 260, 341, 350 in the Grammar. In order to facilitate the reading of the Specimens, I have written get up instead of ger up, wot iz it? instead of wor iz it? etc. See § 290.

III.

Line 4, fot *for it.* 11, jie (§ 337). 17, on forms like we(ə) see § 193. 22, ðiə see § 354. 26, tmītin *class meeting, prayer meeting.* 34, nuən (§§ 357, 399). 37, on wel beside wīl see § 399. 63, sum ən mad (lit. *some and mad,* a very common phrase) *very angry.* 73, sitš ən ə (§ 340). 80, on (see page 73 note). 89, bīzm (lit. *besom) good-for-nothing.* 99, äez read āz *ours.* 100, wi ə tlate(r) *and at the same time inflicted blows upon them.* 101, þinz here used contemptuously of Grace's children. 106, mel nə mak pleonastic for *meddle.* 107, ðe (see page 112). 109, ən oel (§ 399). 118, Džemeekə *Jamaica rum.*

IV.

Line 2, eeləs *ale-house, beer-house.* 3, də (§ 390). 5, ont *of it.* 11, Ned ə oud Bilz *Ned (the son) of old Bill.* 14, tšet (§ 381). 23, seðə (lit. *see thee) look!* 34, dān-tsteez lit. *down the stairs.* 38, strak (§ 363). 52, Bili (§ 339). 88, must (§ 392). 108, let (§ 381). 128, it (§ 351).

V.

Line 14, **tweivin šeed** *the weaving shed.* 25, **tə** *thou* (§ 350). 46, **tes** *thou hast.* 56, **wišt** *hush !* 104, **tentri end** *the end of the passage.* 136, **likə(r)** (lit. *liquour*) *drink.*

VI.

Line 8, **muild ən broild** *struggled hard.* 25, **snikt** *cut.* 32, **wudn ən** (lit. *wooden one*) *coffin.* 42, **if sə ədnt ə ed** (lit. *if she had not have had*) *if she had not had.* This construction only occurs in subordinate sentences, and has probably arisen from contamination with such phrases as, **šud or šəd ə dunt** *she would have done it*; **tladz ed ə guen** *the boys would have gone.* We generally say **ad ə lend jet if jəd nobed ə ast mə** *I would have lent you it, if you had only (have) asked me.* Cp. the end of §§ 389, 397. 48, **we dān ə wun fuit** *was down of one foot,* i. e. *one of her legs was longer than the other.* 59, **kut mi stiks** *make myself scarce.* 86, **ə flī i mi iər-oil** *a box on the ears.* 93, **ðat,** see § 399. 100, **seez** (§ 382). **med** (§ 392).

VII.

Line 53, **stail** is the lit. Engl. form, see § 315. The same is also the case with **midžez** (VIII. 36).

IX.

After line 200 the following four lines have been inadvertently omitted in our Specimen :—

> sez ai, 'a nivə so(ə) ə tšap
> sə iəzifl ən fat ;
> ðal siuəlī len ə elpin and
> tə lift ər of ə tplat.'

INDEX.

antm *anthem*, 57, 286.
anvil *anvil*, 57.
anz *hands*, 302, 310.
ap *to wrap up (with clothes)*, 57, 317.
äp *harp*, 61.
apl *apple*, 57, 247.
apm (lit. *happen*) *perhaps*, 270, 399.
aprən *apron*, 196.
arə *arrow*, 57, 243.
arənd *notoriously bad*, 207.
arənd *spider*, 194, 304.
as *ash, ashes*, 57, 312, 337.
as (aks) *to ask*, 125, 312.
äs *house*, 171, 310.
äsəmivə(r) *howsoever*, 399.
ask *dry, rough, harsh*, 312.
as-midin *ash-pit*, 57, 312.
at *hat*, 57.
ät *heart*, 74.
ät *out*, 171.
ät *thou art*, 61.
avək *havoc*, 194, 322.
avə(r)-məil *oat-meal*, 57.
ävis, ävist *harvest*, 61, 245, 292.
äz *ours*, 352.

bä *to bow*, 171, 315.
bad *bad*, 144, 343.
bad (pret.) *invited*, 57, 373.
bai *to buy*, 315, 382.
baid *to endure, put up with, wait, stop, remain*, 156, 361.
bait *to bite*, 156, 361.
bak *back*, 57.
bäk *bark*, 61, 312.
bäk *to bark*, 74.
bakə *tobacco*, 246.
bakəd *backward*, 243.

bakədz *backwards*, 251.
bäkm *collar of a horse*, 74, 315.
bak-stn *the iron plate on which oat cakes are baked*, 70.
baləks *testiculi*, 243.
bäli *barley*, 61, 245.
bäm *barm*, 74.
ban (pret.) *bound*, 57, 301.
bän *child*, 61, 259, 280.
bän *barn*, 74.
bän *going*, 171, 303.
band *string, cord*, 57.
bäns *to bounce*, 115.
bänti *bounty*, 235.
barə *barrow*, 57, 243.
baril *barrel*, 194.
bas *door mat, hassock*, 57.
bastail *workhouse, union*, 234, 243.
bastəd *bastard*, 195, 243.
bät *about, without*, 171, 242, 246, 289, 400.
baþ *bath*, 57, 306.
bed *bed*, 73.
bed-stəid *bedstead*, 87.
beəbə(r) *barber*, 203.
beəd *to bathe*, 70, 308.
beədž *barge*, 203.
beəgɒ *bargain*, 203, 247, 271.
beək *to bake*, 70, 312.
beəkəs *bakehouse*, 243.
beəkɒ *bacon*, 204, 247.
beəl *bale*, 204.
beəli *bailiff*, 204, 245.
beən *near, direct*, 84.
beə(r) *bare*, 70.
beə(r) (pret.) *bore*, 70, 369.
beəs *bass*, 195.
beet *bait*, 84.
beət *to abate*, 246.

beete(r) *to barter*, 203.
bef *to cough*, 73, 280.
beg *bag*, 59, 315.
beg *to beg*, 73.
beid *bead*, 87.
bek *beck*, 73, 280, 312.
bel *bell*, 73.
bele *to bellow*, 73, 315.
beles-cap *a cap bordered or adorned with lace.*
belesez *bellows*, 73, 338.
beli *belly*, 73, 245.
belt *belt*, 73.
bend *to bend*, 73, 381.
beŋ *to throw, hit violently*, 59, 280.
beŋk *bank, bench*, 59, 73, 312.
beŋ-up *very good, excellent.*
besk *to bask*, 60, 306, 310, 312.
best *best*, 73, 343.
bešfl *bashful*, 197.
bete(r) *better*, 73, 343.
bezl *to embezzle*, 206, 246.
be *by*, 400.
bed *but*, 174, 291, 401.
bēd *bird*, 90, 261.
bēdn *burden*, 120, 306.
be-eev *to behave*, 70.
be-fue(r) *before*, 242, 400.
be-gan *began*, 57.
be-gin *to begin*, 89, 242, 315, 367.
be-gun *begun*, 111.
be-int *behind*, 305, 400.
bēk *birch*, 90, 259, 312.
be-kos *because*, 225, 401.
bēl *to pick out small pieces of straw, etc. from flannel or cloth*, 228.
bēl āt *to draw or pour out (drink to or for any one)*, 120.

be-lief *belief*, 179.
be-līv *to believe*, 150.
bēn *to burn*, 74, 261, 382.
bere *borough*, 113.
beri *berry*, 81, 245, 315.
beri *to bury*, 120, 245, 258, 315.
be-said *besides*, 400.
be-twīn *between*, 187, 400.
bēþ *birth*, 120, 259.
bi *by*, 160, 400.
bī *bee*, 187.
bĭ *to be*, 187, 396.
bid *to invite to a funeral*, 89, 280, 300, 303.
bied *beard*, 68, 259.
biek *beak*, 231, 322.
biem *beam*, 178.
bien *bean*, 179.
bie(r) *to bear*, 75, 260, 369.
bie(r) *beer*, 188.
bies, biest *beast, cow*, 231, 292, 338, 381.
biet *to beat*, 179, 381.
bīf *beef*, 232.
big *big, large*, 89, 315.
bi gou, bi goi *a kind of oath.*
bi gum *a kind of oath.*
bi-int, be-int *behind*, 89, 305.
bīld *to build*, 119, 254, 381.
bin *within*, 89, 268, 400.
bĭn *been*, 187, 396.
bi nā *by this time*, 399.
bind *to bind*, 89, 367.
biŋ *a bin*, 89, 273.
bit *a bit*, 89, 289.
bite(r) *bitter*, 89.
bi tmegs *a kind of oath.*
bitn *bitten*, 89.
bitš *bitch*, 89, 312.
biu *bough*, 164, 315.

breitš *a breach*, 87, 312.
brek *to break*, 88, 258, 312, 369.
breŋ (pret.) *brought*, 59, 368.
brest *breast*, 192.
brīd *to breed*, 147, 381.
bried *bread*, 179.
bried-fleik *a hurdle on which oat-cakes are dried*, 87, 312.
briedþ *breadth*, 137.
brieþ *breath*, 131.
brieð *to breathe*, 131, 306.
brig *bridge*, 117, 280, 315.
brigz *a trivet*, 315, 338.
brim *brim*, 117.
brim *to put the boar to the sow*, 89, 263.
brimstn *brimstone*, 117, 247.
briŋ *to bring*, 89, 258, 273, 367, 368.
brīt *bright*, 93, 261, 318.
britš *breech*, 312.
britšez *breeches*, 149.
briu *to brew*, 190, 256, 382.
briuk *brook*, 164, 312.
brium *broom*, 164.
broitš *to broach*, 219.
brok *badger*.
brokŋ *broken*, 100, 247, 271.
broþ *broth*, 100, 338.
brout *brought*, 167, 318.
brued *broad*, 122.
bruetš *brooch*. 218.
bruid *brood*, 163.
bruslz *bristles*, 121, 287.
brusn (pp.) *burst*, 287.
brust *to burst*, 261, 367.
bruðe′r) *brother*, 169.
bued *board*, 104, 259.
buekŋ *to belch, retch*, 105, 271.

buən *bone*, 122.
bue(r) *boar*, 122.
buet *boat*, 122.
bueþ *both*, 122.
buin *boon*, 163.
buit *to boot*, 163.
buit *boot*, 221.
buið *booth*, 163, 306.
buizm *bosom*, 163, 247.
buk *buck*, 111.
būk *book*, 164.
būk (būkþ) *bulk, size*, 112, 256.
bukit *bucket*, 226.
bul *bull*, 111.
buldž *to bulge*, 226.
bulek *bullock*, 111, 243.
bulit *bullet*, 227, 245.
bum-beeli *bailiff*, 204.
bun (pp.) *bound*, 111, 280, 301.
būn *above*, 283, 400.
bunl *bundle*, 121.
busk, *to go about from place to place singing and playing for money*, 174, 312.
busl *to bustle*, 111, 287.
bušl *bushel*, 227.
bute(r) *butter*, 111, 243.
butn *button*, 226.
butše(r) *butcher*, 227.
buzed *butterfly*, 226, 243, 291, 310.

-d *had*, 395.
-d *would*, 256, 397.
dāe(r) *to dare*, 61, 390.
daft *foolish, silly, cowardly*, 57.
daik *dike, ditch*, 156, 312.
daiv *to dive*, 175, 283, 295, 361.

dăk *dark*, 74.
dākᴅ *to enter*.
dālin *darling*, 189, 259.
dam *large pond of water*, 57.
damidž *damage*, 194, 245, 328.
dān *to darn*, 61.
dān *down*, 171, 400.
dān-reit *downright*.
dāst *dust*, 171.
dāt *doubt*, 235.
dee *day*, 65, 315.
deel *dale*, 70.
deendže(r) *danger*, 204.
deenti *dainty*, 204.
deet *to dart*, 203.
deet *date*, 204.
deevi *affidavit*, 204, 246.
deezi *daisy*, 65.
deg *to sprinkle with water*, 59, 315.
dein *dean*, 234.
delf *a stone quarry*, 73, 283.
delv *to delve*, 73, 283.
demek *potato disease*, 206, 246.
demekt *diseased (of potatoes)*, 206.
deᴅ (pret.) *reviled, reproached*, 59, 367.
depþ *depth*, 192.
det *debt*, 206.
deu *dew*, 180, 250, 295.
de *do*, 398.
dēent *durst not*, 287.
dēst *durst*, 113, 259, 390.
di *do*, 398.
dī *to die*, 79, 295.
dī *to dye*, 150, 315.
did *did*, 117.
didl *to cheat, deceive*, 117.
died *dead*, 179, 295.

dief *deaf*, 179.
diel *deal, to deal*, 137, 382.
die(r) *dear*, 188.
dieþ *death*, 179, 306.
dif-rnt *different*, 247.
dig *to dig*, 89, 315, 373.
dim *dim*, 89.
dīm *to deem*, 147.
din *din*, 117.
dine(r) *dinner*, 211.
dinᴅ up *to reproach, revile*, 76, 367, 368.
dip *to dip*, 117.
dīp *deep*, 187.
disiet *deceit*, 231, 234.
disiev *to deceive*, 231, 244.
distēb *to disturb*, 228.
diš *dish*, 89.
diðə(r) *to tremble, shiver with cold*, 89, 297.
diu *to do*, 164, 398.
diu *due*, 237.
dium *doom*, 164.
diuti *duty*, 237.
divāe(r) *to devour*, 236.
divl *devil*, 192.
dizaie(r) *desire*, 230.
dizi *dizzy*, 117, 245, 315.
dizml *dismal*, 211.
dlad *glad*, 57, 315.
dlaid *to glide*, 156, 361.
dlāmi *sad, downcast*, 171, 315.
dlas *glass*, 57, 310, 315.
dlazn *to glaze*, 57, 310.
dlazne(r) *glazier*, 57.
dlee(r) *to stare hard*, 70.
dlī *glee*, 187.
dliem *gleam*, 137.
dlite(r) *to glitter*, 89.
dlium *gloom*, 164, 315.
dlou *to glow*, 166, 250.

dlue(r) *to stare,* 165, 260, 315.
dlueri *glory,* 224.
dlumpi *sulky, morose,* 315.
dlutn *glutton,* 226.
dluv *glove,* 169.
doeb *to daub, smear,* 225.
Doed *George,* 329.
doen *dawn, to dawn,* 63, 315.
doen *down, feathers,* 173.
dof *to undress,* 100, 295.
dog *dog,* 100, 315.
doi *joy, darling,* a pet word applied to children, 329.
doit *to dote,* 219.
dokᴅ *a dock,* 100, 247.
dolep *lump of dirt,* 278.
dolt *lump of dirt,* 100.
don *to dress,* 100, 268, 295.
dons *dance,* 200.
doudi *a scolding, irritable woman.*
doute(r) *daughter,* 101, 318.
draft *draught, draft,* 57, 319.
drai *dry,* 175, 315.
draip *to drip,* 175, 278.
draiv *to drive,* 156, 283, 361.
dránd *to drown,* 115, 304.
drázi *drowsy,* 171.
dreeg *to drawl,* 70, 315.
dreek *drake,* 70, 312.
dreet *to drawl,* 295.
dreg *to drug,* 59, 315.
dregᴅ *dragon,* 197.
dregz *dregs,* 73, 315.
drenš *to drench,* 73, 277, 312.
drenk *drank,* 59.
drī *dreary, gloomy, tedious,* 150, 315.
dried *to dread,* 131.

driem *dream,* 179, 382.
drieri *dreary,* 188.
drift *drift,* 89.
drink *to drink,* 89, 273, 312, 367.
driu *drew,* 164, 315.
drivm *driven,* 89.
droe *to draw,* 63, 315, 375.
drop *drop,* 100.
druen *drone,* 122.
druev (noun) *drove,* 122.
druft *drought,* 174, 315.
drukᴅ *drunk, drunken,* 111, 247, 368.
dub *a small pool of water,* 111.
dubl *double,* 226, 348.
dudz *clothes.*
due *doe,* 122.
Dued *Joe,* 329.
duef *dough,* 122, 315.
duefl *cowardly,* 122, 315.
duel *dole,* 122.
due(r) *door,* 113.
Duez, Duezi *Joshua,* 329.
duin *done,* 163, 398.
dul *dull,* 107.
dum *dumb,* 111.
dun *to urge for payment,* 111.
dun *done,* 398.
dunᴅ *dung,* 111.
duv *dove,* 174, 283.
duz *dost, does,* 169, 310.
duzn *dozen,* 226.
dwáf *dwarf,* 74, 250, 315.
dwinl *to dwindle,* 160, 250, 266, 298.
džais *joist,* 229, 292, 310, 328.
dželes *jealous,* 206, 243, 328.
dželi *jelly,* 206, 328.

fāl *fowl,* 114, 315.

fale *fallow,* 57, 243.

fan *fan,* 57.

fan (pret.) *found,* 57, 301.

fān *fern,* 61.

fasn *to fasten, conclude a bargain by paying earnest money,* 57, 247, 287, 310.

fat *fat,* 144, 289.

fāt *pedere,* 74.

faðe(r) *father,* 71, 243, 283, 297.

fed *fed,* 148.

feed *to fade,* 204.

feek *trick, deception,* 127.

feel *to fail,* 204.

feen *fain, glad,* 65, 315.

feent *to faint,* 204.

fee(r) *fair,* 65, 315.

fee(r) *to fare,* 70.

fees *face,* 204.

feep *faith,* 204.

feeve(r) *to favour, resemble in appearance or manners,* 204.

feeve(r) *fever,* 84.

feit *to fight,* 86, 289, 318, 367.

fel *to fell,* 73.

fel (pret.) *fell,* 192.

felt (noun) *felt,* 73.

felt (pret.) *felt,* 148.

felte(r) *to entangle.*

fend *to provide for oneself,* 206.

fent *remnant of a piece of cloth,* 206.

fešn *fashion,* 197, 247, 269, 327.

fest *fast, firm,* 60.

feðe(r) *feather,* 73, 306.

feu *few,* 180, 250, 283, 357.

fezn *pheasant,* 206, 269, 293, 310.

fēd *third,* 306.

fe-getn (pp.) *forgot,* 242.

fēniš *to furnish,* 228.

fēnite(r) *furniture,* 228, 243, 288.

fe(r) *for,* 400.

fere *furrow,* 113, 243, 258, 318.

feri *first,* 346.

ferin *foreign,* 224, 245.

ferinez *foreigners.*

fe-sak *to forsake,* 376.

fe-seen *forsaken,* 312.

fēst *first,* 120, 309, 344.

fīd *to feed,* 147, 381.

fidl *fiddle,* 89, 296.

fiebl *feeble,* 231.

fie(r) *fear,* 131.

fies *fierce,* 233.

fiest *feast,* 231.

fiet *feat,* 231.

fiete(r) *feature,* 231, 288.

fift *fifth,* 160, 289, 309, 344.

fifti *fifty,* 160, 344.

fiftīn *fifteen,* 344.

fiftīnt *fifteenth,* 344.

fiftit *fiftieth,* 344.

fig-wet *figwort,* 120, 243.

fikl *fickle,* 89, 312.

fil *to fill,* 117.

fīl *to feel,* 147, 382.

fīld *field,* 78, 254.

filep *to beat, flog,* 278.

film *film,* 89, 264.

filþ *filth,* 177.

fin *fin,* 89.

find *to find,* 89, 300, 367, 368.

fīnd *fiend,* 187.

finiš *to finish,* 211, 327.

fouet *fourth*, 190, 309, 344.
fouetīn *fourteen*, 190, 344.
fouetīnt *fourteenth*, 344.
fouk *folk*, 103, 283.
fout *fault*, 199, 256, 283.
frai *to fry*, 229.
fraide *Friday*, 156.
frān *to frown*, 235.
fratš *to quarrel.*
fre *from*, 400.
freem *to make a start* or *beginning*, 70, 283.
frend *friend*, 192.
frenz *friends*, 302.
freš *fresh*, 73, 312.
fre *from*, 400.
frī *free*, 187.
friet *to fret, mourn over*, 82, 381.
frig *coire*, 315.
frīt *fright*, 118, 261, 318.
friut *fruit*, 239.
frīz *to freeze*, 187, 365, 366.
froed *fraud*, 225.
frog *frog*, 100, 315.
frost *frost*, 100.
froþ *froth, to foam*, 100, 306.
frozn *frozen*, 100, 247, 269, 310.
frunt *front*, 226.
fudl *to confuse*, 283.
fuedž *to forge*, 223, 328.
fuem *foam*, 122.
fue(r) *before*, 400.
fues *force*, 223.
fuid *food*, 163.
fuil *fool*, 221.
fuit (pl. **fīt**) *foot*, 163, 336, 337.
ful *full*, 111.
fulle(r) *fuller*, 111.
fuml *to fumble*, 282.
fun (pp.) *found*, 111, 301.
fus *fuss*, 174.
fuzi *soft, spongy*, 283, 310.

ga *gave*, 283.
gab *impudence*. 57, 280, 315.
gad *to gossip*, 57.
gāl *the matter which gathers in the corner of the eye*, 326.
galek *lefthand*, 194, 248, 326.
galep *to gallop*, 194, 243.
gales *gallows*, 57, 315.
galesez *braces*, 254, 328.
galn *gallon*, 194, 337.
gam *game, to gamble*, 57, 263.
gami *lame*, 263.
gān *gown*, 235.
gane(r) *gander*, 57, 243, 298, 315.
garit *garret*, 194, 326.
gat (pret.) *got*, 57.
gāt *gout*, 235.
gavlek *crowbar*, 71, 315.
gee *gay*, 204.
geed *guard*, 203.
geedn *garden*, 203.
geen *gain*, 315.
geen *near, direct*, 84, 315.
geep *to gape*, 70, 315.
geet *gate*, 70, 315.
geete(r) *garter*, 203, 326.
geg *to gag*, 59, 315.
geŋ *gang*, 59.
geŋ-wee *thoroughfare, passage*, 59.
ges *to guess*, 206.
gest *guest*, 315.
get *to get*, 88, 315, 372.
getn (pp.) *got*, 73, 286.
geðe(r) *to gather*, 60, 243, 297.
gezlin *gosling*, 148, 245, 276.
gēd *fit, bout.*

gēdl *girdle*, 120.
gēn *to grin*, 74, 261.
gēs *grass*, 69, 261.
gēsl *gristle*, 90, 261, 286, 315.
gēt *great*, 185, 261, 289.
gēts lit. *greats*, 177.
gēþ *girth*, 306.
gi *give*, 283.
gidi *giddy*, 89.
giən *against*, 400.
giə(r) *gear*, 68.
gift *gift*, 89, 283.
gīld *to gild*, 119.
gilt *a young female pig*, 89, 315.
gimlit *gimlet*, 211, 243.
gīn *given*, 79, 283.
ginl *a long narrow uncovered passage*, 247.
gīs *geese*, 147, 310.
gium *gum*, 164.
giv, gi *to give*, 77, 315, 372.
gizn *to choke*, 211, 326.
gizn *gizzard*, 211.
God *God*, 100.
goəki *left-handed*, 198.
goəl *gall*, 62.
goəm *heed, care, attention*, 184.
goəmləs *silly, stupid*, 184.
goit *channel, mill-stream*, 109, 289, 315.
gol *goal*, 217, 326.
gosəp *gossip*, 91.
gospl *gospel*, 100.
goud *gold*, 103, 315.
graim *soot (on the kettle)*, 156.
graip *to gripe*, 156.
gran-faðe(r), gram-faðe(r) *grandfather*, 194, 299.
grant *to grant*, 195, 326.
grēē *gray*, 133, 315.

greənz (pl.) *malt which has been used in brewing beer*, 204, 338.
greəs *grace*, 204.
greət *grate*, 204.
greəv *grave*, 70, 283.
greəz *to graze*, 70, 310.
grīdi *greedy*, 130.
griəs *grease*, 231.
grīf *grief*, 232.
grīn *green*, 147, 315.
grind *to grind*, 89.
grip *grip*, 89.
grīt *to greet*, 147.
griu *grew*, 190.
griuil *gruel*, 239.
grou *to grow*, 166, 250, 378.
gruən *to groan*, 122.
gruəp *to grope*, 122.
gruəv *grove*, 122.
gruin *snout of a pig*, 221, 268.
gruml *to grumble*, 226, 247.
grund *to grind*, 381.
grund *ground*, 111, 300, 315.
grun-sil *groundsel*, 89, 111, 251, 299.
grunt *to grunt, grumble, find fault*, 111.
grunz (pl.) *sediment*, 111, 302, 338.
guə *to go*, 122, 382.
guəd *goad*, 122.
guən *gone*, 122.
guə(r) *gore*, 122.
guəst *ghost*, 122.
guət *goat*, 122, 315.
guid *good*, 163, 315, 343.
guis (pl. gīs) *goose*, 163, 336.
gulit *gullet, channel for water*, 226, 245.
gust *gust*, 111.
gutə(r) *gutter*, 226.

iuneti *unity*, 237, 253.
iunien *union*, 237.
ius *use*, 237, 253.
iusfl *useful*, 237.
iusles *useless*, 237.
iuz *to use*, 237, 310.
ive(r) *ever*, 145, 283, 399.
ivri *every*, 145, 357.
iz *his*, 89, 351, 352.
iz *is*, 89, 310.
iz *he has, he is*, 310.

jād *yard*, 61, 315.
jāe(r) *your*, 190, 350.
jān *yarn*, 61, 315.
jare *yarrow*, 57, 243, 250.
jāz, *yours*, 352.
jel *yell*, 73, 315.
jelp *yelp*, 73, 315.
je *ye, you*, 252, 350.
je(r) *your*, 351.
jes *yes*, 91, 399.
jesen, jesel, jeseln *yourself, yourselves*, 353.
jesenz *yourselves*, 353.
jest *yeast*, 81, 315.
jestede *yesterday*, 81, 243, 315, 399.
jestenīt *last night*, 399.
jet *yet*, 81, 399.
jĭ *ye, you*, 155, 252, 350.
jied (3 feet) *yard*, 74, 337.
jien *to yearn*, 74.
jie(r) *year*, 131, 252, 337.
jīld *to yield*, 78, 315.
jiuþ *youth*, 190.
joen *to yawn*, 80, 315.
jole *yellow*, 80, 243, 254, 315.
jon, jond *yon*, 80, 252, 354.
jondeli *vacant, beside oneself*.
jonde(r) *yonder*, 399.

juek *yolk*, 83, 105, 252, 315.
juŋ *young*, 111, 252.

kā *cow*, 171, 312.
kāe(r) dān *to bend down, sit down*, 172.
kaf *chaff*, 57, 283. 312.
kaind *kind*, 312.
kait *kite*, 175, 312.
kākume(r) *cucumber*, 237, 263, 282.
kal *to gossip*, 57, 312.
kāl *cowl, to frown*, 114, 254, 315.
kan *can*, 57.
kan (verb) *can*, 57, 389.
kani *knowing, skilful, nimble*, 57, 245.
kanl *candle*, 57, 247, 266, 298, 312.
kānsl *to counsel*, 235.
kānt *to count*, 235.
kap *cap*, 57, 194.
kap *to surprise*.
kapil *a piece of leather sewn over a hole in a boot or shoe*, 194.
karit *carrot*, 194, 245.
kasl *castle*, 57, 286.
kā-slip *cowslip*, 117.
kat *cat*, 57.
kāt *cart*, 61, 312.
katš *to catch*, 383.
kātš *couch*, 235.
kāv *to carve*, 74, 283, 312.
keed *card*, 203, 322.
keedž *cage*, 204.
keek *bread of any kind*, 70, 312.
keekes *body, carcase*, 203, 322.
kee(r) *care*, 70, 312.

kees *case*, 204, 322.

kei *key*, 139, 312, 315.

keišn (lit. *occasion*) *need, necessity*, 322.

kek *hemlock*, 312.

kemp *short coarse white hairs in wool*, 73, 312.

kenke(r) *to rust, corrode*, 59, 197, 243.

kep *to catch* (*a ball*), 278, 312.

kept *kept*, 148.

kest *to cast*, 60, 312, 381.

ketl *kettle*, 73, 247, 312.

ked *could*, 389.

kē-get *kirkgate*, 90, 312, 313.

ken (verb) *can*, 389.

kēn *currant*, 228, 259, 292.

kēnl *kernel*, 120, 312.

kēs *to curse*, 113, 310, 312.

kēsmes *Christmas*, 161, 243, 261, 312.

kēsn *to christen*, 161, 261, 310.

kid *kid*, 89.

kil *to kill*, 77, 250, 312.

kīl *to cool*, 147, 312.

kiln *kiln*, 117, 312.

kīn *keen*, 147, 312.

kindm *kingdom*, 264, 273 note, 312.

kinl *to bring forth* (*of rabbits*), 117.

kinlin *firewood*, 117, 298.

kin *king*, 117.

kink *to cough* (of whooping cough), 89.

kin-kof *whooping cough*, 89, 312, 313.

kīp *to keep*, 147, 312.

kist *chest, box*, 89, 310.

kit *a pail*, 89, 312.

kitl *to tickle*, 89, 257, 312.

kitl *to bring forth kittens*, 312.

kitlin *kitten*.

kitšn *kitchen*, 117, 312.

kiue(r) *cure*, 238.

kn weak form of kan *can*, 271, 359.

kob-web *cob*, 100.

kod *cod*, 100.

koef *calf*, 62, 312.

koef *calf* (*of the leg*), 62.

koel *to call*, 62, 312.

koen *corn*, 104, 312.

koene(r) *corner*, 223.

koese *causeway*, 225, 243, 322.

kof *cough*, 100, 319.

koil *coal*, 109, 254.

koiles *coalhouse*, 243.

koit *quoit, coit*, 216.

koit *coat*, 219, 312.

kok *cock*, 100, 312.

kokl *cockle*, 100, 312.

kolep *slice of bacon*, 100, 243.

kole(r) *collar*, 214.

kom *came*, 169.

konsān *concern*, 207.

konséet *conceit*, 234.

konsiðe(r) *to consider*, 211, 297.

kontráiv *to contrive*, 229, 361, 364.

kontréeri *contrary*, 204 note, 322.

kope(r) *copper*, 100.

kos *because*, 225, 242, 246, 401.

kost *to cost*, 381.

kot *staples of wool tightly entangled together*, 289.

232

INDEX.

kweet *quart*, 203, 250, 259, 322, 337.
kweete(r) *quarter*, 203, 347.
kwīn *queen*, 147.

-l *will*, 397.
lā *to allow*, 235.
lad *lad*, 57.
lād *loud*, 171.
laf *to laugh*, 57, 319.
lafte(r) *laughter*, 57, 319.
laif *life*, 156.
laik *like*, 156.
laim *lime*, 156.
lain *line*, 156.
lais *lice*, 175.
lam *lamb*, 57, 66, 281.
lamp *lamp*, 194.
land *land*, 57.
lanloed *landlord*, 299.
lāns *an allowance of refreshment or money*, 235, 246.
lap *lap, lappet*, 57.
lap *to wrap up*, 57, 254.
laps *a kind of woollen waste made in spinning*, 338.
lari *last*, 346.
las *lass, girl*, 57.
lās (pl. **lais**) *louse*, 171, 310, 336.
last *last, latest*, 57, 343.
lat *late*, 57, 254, 289, 343.
lat *lath*, 57, 289.
late(r) *latter, later*, 57, 343.
latist *latest*, 343.
latš *latch*, 312.
laðe(r) *ladder*, 144, 297.
laðe(r) *lather, foam, froth*, 71, 186, 306.
lavrek *lark*, 125, 243, 312.
lee *to lay*, 84, 315, 382.

leed *laid*, 84, 315.
leedi *lady*, 141, 245, 283.
leedl *ladle*, 70.
leek *to play*, 127, 312.
leelek *lilac*, 229, 243, 322.
leem *lame*, 70.
leen *lain*, 84, 315.
leerem *alarum*, 195.
lees *lace*, 204.
leeð *barn*, 70, 306.
leev *barn*, 306.
left (pret. and pp.) *left*, 143.
leg *leg*, 73, 315.
lein *to lean*, 139, 382.
leitš *leech*, 132, 312.
lek *to leak*, 88, 312.
lek *leek*, 186.
len *to lend*, 143, 268, 303, 382.
lenit *linnet*, 99, 212, 245.
lent, lend (pret. and pp.) *lent*, 143.
lenþ *length*, 73, 275.
leŋ (**loŋ**) *long*, 59.
leŋ *to long for*, 59.
leŋki *tall and thin*.
leŋ-setl *a long bench with a high back*, 59.
leŋwidž *language*, 197, 328.
les *less*, 143, 343.
leš *to comb the hair of the head*, 59.
let *to let*, 134, 381.
let (pret.) *let*, 154.
lete(r) *letter*, 206.
letis *lettuce*, 206, 245.
leðe(r) *leather*, 73, 306.
levm *eleven*, 246.
lī *to tell a lie*, 187, 315.
lid *lid*, 89.
lied *lead*, 179.
lied *to lead*, 137, 381.

liede(r) *tendon*, 137.
lief *leaf*, 179.
lien *lean*, 137.
lien *to learn*, 74, 382.
liest *least*, 137, 343.
liev *to leave*, 137, 382.
lif *soon*, 187.
lift *to lift*, 117.
lig *to lie down*, 89, 254, 315, 382.
lik *to lick*, 89, 312.
lim *limb*, 89.
limit *limit*, 211.
linin *linen*, 160.
lints *lentils*, 209.
liꞃ *heather*, 117, 273.
liꞃe(r) *to linger*, 76.
lip *lip*, 89.
lisn *listen*, 117, 287.
list *list*, 211.
list *to enlist*, 211, 246.
līt *light, levis*, 93.
līt *light, to light*, 187, 381.
litl *little*, 177, 343.
lītnin *lightning*, 150.
lits *lit. littles*, 177.
līts *the lungs of animals*, 93, 318, 338.
liuk *to look*, 164, 312.
lium *loom*, 164, 254.
liv *to live*, 89, 283.
live(r) *to deliver*, 211, 246.
live(r) *liver*, 89, 283.
lodž *to lodge*, 214.
loe *law*, 63, 315.
loed *lord*, 283.
loft *loft*, 100.
loin *lane*, 69, 109, 254.
loin *loin*, 216.
loitš *loach*, 219.
loiz *to lose*, 109, 310, 382.
lok *lock*, 100, 312.

loks *small pieces of wool which have been detached from the fleece*, 100, 338.
loꞃ (leꞃ) *long*, 59.
lop *flea*, 100, 278.
loped *clotted, covered with dirt*, 100, 243.
lopste(r) *lobster*, 100, 278.
lost *lost*, 100.
lot *lot*, 100.
lotments *allotments*, 246.
lou *low*, 124, 315.
loup *to leap, jump*, 184, 317.
lous *loose*, 184.
lued *load*, 122.
luef *loaf*, 122, 317.
luen *loan*, 122.
luensm *lonely*, 122, 247.
lueþ *loath*, 122.
lueð *to loathe*, 122.
lug *to pull the hair of the head*, 111, 315.
luꞃ *lung*, 111.
luv *love*, 111.

m *them*, 350.
mad *mad*, 144.
madlin *a bewildered or confused person*, 144.
mai *my*, 156, 351.
maie(r) *mire*, 176.
maiklskoup *microscope*.
mail *mile*, 156, 337.
main *mine*, 156, 352.
mais *mice*, 175.
mait *mite*, 156.
mak *to make*, 71, 312, 383.
māk *mark*, 61, 312.
man (pl. men) *man*, 57, 336.
mane(r) *manner*, 194.
mānt *to mount*, 235.
map *a mop*, 194.

mare *marrow*, 57, 243, 315.

mare *to match a pattern*, 194, 243.

mās (pl. **mais**) *mouse*, 171, 310, 336.

mat *mat*, 289.

māt *to moult*, 235, 256.

māþ *mouth*, 171.

mebi (lit. *may be*) *perhaps, possibly*, 65, 399.

mede *meadow*, 134, 243.

mee (verb) *may*, 65, 315, 393.

meed (pret. and pp.) *made*, 70, 312.

meeg *maw*, 70, 315.

meelek *trick, to play tricks upon a person.*

meen *main*, 65, 315.

meen *mane*, 70.

mee(r) *mare*, 75.

meesn *mason*, 204.

meeste(r) *master*, 195.

meet *mate*, 70.

meil *meal, flour*, 87.

meit *meat*, 87.

meitš *to measure*, 312.

mel *mallet*, 206.

mel *to meddle*, 206.

melt *to melt*, 73, 381.

men *men*, 73.

mend, *to mend*, 206.

mens *neatness, tidiness*, 73, 312.

ment *meant*, 143.

meš *mash*, 59, 125.

mešt *smashed, broken in pieces.*

met *met*, 148.

meze(r) *measure*, 206, 243, 310.

mezlz *measles*, 234, 338.

me (verb) *may*, 393.

me *me*, 350.

med (verb) *might*, 393.

mēki *mirky*, 120.

men *man*, 249.

men *must*, 392.

meníue(r) *manure*, 238, 242.

meraine *merino wool.*

meri *merry*, 120, 245.

mēðe(r) *to murder*, 120, 297.

mi *my*, 351.

mī *me*, 155, 350.

midif *midwife*, 160, 251.

midin *dunghill*, 276, 296.

midl *middle*, 89, 296.

mīdles *troublesome, tiresome, impatient, to no purpose*, 154.

miel *meal, repast*, 131.

mien *mean*, 137.

mien *to mean, intend*, 137, 382.

mig *midge*, 117, 315.

miks *to mix*, 89, 312.

mīld *mild*, 92, 254.

mil-deu *mildew*, 89.

milk *milk*, 77.

miln *mill*, 117, 269.

ministe(r) *minister*, 211, 244.

mins *mince*, 211.

mint *mint*, 89.

minl *to mingle*, 76, 273.

mis *miss*, 89.

misen, misel, miseln, *myself*, 353.

mist *mist*, 89.

mistl *cow-house*, 263, 287.

mistšif *mischief*, 211.

mīt *to meet*, 147, 289, 381.

mīt (noun) *might*, 93, 318.

mitš *much*, 89, 312, 343.

miul *mule*, 237.

miuld *angry.*

miuzik *music*, 237.
mizl *to drizzle (of rain)*, 263, 310.
mizl-tuə *mistletoe*, 89.
moə *to mow*, 123, 377.
moək *maggot*, 63, 306, 312.
moən *morning*, 104.
moəndə(r) *to wander about without any definite aim in view.*
moəndž *mange*, 196, 328.
moəndži *mangy, peevish*, 328.
moənin *morning*, 104.
moist *moist*, 216.
moistə(r) *moisture*, 216, 243, 288.
moit *mote*, 109.
moiðə(r) *to ponder over, be anxious*, 297.
molt *malt*, 58, 254.
moni *many*, 58, 245, 315, 343, 357.
mos *moss*, 100.
mot, moti *a mark at quoits*, 214.
moþ *moth*, 100.
moud *mould, model*, 220.
moud-wåp *a mole*, 103.
mud (verb) *might*, 393.
mūd *crowded, crammed*, 263.
muən *to moan*, 122.
muən *to mourn*, 113.
muənt *must not*, 392.
muə(r) *moor*, 165.
muə(r) *more*, 122, 343.
muəst *most*, 122, 343.
mūfin *muffin*, 112.
muid *mood*, 163.
muild *confusion, bad temper*, 163.
muild ən teu *hard labour, continuous toil.*

muin *moon*, 163, 263.
muk *muck*, 121, 312.
muml *to mumble*, 111, 263, 288.
mun *must*, 111, 263, 392.
mundə *Monday*, 169.
muni *money*, 226.
muns *months*, 307, 310.
munþ *month*, 169, 337.
munə(r) *monger*, 59.
munril *mongrel*, 226.
musl *muscle*, 310.
musl *mussel*, 111, 312.
must *must*, 392.
musted *mustard*, 226, 243.
mutn *mutton*, 226, 247.
muðə(r) *mother*, 169, 297.
muzl *muzzle*, 226.

nā *now*, 171, 399.
naif *knife*, 156.
nain *nine*, 344.
naint *ninth*, 309, 344.
nainti *ninety*, 344.
naintīn *nineteen*, 344.
naintīnt *nineteenth*, 344.
naintit *ninetieth*, 344.
nais *nice*, 229.
nap *nap*, 57.
narə *narrow*, 57, 243.
nat *gnat*, 57, 315.
natə(r) *to gnaw, nibble*, 265.
natərin *scolding, fault-finding in a small vexatious manner.*
nati *neat, tidy, dexterous (of old people)*, 265, 286.
nat-rl, nat-rə-bl *natural*, 194, 247, 288.
navi *canal*, 247, 265.
neb *bill, beak*, 73, 280.
neə *nay*, 84, 399.

nuen-keet *silly foolish person.*
nuetis *notice,* 218.
nuez *nose,* 105, 310.
nuin *noon,* 163, 268.
num *numb,* 111.
nume(r) *number,* 226, 282.
nut *nut,* 111, 317.
nuvis *novice,* 215.
nuvl *novel,* 215.

óbstakl *obstacle,* 214, 243.
od *odd,* 100.
od *to hold,* 64, 300, 381.
od, rot it *a passionate rebuke or remonstrance.*
oef *half,* 283.
oek *hawk,* 63, 283.
oeked *awkward,* 243, 251.
oekedli *awkwardly,* 399.
oel *all,* 62, 357.
oel *hall,* 62.
oemend *almond,* 198, 255.
óeminak *almanac,* 198, 243, 255.
oen *horn,* 104.
oen *own,* 124, 315.
oepeþ *halfpennyworth,* 62, 243, 247, 251, 272.
oepni *halfpenny,* 62, 245, 283.
oes *horse,* 104, 261, 310.
oeðe(r) *either,* 123, 243, 357, 401.
oeðe(r) *order,* 223, 258, 297.
ofl *offal,* 100.
ofld *disreputable.*
oft *oft, often,* 100, 399.
og *the first year's wool of a sheep,* 100, 315.
oil *hole,* 109, 317.
oil *oil,* 216.

ointment *ointment,* 216.
oiste(r) *oyster,* 216.
oke-daik *small stream of iron-water,* 214.
oks (pl. oksn) *ox,* 100, 320, 334.
ole *hollow,* 100, 243, 318.
oles *always,* 58, 243, 251, 399.
olin *the holly-tree, twig of the holly-tree,* 100, 245, 268.
olt *halt,* 58.
omes, omest *almost,* 58, 243, 255, 292, 399.
on *on, of,* 100, 249 note, 400.
one(r) *honour,* 214.
oni *any,* 146, 245, 315, 357.
onibodi *anybody,* 357.
oniwie(r) *anywhere,* 399.
ont *aunt,* 200.
op *to hop,* 100.
opm *open,* 100, 270.
o(r) *or,* 401.
ote(r) *otter,* 100.
otšed *orchard,* 100, 243.
ou *to owe,* 124, 315.
oud *to hold,* 64.
oud *old,* 64, 300.
oue-kesn *overcast, gloomy (of the sky),* 287.
oue(r), ove(r) *over,* 283, 400.
oue(r)-welt *to upset,* 73.
out *ought,* 124, 318, 394.
out *holt,* 103, 289.
ovl *hovel,* 100.

pāe(r) *power,* 236.
pai *pie,* 229.
paik *pike,* 156.
paik *to pick, choose, select,* 229, 322.
pail *pile,* 156.

roul *to roll*, 220.
rout *wrought*, 101, 318.
rubiš *rubbish*, 226.
rudi *ruddy*, 111, 245, 315.
rueb *robe*, 218.
rued *road*, 122.
rueg *rogue*, 218.
ruep *rope*, 122.
rue(r) *to roar*, 122.
ruez *rose*, 105, 310.
ruf *rough*, 174, 319.
ruid *rood*, 163.
ruif *roof*, 163, 283.
ruit *root*, 163.
run *to run*, 367, 368.
runin *running*, 245, 276.
run *wrung*, 111.
rust *rest, repose*, 310.
ruš *rush*, 97.

s *shall*, 256, 312, 391.
s *us*, 350.
sā *a drain, sough*, 310, 315.
sā *sow*, 114, 315.
sad *sad*, 57.
sadl *saddle*, 71, 296.
sādžn *sergeant*, 207, 292.
sāe(r) *sour*, 172.
said *side*, 156.
saieti *society*, 246.
sail *to strain through a sieve*, 156, 315.
sailm *asylum*, 229, 246.
sain *sign*, 229.
saip *to ooze or drain out slowly*, 156.
saiδ *scythe*, 156, 306, 315.
saizez *assizes*, 229, 246.
sāk *to suck*, 171, 310, 312.
sakles *simple, silly*, 57, 243.
sal *shall*, 57, 312, 391.
sale *sallow*, 57, 243.

saleri *celery*, 210.
salit *salad*, 194, 245.
sāmen *sermon*, 207.
sam up *to pick up, gather together*, 57, 263, 310.
sand *sand*, 57.
sānd *sound, noise*, 235.
sant *saint*, 204, 249.
sānt *shall not*, 256, 391.
sap *sap*, 57.
sare (sāv) *to serve*, 207, 243, 258.
sat *sat*, 57.
satl *to settle*, 57, 257.
sāþ *south*, 171.
sāvis *service*, 207.
sāvnt *servant*, 207, 247, 259.
sed *said*, 134, 315.
see *to say*, 84, 315, 382.
seef *safe*, 204.
seeg *a saw*, 70, 315.
seek *sake*, 70, 312.
seekrid *sacred*, 204.
seel *sail*, 84, 315.
seel *sale*, 70.
seem *lard*, 204, 310.
seem *same*, 70.
seent (sant) *saint*, 204.
seev *to save*, 204.
seg *to distend*, 59, 315.
seg *sedge*, 73, 315.
sek *sack*, 73, 312.
seki *second*, 346.
seknd *second*, 344.
sel (sen) *self*, 73, 283.
sel *to sell*, 73, 382.
seldn *seldom*, 73, 247, 269.
self *self*, 353.
sen (sel) *self*, 73, 283.
send *to send*, 73, 381.
sens *sense*, 206.
sent *sent*, 73.

R

skai *sky*, 175, 312.
skeelet *scarlet*, 203, 322.
skeelz *scales*, 70, 204, 312.
skelp *to beat, flog*, 73, 312.
skep *a large wicker basket for holding spinning bobbins*, 73, 312.
skēf *scurf*, 113, 312.
skift *to shift, remove*, 89, 312.
skil *skill*, 89, 312.
skin *skin*, 89, 312.
skoud *to scald*, 199, 322.
skoup *scoop*, 168, 312.
skraml *scramble*, 57, 312.
skrat *to scratch*, 57, 312, 381.
skriptə(r) *scripture*, 211.
skreep *to scrape*, 70, 312.
skriem *to scream*, 312.
skrīk *to shriek*, 158, 312.
skuə(r) *score*, 337.
skuft *the nape of the neck*, 111, 312.
skuil *school*, 163, 312.
skul *skull (of the head)*, 111, 312.
skutə(r) *to spill*, 111, 243, 312.
sl *shall*, 312, 391.
slaftə(r) *to slaughter*, 57, 319.
slaid *to slide*, 156, 361.
slaim *slime*, 156.
slaip *to take away the skin or outside covering*, 156.
slak *slack*, 57.
slām *slumber*, 171.
slāt *to bedabble*, 289.
slatə(r) *to spill*, 310.
slavə(r) *slaver*, 57.
slee *to slay*, 65, 375.
sleen *slain*, 65, 315.
slek *small coal*, 73, 312.

slek *to extinguish a fire, etc., with water*, 73, 312.
slen (pret.) *slung*, 59.
slenk (pret.) *slunk*, 59, 367.
slept *slept*, 134.
slī *sly*, 147, 315.
slidn (pp.) *slid*, 89, 247.
slin *to sling*, 76, 367, 368.
slink *to slink*, 89, 367.
slink *a sneak*.
slip *to slip*, 89.
slīp *to sleep*, 130, 383.
slipi *slippery*, 89, 245.
slit *to slit*, 373.
slitn (pp.) *slit*, 89.
sliu *slew*, 164, 315.
slīv *sleeve*, 150.
sloe *slow*, 123, 250.
slop *the leg of a pair of trousers*, 100.
slot *bolt of a door*, 100.
sluf *slough*, 169, 315.
slukn *slunk*, 274, 368.
slumek *a dirty, untidy person*, 312.
slumə(r) *slumber*, 243, 282.
slun *slung*, 111.
smait *to smite*, 156.
smāt *smart*, 74.
smel *to smell*, 73, 382.
smelt *to smelt*, 73.
smeš *smash*, 59.
smiə(r) *to smear*, 75.
smitl *to infect*, 89, 247.
smitn *smitten*, 89.
smiþ *smith*, 89, 306.
smiði *smithy*, 89, 306.
smivi *smithy*, 306.
smoel *small*, 62.
smok *smock*, 100.
smuə(r) *to smother, suffocate*, 104, 260.

spuin *spoon*, 163.

spun *spun*, 111.

st *should*, 256, 305, 312, 391.

stāe(r) *star*, 74.

staf *staff*, 57.

stak (pret.) *stuck*, 57.

stāk *very, quite*, 312.

stāk mad *very angry*, 61.

stākɒ *to grow stiff, stiffen*, 61, 271.

stamp *to stamp*, 57.

stand *to stand*, 57, 375.

stapl *staple*, 71, 196.

stāt *stout*, 235.

stati *statue*, 245.

stāv *to starve*, 74, 283.

stedi *steady*, 310.

steebl *stable*, 204.

steek *stake*, 70, 84, 312.

steel (pret.) *stole*, 70.

stee(r) *to stare*, 70.

steevz *staves*, 70.

steez *stairs*, 141.

stege(r) *to stagger*, 59.

steil *to steal*, 87, 369.

steil *the handle of a pot or jug*, 87.

steim *to bespeak*, 87, 283, 310.

stem *stem*, 73.

stenɒ (pret.) *stung*, 59.

stenk (pret.) *stunk*, 59.

step *step*, 73.

step-faðe(r) *step-father*, 192.

stepsez *steps*, 338.

stē(r) *to stir*, 120.

sterek *heifer*, 91, 248.

sterep *stirrup*, 162, 243, 315.

stī *sty, ladder*, 94, 158, 315.

stī *sty*, 125.

stī *stile*, 315.

stied e *instead of*, 400.

stiem *steam*, 179.

stiep *steep*, 179.

stie(r) *to steer*, 151.

stif *stiff*, 160.

stik *stick*, 89.

stik *to stick*, 89, 373.

stil *still*, 89.

stīl *steel*, 150.

stīl *stile*, 94, 315.

stint *to stint*, 117.

stinɒ *to sting*, 89, 367.

stink *to stink*, 89, 367.

stīpl *steeple*, 150.

stitš *to stitch*, 89, 312.

stiupid *stupid*, 237.

stoek *stalk, stem*, 62.

stoel *stall*, 62.

stoeleisn *satiation*.

stoem *storm*, 104.

stok *stock*, 100.

stop *to stop*, 100.

stou *to stow*, 166.

stoun *stolen*, 103.

straid *to stride*, 156, 361.

straik *to strike*, 156, 361, 363.

straiv *to strive*, 229, 361, 364.

streendž *strange*, 204.

streit *straight*, 86, 318.

strenþ *strength*, 73, 275.

strenɒ (stroɒ) *strong*, 59.

stretš *to stretch*, 73, 312.

streu *to strew*, 85, 250, 382.

strie *straw*, 179, 310.

striek *streak, stripe*, 98.

striem *stream*, 179.

strikɒ *stricken*, 89.

strinɒ *string*, 76.

strinɒ *to string*, 367.

strip *to strip*, 150 note.

strīt *street*, 130.

tă *thou,* 350.

tăd *towards.*

tādz *towards,* 61, 243, 251.

tāe(r) *tar,* 75.

tāe(r) *tower,* 236.

taid *feast time,* 156, 285.

taidin *a present from the feast,* 156.

taik *a low fellow,* 156.

tă-il (also tail) *towel,* 235.

taim *time,* 156.

tairen *tyrant,* 293.

tais *to entice,* 229, 246.

tait *soon,* 156.

tak *to take,* 71, 312, 375.

tale *tallow,* 57, 243, 315.

tăli *to agree, be right,* 194, 245.

tan *to tan,* 57.

tān *town,* 171.

tap *tap,* 57.

tarie(r) *terrier dog,* 208, 243.

tate(r) *tatter,* 57.

teebl *table,* 204.

teel *tail,* 65, 315.

teel *tale,* 70, 254.

teele(r), teelje(r) *tailor,* 204.

teem *tame,* 70, 285.

teen *taken,* 70, 312.

teest *taste,* 204.

teestril *rascal, good-for-nothing.*

teitš *to teach,* 138, 312, 383.

tel *to tell,* 73, 382.

tem *poured out,* 148.

tem-ful *brimful,* 148.

temz *a coarse hair sieve,* 73, 285, 310.

ten *ten,* 192, 344.

tent *tenth,* 309, 344.

teᴅ *a sting, to sting,* 59.

teᴅz *tongs,* 59, 273, 338.

teu *to work zealously,* 180, 285.

te, tev *to,* 283, 400.

te *thou,* 306, 350.

tĕd *turd,* 120.

te-dee *to-day,* 399.

tĕf *turf,* 113, 283.

te-geðe(r) *together,* 60, 297.

te-moen *to-morrow,* 104, 242, 399.

te-moen-tnīt *to-morrow (the) night,* 399.

tĕn *bout, turn, to turn,* 113, 228.

tĕnep *turnip,* 228, 243.

te-nīt *to-night,* 399.

tī *to tie,* 150.

tie *tea,* 231.

tiem *team,* 179.

tiez *to tease,* 137.

tift *condition, state, order,* 211.

tik *tick,* 89, 312.

til *to till,* 89.

tīl *tile,* 94, 315.

tīm *to pour out,* 147, 381.

tin *tin,* 89.

tit (titi) *breastmilk,* 89.

tīt *tight,* 93, 318.

tīp *teeth,* 147.

tiu *too, also,* 164, 399.

tiuk *took,* 164, 312.

tiuzde *Tuesday,* 159.

tlād *cloud,* 171, 312.

tlāk *clerk,* 207, 323.

tlam *to famish,* 57, 312.

tlap *clap,* 57.

tlap *to place, put down.*

tlāt *clout,* 171, 312.

tlate(r) *to clatter,* 57.

tlee *clay,* 315.

tleem *to claim,* 204, 323.

trof *trough*, 100, 315.

trolǝp *a dirty, untidy person*, 285.

trons *trance* 200.

trubl *trouble*, 226.

trunl *trundle*, 121.

truɒk *trunk*, 226.

trūzǝz *trousers*, 235, 338.

tšaid *to chide*, 312.

tšap *chap*, 186, 312.

tšapil, tšapl *chapel*, 194, 330.

tšavl *to nibble at, gnaw, chew*, 57, 312.

tšeedž *charge*, 203, 330.

tšeef *to chafe*, 204.

tšeemǝ(r) *chamber*, 204, 263, 282, 330.

tšeendž *change*, 204, 328.

tšee(r) *chair*, 205.

tšeltǝ‚r) *to clot, coagulate (of blood)*, 254.

tšeu *to chew*, 190, 312, 382.

tšerǝp *to chirp*, 91, 248, 312.

tšeri *cherry*, 207, 311, 330.

tšētš *church*, 90, 312.

tšiǝnǝ *chinaware*, 229.

tšiǝp *cheap*, 179, 312.

tšiǝt *to cheat*, 231, 381.

tšīk *cheek*, 181, 312.

tšikin *chicken*, 89, 312.

tšildǝ(r) *children*, 89, 92, 312, 335.

tšimli *chimney*, 211, 330.

tšin *chin*, 89, 312.

tšiuz *to choose*, 187, 312, 365, 366.

tšiuz-wot *whatever*, 357.

tšīz *cheese*, 130, 312.

tšoǝk *chalk*, 62, 312.

tšois *choice*, 216, 330.

tšons *chance*, 200, 330.

tšont *chant*, 200, 330.

tšoul see § 312.

tšozn *chosen*, 100, 247.

tšuǝk *to choke*, 105, 312.

tšuf *proud, haughty*, 111, 312.

tšuk *to throw, pitch*, 226.

tū *two*, 129, 250, 344.

tub *tub*, 111.

tuǝ *toe*, 122.

tuǝd *toad*, 122.

tuǝkɒ *token*, 122, 247.

tuǝn (lit. *the one*) *one of two*, 122, 345.

tug *to tug, plod*, 111, 315.

tug ǝn teu (words of nearly the same signification, coupled for the sake of emphasis) *to work hard and strive*.

tuil *tool*, 163.

tuiþ (pl. tīþ) *tooth*, 163, 336.

tul *to*, 97, 285, 400.

tuml *to tumble*, 111, 263, 282.

tun *tun*, 111, 226.

tuɒ *tongue*, 111.

tup *a ram*, 111.

tupms *twopence*, 349.

tusk *tusk*, 111.

tutš *to touch*, 226.

tūpri (lit. *two or three*) *few*, 192, 349.

tuðe(r) *the other*, 169.

twain *twine*, 156.

twais *twice*, 156, 250, 348.

twelft *twelfth*, 73, 289, 309, 344.

twelv *twelve*, 73, 283, 344.

twenti *twenty*, 73, 344.

twentit *twentieth*, 344.

twig *twig*, 89, 315.

twil *quill, pen*, 324.

twilt *quilt*, 211, 254, 324.
twilt *to beat, thrash*, 324.
twin, *twin*, 89.
twīn *between*, 246, 400.
twiŋkl *to twinkle*, 89, 312.
twist *twist*, 89.
twot *pudendum fem.*, 250.

þak *thatch*, 57, 306, 312.
þāzn *thousand*, 171, 247, 301, 302, 310, 344.
þāznt *thousandth*, 344.
þəd *third*, 90, 261, 344.
þədi *third*, 346.
þeŋk *to thank*, 59.
þəti *thirty*, 90, 245, 344.
þətīn *thirteen*, 344.
þətīnt *thirteenth*, 344.
þətit *thirtieth*, 344.
þəzdə *Thursday*, 172.
þī *thigh*, 187, 318.
þibl *a smooth round stick used to stir porridge with.*
þīf *thief*, 187, 283.
þik *thick, friendly, in love with*, 89 312.
þiml *thimble*, 177, 247, 282.
þin *thin*, 117.
þiŋ *thing*, 86, 273.
þiŋk *to think*, 76, 273, 306, 312, 383.
þisl *thistle*, 89.
þoe *to thaw*, 123, 377.
þoen *thorn*, 104.
þoil *to give ungrudgingly*, 109, 306.
þout *thought*, 167, 318.
þraiv *to thrive*, 156, 283, 306, 361.
þrast (pret.) *thrust*, 57.
þreŋ *busy, throng*, 59.

þrepms *threepence*, 192, 270, 349.
þreš *to thresh*, 73.
þrešld *threshold*, 73.
þrə *through, from*, 400.
þrī *three*, 187, 344.
þribl *threefold*, 209, 348.
þrīd *thread*, 130.
þriəp *to dispute, contradict*, 179, 306.
þriətn *to threaten*, 179.
þrif *through*, 319.
þrift *thrift*, 89.
þrift (þriu) *through, from, on account of*, 116.
þriu *threw*, 190.
þriu (þrift) *through, from, on account of*, 116, 319.
þroe *to throw*, 123, 377.
þroit *throat*, 109.
þrosl *thrush*, 100, 287, 310.
þrotl *to press on the windpipe, choke*, 100.
þrusn (pp.) *thrust*, 287.
þrust *to thrust*, 178, 367, 368.
þum *thumb*, 174.
þune(r) *thunder*, 111, 243, 266, 298.

ðă *thou*, 171, 306, 350.
ðai *thy*, 155, 351.
ðain *thine*, 156, 352.
ðat (demon. pr. and conj.) *that*, 57, 306, 354. Cp. also 399.
ðăz *thou hast*, 310, 395.
ðe *they*, 350.
ðee *they*, 84, 350.
ðee(r) *their*, 84, 351.
ðeez *theirs*, 352.
ðem (demon. and pers. pr.) *them, those*, 306, 350, 354.

ðen *then*, 108, 306.
ðe *the*, 241.
ðe *thee*, 350.
ðe *they*, 350.
ðe(r) *their*, 351.
ðe(r) *there*, 399.
ðesen, ðesel, ðeseln, ðesenz *themselves*, 353.
ði *thy*, 306, 551.
ðī *thee*, 155, 350.
ðie(r) *there*, 131, 306, 354, 399.
ðiez *these*, 98, 354.
ðis *this*, 89, 310, 354.
ðisen, ðisel, ðiseln *thyself*, 353.
ðoe *although*, 401.

ue *who*, 122, 250, 355.
ued *hoard*, 104.
u(e)-ive(r) *whoever*, 357.
uek *oak*, 122.
uel *whole*, 122, 317.
ueli *holy*, 122, 245.
uem *home*, 122.
uenli *lonely*, 122, 245.
uep *hope*, 105.
ue(r) *oar*, 122.
ue(r) *hoar*, 122.
ues(t) *hoarse*, 122, 310.
uets *oats*, 122.
ueþ *oath*, 122.
uez *whose*, 355.
uf *displeasure, an offended manner, rage*, 315.
ug *to carry*, 111, 315.
ugli *ugly*, 111.
ugɒ *hip*, 111, 247, 271.
uid *hood*, 163.
uif *hoof*, 163, 283.
uin *to harass, treat badly*, 163.

ulet *owl*, 174, 243.
ulz *bean-swads*, 111.
umbugz *sweets*.
uml *humble*, 226, 247, 263, 282.
umpaie(r) *umpire*, 230.
unded *hundred*, 111, 243, 299, 344.
unde(r) *under*, 111, 400.
undet *hundredth*, 299, 344.
uni *honey*, 111.
unien *onion*, 226.
uni-sukl *honeysuckle*, 174.
unsiue(r) *uncertain*, 240, 243.
unt *to hunt*, 111.
unɒe(r) *hunger*, 111, 243, 273.
unɒkl *uncle*, 226.
up *up*, 174, 400.
upodn *upholden*.
up-reit *upright*.
ut *hot*, 126, 317.
uðe(r) *other*, 169, 357.
uðe(r) *udder*, 174, 297.
uvm *oven*, 107, 270.
uz *us*, 174, 310, 350.
uzbn *husband*, 174, 301, 302, 310.

-v *have*, 395.
vā *vow*, 235.
vaielet, *violet*, 230.
vale *value*, 194, 243.
vali *valley*, 194, 245.
vāment *vermin*, 207, 294.
vāniš *varnish*, 207, 327.
vantidž *advantage*, 246.
vari *very*, 208, 245, 250, 258, 399.
veen *vein*, 204.
vente(r) *to venture*, 206, 288.
vesl *vessel*, 206.

viel *veal*, 231, 250.
viu *view*, 237, 253.
vois *voice*, 216, 250.
voiðe(r) *large clothes' basket*, 216, 250, 297.

wa *why*, 249.
wād *ward*, 61,
wāe(r) *worse*, 74, 260, 343.
wāf *wharf*, 61, 317.
waid *wide*, 156.
waie(r) *wire*, 157.
waif *wife*, 156, 283.
wail *while, time*, 156.
wain *wine*, 156.
waip *to wipe*, 156, 250.
wait *white*, 156.
wait ali, see § 346 note.
waiz *wise*, 156.
wak *to beat, flog*, 250, 306.
wāk *pain, to ache*, 61, 312.
wāk (noun) *work*, 74, 250, 259, 312.
wākes *union, workhouse*, 243.
walep *to beat, flog*, 202, 250.
wām *warm*, 61.
wan (pret.) *wound*, 301.
wān *to warn*, 61.
wap (wop) *to hit, throw*.
wāp *warp*, 61.
warend *to warrant*, 202, 250, 291.
wāst *worst*, 343.
wāt *wart*, 61.
wāte *weekday*, 74, 243, 305, 313.
web *web*, 73, 280.
wed *to wed, marry*, 73, 381.
wednzde *Wednesday*, 170.
wedž *wedge*, 73.
wee *way*, 84, 315.

weed *to wade*, 70, 250.
weedž *wage*, 250.
week *weak*, 127.
weel *whale*, 70.
ween *to wane*, 70.
wee(r) *to spend* or *lay out money*, 70, 250.
weest *waste*, 149.
weeste(r) *a silly, stupid fellow*.
weet *to wait*, 204, 250.
weev *wave*, 70, 133.
weeve(r) *to waver*, 70, 250.
weft *weft*, 73, 283.
weg *to wag*, 59, 315.
wegn *wagon*, 59, 247, 271.
wei *to weigh*, 87, 315.
weik *the wick of a lamp* or *candle*, 87, 312.
weit *weight*, 93, 318.
weiv *to weave*, 87, 283, 372.
wel (noun) *well*, 73.
wel (adv.) *well*, 399.
welp *whelp*, 73.
wen *when*, 108, 317.
went, *went*, 73.
wen *thong*, 59, 250, 273, 306.
wesp *wasp*, 60.
west *west*, 73.
weš *to wash*, 59, 312, 383.
wešes *washhouse*, 243.
wet *wet*, 134, 289, 381.
wetstn *whetstone*, 73.
weðe(r) *weather*, 73, 297.
weðe(r) *whether*, 60.
weðe(r) *the wool of a sheep which has already been shorn at least once before*, 73, 306.
we *we*, 350.
wed *would*, 256, 397.
wōd *word*, 104.

wŏk *to work*, 120, 312, 383.
wēl *to whirl*, 90.
wēld *world*, 104.
wĕm *worm*, 120.
we(r) *our*, 351.
we(r) *was, were*, 396.
weri *to worry*, 120, 245, 315.
wesen, wesel, weseln, wesenz
    ourselves, 353.
wēsit *worsted*, 305.
wēþ *worth*, 74, 306.
wi *with*, 89, 307, 400.
wĭ *we*, 155, 350.
wīd *weed*, 187.
wide *widow, widower*, 89,
    243, 250, 296.
wient *will not*, 256, 397.
wiepm *weapon*, 131, 247,
    270.
wie(r) *to wear*, 75, 369, 371.
wie(r) *where*, 131, 317.
wieri *weary*, 149.
wiet *wheat*, 137, 317.
wiez *to wheeze*, 131.
wik *quick, alive*, 89, 250,
    312.
wik *week*, 89, 337.
wīl (adv.) *well*, 79, 399.
wīl *wheel*, 187, 250.
wil *will*, 89, 397.
wīld *to wield*, 78.
wīld *wild*, 92, 254.
wile *willow*, 77, 243.
wimin *women*, 160, 283.
win *to win*, 89, 367.
wind *wind*, 89.
wind *to wind*, 89, 367, 368.
winde *window*, 89, 243, 250.
winte(r) *winter*, 89.
wiŋ *wing*, 76, 250.
wiŋk *to wink*, 89.
wīp *to weep*, 147.

wisl *to whistle*, 89, 287.
wisnde *Whitsuntide*, 287.
wisnde sunde *Whitsunday*,
    287.
wispe(r) *to whisper*, 89.
wiš *to wish*, 177, 312.
wišin *cushion*, 325.
wišt *silent, quiet*.
wit *wit*, 89.
wită, wite? *wilt thou?* 256,
    397.
witek *wicket*, 286.
witl *large carving knife*, 89,
    250, 306.
witš *which*, 77, 256, 312,
    355.
witš *witch*, 89.
wiðăt *without*, 400.
wiðe(r) *to hurl, throw*, 250.
wiu-in *whistling* (*of the
    wind*).
wizdm *wisdom, wise*, 160,
    247.
wīzl *weazel*, 79.
wizn *to wither*, 89, 310.
wod *would*, 256, 397.
woef (woefl) *sickly to the
    smell, insipid to the taste*,
    62, 250, 319.
woek *to walk*, 62, 312.
woel *wall*, 62.
wokn *to waken*, 58, 247, 271,
    312, 382.
woks *wax*, 58.
woks *to grow*, 320.
wol *until*, 249, 401.
wonde(r) *to wander*, 58.
wont *want*, 58, 250.
wop (wap) *to hit, throw*.
wo(r) *was, were*, 58, 396.
wot (wor) *what*, 58, 250,
    317, 355.

Oxford

HORACE HART, PRINTER TO THE UNIVERSITY

13

www.ingramcontent.com/pod-product-compliance
Lightning Source LLC
Chambersburg PA
CBHW030352270326
41926CB00009B/1076